MOBILIZING MOVEMENTS

ENDORSEMENTS

An invaluable contribution—comprehensive, inspirational, and practical—for all of us who long to see the kingdom of God expanded by seeing whole nations discipled. Backed by a life of experience, Murray uses his pastoral heart to relate the nitty gritty of how to develop effective national church-planting processes around the world.

RON ANDERSON
catalyst, Lausanne Church Planting Issue Network

Moerman has offered the global church a great gift, the gift of synthesis. Learning from forty years of church planting strategies, looking at current trends in DMM and CMP, and discerning the challenges of our time for missions engagement, Moerman offers a practical guide for denominational leaders, church planters, and apostolic leaders to think critically about how their praxis can contribute to the goal of discipling all nations. A must read!

DR. RAPHAËL ANZENBERGER
leadership team, PC2P.org facilitator, Global SCP Taskforce

Multiplying Movements—applied in the power of the Spirit—can unleash a cascade of church planting among least-reached peoples and places. I experienced these principles firsthand in Zimbabwe, where sixty denominations came together in a national process, resulting in ten thousand churches planted within a decade. Had this book been available, the momentum would have flowed even further. Glean from these global insights, and you'll be propelled in the discipling of nations!

DR. DEAN CARLSON
president, One Challenge
international liaison, Movement for African National Initiatives

In *Mobilizing Movements*, Murray Moerman fills an important gap in kingdom literature. Few people have written books on saturation church planting (SCP) in recent years, and even fewer on the role of movements in SCP. These two massively important topics are made for one another. SCP is an important goal, and movements are the primary means by which to achieve this goal. To consider either without the other is to miss a key connection for achieving the advance of the kingdom and the completion of the Great Commission. Murray writes from a position of considerable experience on several levels, most notably in his leadership of the Global Church Planting Network.

DR. CURTIS SERGEANT
founder, MetaCamp; leader, Zúme; co-facilitator, 24:14

Mobilizing Movements is a book for our time. It's a practical tool to empower leaders in multiplying disciples that will transform this world so needy for our Lord Jesus Christ. World Evangelical Alliance (WEA) recognizes that discipleship is core to the mission of Jesus. That's why it works toward instilling disciple-making as an evangelical DNA and welcomes discipleship resources like *Mobilizing Movements*.

BISHOP EFRAIM TENDERO
secretary general, WEA

MOBILIZING MOVEMENTS

LEADERSHIP INSIGHTS FOR DISCIPLING WHOLE NATIONS

MURRAY MOERMAN

WILLIAM
CAREY
PUBLISHING

Available at missionbooks.org

Published by William Carey Publishing
10 W. Dry Creek Cir
Littleton, CO 80120 | www.missionbooks.org

William Carey Publishing is a ministry of Frontier Ventures
Pasadena, CA 91104 | www.frontierventures.org

Cover and Interior Designer: Mike Riester
Copyeditor: Andy Sloan
Managing Editor: Melissa Hicks

ISBNs: 978-1-64508-229-3 (paperback), 978-1-64508-231-6 (mobi), 978-1-64508-232-3 (epub)

Printed Worldwide

25 24 23 22 21   1 2 3 4 5   IN

Library of Congress data on file with publisher

DEDICATION

To all my brothers and sisters in the emerging generation,
known and unknown to me, committed to God's eternal redemptive purpose
that the earth "be filled with the knowledge of the glory of the Lord
as the waters cover the sea." (Hab 2:14)

May God the Father, Son, and Holy Spirit fill you
with vision, strength and courage!

CONTENTS

Tables

Figures

ACKNOWLEDGMENTS

This book could not have been written without the shared ministry experience of colleagues and teammates from around the world for the past thirty years. These include:

Canadian teammates forging the movement birthed as Church Planting Canada: Ron Bonner, John Caplin, Glenn Gibson, Lorne Hunter, Dave McCann, Jay Pinney, Cam Roxburgh, and so many more. Thank you for your support, patience, hard work, and prayer.

Friends and colleagues in OC, my sending mission whose acronym goes by many names, including One Challenge, OC International, and Outreach Canada. Thank you for your friendship, support, and vision, and for being a strong and faithful "home base" over the years. I won't even begin to try to list the scores of dedicated friends.

Friends and colleagues in Dawn Ministries, including its founder, Jim Montgomery, and subsequent leaders Stephen Steele, Ngwiza Mkandla, and Bernardo Salcedo, along with friends from whom I have learned tools and resources—such as Roy Wingerd, Bob Waymire, and too many others to mention.

Friends and colleagues in Europe who are committed to the vision and strategy of national church-planting processes, including Reinhold Scharnowski and Wolfgang Fernandez in days past, and the current NC2P team, including Ron Anderson, Raphael Anzenberger, Øivind Augland, Jürgen Eisen, Craig Hamer, Christian Kuhn, Tom McGehee, Martin Robinson, Dietrich Schindler, Jennifer Williamson, and others.

Friends and colleagues in the Global Church Planting Network, which I was privileged to help initiate with Steff Nash, Dean Carlson, Alex Abraham, Joshua Pillai, David Watson, Dick Grady, Ric Escobar, Pat Roberson, Trevor Betts, Markos Zemede, Medhat Aziz, Yerry Tawalujan, Brian Mills, and the scores who continue to carry the torch.

Other friends and acquaintances helped bring this book into reality. Thank you for your invaluable advice and editorial input, along with your perspective, perseverance, and so much more—including a key research chapter written by Russ Mitchell. My heart is also grateful for Larry Kraft, Chris Maynard, and Gordon Jackson. Thank you, John Huschka, for "teaching me to fish," using tools in MS Word. Thank you, Jan Henderson, for your painstaking proofreading, reminding me, "You asked for it!" Thanks, Raymond Trembath, for your eagle eye also. Finally, the fabulous team at William Carey Publishing: Melissa Hicks, Katie McGaffey, Andrew Sloan, Mike Riester, and director, DG Wynn. Every question was opportunity for improvement. All errors in content or detail remain my own.

Thank you to the contributions of many friends and practitioners over the years who participated in peer-learning conversations, sharing challenges and mistakes to help us all become more fruitful servants of the King. Thank you too to the Focus on Fruit Team, devoted disciple-makers in a challenging environment, from whom so much has been learned.

There is no way to say thank you to my wife and kingdom mission partner, Carol, who has prayed with me, encouraged me, and offered wisdom and the occasional push in the right direction. She is the beloved mother of our five children and the beloved grandmother of our eleven grandchildren—our joy and delight.

PREFACE

John Wesley famously said, "Give me one hundred men who fear nothing but sin and desire nothing but God, and I care not whether they be clergymen or laymen, they alone will shake the gates of Hell and set up the kingdom of Heaven upon Earth."

An Ethiopian friend breathed, "Dear God, help me to be one of them."

My heart gives that same cry, and yet it's clear now that we need not ninety-nine more (Sorry, John Wesley), but many more of such fearless, focused, sold-out men and women. A strategically specific and relatively well-accepted ratio is *one church for every thousand people on the planet.*

With that goal in mind, we keep a laser focus on what matters most: God graciously became incarnate in Christ because he wants to live among us and in us for our redemption. He removed the barriers of sin, shame, and guilt on the cross, so that as we're reconciled to the Father, his transforming life could enter us and through us bring healing and transformation to the *ethne*—the families, communities, and peoples of the world.

Jesus commanded us to make disciples in whom he can live and through whom he can bring transformation. These disciples live and work in community. The New Testament calls this community "church." The church supports disciples in their life and work for transformation.

As disciples are made, churches are formed. As churches are formed (hopefully), disciples are made. To help people respond to Christ, disciple-making and church planting must extend to the extremities of every people group and nation. The aim of this book is to advance the vision and reality of Christ incarnate in his church in every nation, living out the transformation that comes from the *missio Dei.*

This book assumes that you are sold out to obey Jesus Christ in his call to disciple the nations. It assumes your passion is lifelong and that throughout your long obedience you want to grow in effectiveness and impact—locally, nationally, and beyond. Some concepts may be challenging at one stage of experience or leadership development. Yet we grow and the Lord calls us forward, equipping us for a broader scope of ministry than we could have envisioned in an earlier stage.

The promise of Scripture is that those who delight in the Lord will continue to bear fruit in every season of life (Ps 1:2–3). When Moses questioned God's calling him to a scope of ministry beyond his faith and courage, the Lord asked, "What is that in your hand?" (Ex 4:2). What the Lord puts in our hand will prepare us, by his grace and power, for the next level of leadership or scope of ministry to which he calls us.

As such, through this book I hope to offer help and encouragement at the stage you are now facing, as well as in future stages when you come back to reread a chapter that initially seemed beyond where you were at.

Movements to Christ are needed in every ethnic, geographic, and cultural space. Since the goal is to ensure that everyone in a nation has equal opportunity to know him who is eternal life (John 17:3), these disciple-making and church-planting movements must be seen in their national context. In every nation. Globally.

Essential to laying this foundation for the book's global aim is to familiarize you, at the outset, with a concept a friend and mentor introduced me to thirty years ago. James Montgomery published *DAWN 2000: 7 Million Churches to Go* in 1989. This book painted a challenging vision and mission strategy born in the Philippines. Montgomery's acronym came from the strategy of Discipling a Whole Nation (DAWN). Though revolutionary in many ways, the strategy wasn't perfect, of course, and new insights have—and will be—developed.

Yet the high-level, strategic thinking found in the original DAWN strategy has grown, morphed, and been modified over the ensuing decades. As a result, you may recognize some of its core ideas in terms having grown out of this soil, like:

- **Saturation Church Planting (SCP)**—which highlights church planting as the *means* to mobilize the "whole church" in the "whole nation."
- **Strategic Church Planting**—which employs the same SCP acronym, but uses the term *strategic* to focus on the deliberate and purposeful prioritization of the most difficult or needed harvest fields yet to know Christ within the whole nation.
- **National Initiatives**—which is the term favored by the Movement for African National Initiatives (MANI) to emphasize the proactive nature of national partnerships in obedience to the Great Commission. The term includes church planting among the least-reached and the impact of healthy churches.
- **National Church Planting Process (NC2P)**—which is a term used in Europe to underscore the reality that a national movement is not simply an event but a long-term committed process. National church planting processes tend to be less goal-oriented and more organic, recognizing that the process may well take an undefined period of time.

The essential *whole nation* concept and approach is seen, even thirty years later, in the core passion of each of these strategies, and therefore is the framework in which the specific tactics in this book can be worked out. It is both flexible and comprehensive in scope, as Jesus' Great Commission requires, and has a collaborative approach to disciple-making and church planting that speaks to the unity the Lord wants from his church.

The thesis of this book is that every nation needs a well-led national church-planting process. With adaptation, this is possible in every county and city in the radically diverse contexts of our globe, and led wisely will greatly accelerate the penultimate step toward completion of the Great Commission.

A fly-over view of the flow of this book is one of water flowing from foothills into a river. Chapter 1 overviews the "big idea" of mobilizing the whole church to disciple the whole nation, as well as a brief history of the "streams" flowing towards it. Part 1 highlights lessons learned, as well as accelerants that have been identified in movements gleaned from practitioners around the world. Moving from the past to the reader's present, Part 2 dives into practical wisdom for practitioners wanting to get started in their unique setting. Part 3 embraces the longer-term work in the nations—both challenges to be resolved and polarities to be held in tension in a leadership process that calls for a long obedience in the same direction. Part 4 examines the fruitful interaction between national and church-planting facilitators—indigenous and expatriate.

National disciple-making and church-planting processes are inevitably and intensely practical. Consequently, this is a hands-on book that shares hard-won lessons of a lifetime.

While many leaders assume that mission planning is beneficial, other Christians view planning as getting in the way of following the guidance of the Holy Spirit. The balance struck in this volume is one which believes God creatively guides hearts that are humble and open, even as we pursue useful strategies toward the *missio Dei* goals voiced in Scripture. Paul's openness to the dream that diverted his path to Macedonia (Acts 16) is an example of a man who both devises the best plan he can and diverts from the plan at the point God directs. Wandering in the wilderness (Numbers 14 to Deuteronomy 34), however, is *not* God's normal plan for his people. Vision, goals, and planning are valuable work—and not in opposition to continually seeking the guidance and direction of the Holy Spirit.

My hope, desire, and prayer is that a new generation of emerging mission leaders will become acquainted with the vision and beauty of the whole-nation strategy, see it as the spiritual work it is, and build on the experiences of those who have gone before. Further, my prayer and invitation is that you, the reader, will open your heart to the call of God. It was this that broke John Knox's heart on seeing the plight of his nation, pleading "Lord, give me Scotland, or I die." This is a costly call. But in my experience it is a costly call that, by the grace of God, reshapes women and men to give their lifelong, sustained best through hardship, opposition, and spiritual warfare—to the glory of our King and only Savior.

MURRAY MOERMAN
Vancouver
August, 2020

GLOSSARY: TERMS AND ACRONYMS

4–14 Window—This refers to children aged four to fourteen who warrant special attention in evangelism and discipleship. This is not a geographic designation, like the 10–40 Window.

4G—This refers to four generations of believers related to one another spiritually. These may be new disciples, discipling-making groups, or church plants. A first spiritual generation leads others to Christ, thereby creating a second-generation disciple, discipling-making group, or church plant. These second-generation believers in turn lead others to Christ, creating a third spiritual generation, which then leads to a fourth spiritual generation in Christ. Not always, though ideally, those in each spiritual generation lead not just one person to Christ but two or more new disciples, groups, or church plants.[1]

10–40 Window—This refers to an area from West Africa to Japan that is between 10 degrees north latitude and 40 degrees north latitude. Most of the world's unreached peoples, as well as most of those living in poverty and illiteracy, reside here.

24:14—This refers to the 24:14 Network, which aims, in response to the words of Jesus in Matthew 24:14, to start disciple-making movements in every segment of the globe. See chapter 19.

AAGR—Annual average growth rate calculations are vital for objective reflection on the health and growth of a church, denomination, or movement. For help in making AAGR calculations, see *Church Growth Survey Handbook*, which is listed in the "Strategic Information" section of the bibliography.

Congress—This refers to a national gathering of church leaders sharing a vision of multiplying disciples and planting churches among the least-reached so that every people group and person in the country has equal opportunity to be transformed by the knowledge of Jesus Christ. The term, admittedly Western, highlights the purpose of gathered leaders not only to *confer* (conference), but in addition to *decide together* (congress). Research updates, highlighting both progress and the work yet remaining, as well as case studies of planting models that are taking root and multiplying among those who have had the least opportunity to be engaged by winsome followers of Christ, are important to share in these regular national gatherings. Similar gatherings can take place at a state or provincial level.

Constantinian (era and model of church)—Emperor Constantine, most historians believe, intended to do the church a great favor in about 313 AD when he diverted Roman state income from pagan temples to the Christian church. The net effect, however, was counterproductive. Clergy began to be paid and became a special class. Church buildings were constructed and furnished more like pagan temples from the era preceding Christ, complete with altars and vestments, than the simple missional communities formed by Jesus' first followers. The Protestant Reformation, when it finally took hold, was a reformation of theology that did not touch the clergy/laity distinction or the budget priority of buildings, programs, and salaries. The Constantinian model was challenged in the modern era in fits and starts, first by the Pentecostal movement, which started in the early 1900s, and then by the subsequent charismatic renewal. Contemporary house-church and disciple-making movements are also a challenge to the Constantinian-era model of church.

CPM—Church-planting movements can be viewed as a comparatively simple church-planting approach, popularized by the research of David Garrison in 1999. It refers to practical principles found in common among churches that plant churches that plant churches into the third and fourth generations. These principles emphasize prayer and the biblical simplicity of obedience, lay leadership, and the intentional, frequent planting of small churches.[2] Many of these principles have been in use by other noninstitutional approaches throughout church history and brought to the attention of the West by George Patterson during his missionary service in Central America.

DAWN—Discipling a whole nation is a vision and macro strategy developed by Jim Montgomery of Dawn Ministries. The strategy focuses on rallying the church in a given nation to plant churches in the least-reached communities and bring people groups to a "saturation" level of a church for every one thousand people in the general population. This is considered the "penultimate" goal before a nation can be discipled.

DMM—Disciple-making movements is a micro strategy focused on obedience-based responses to Scripture in small discussion and accountability groups. Small groups aim to begin other groups rather than enlarge. Many DMM practitioners view four spiritual generations of disciple-making groups as foundational. David Watson is often associated with the early development of this movement.[3]

GACX—Global Alliance for Church Multiplication is a network of churches and mission organizations committed to the goal of one church for every thousand persons in every physical and cultural space.

GCPN—Global Church Planting Network is a collaborative relational network aimed at accelerating church planting in every global region.

Harvest Force—The harvest force in every nation includes disciples of Christ who are or could be mobilized to work in the harvest field to win the lost to Christ. Organizationally, the harvest force is composed of denominations, parachurch organizations, local congregations, and mission agencies. Theologically, the harvest force is the body of Christ. The biggest challenge to the harvest force today is nominal Christendom.

Harvest Field—The harvest field includes those who do not yet know or have not yet positively responded to the claims of Christ. Study of the harvest field includes better understanding of the demographics and geography encompassing those yet outside the gospel in ways that will help those who follow Christ lead others to him through disciple-making, church planting, and church-planting movements.

John Knoxer—A person with the heart of John Knox for his or her nation. John Knox was reported to have agonized in prayer, "Lord, give me Scotland, or I die." This passion for the gospel and for the lost is the heart of a national process leader.

---

3 DMM-related sites include www.contagiousdisciplemaking.com and http://zumeproject.com. See bibliography for additional resources.

Least-reached—People groups that contain committed Christians, but not in adequate numbers to be able to complete the Great Commission within their people group.[4]

Movements—Movements were long-defined simply as a group of people working together to advance their shared political, social, religious, or artistic vision. Movements to Christ, however, are being defined more precisely today than in previous generations. This enables mission research to more accurately track and celebrate mission fruitfulness in various settings. Movements are now defined as a minimum of one thousand persons who have come to Christ within multiple streams to a fourth generation. A fourth-generation church is one that came into being when new believers (first generation) won new believers to Christ (second generation) who in turn won new believers (third generation) who in turn won new believers incorporated into a spiritual fourth-generation small group or church.

NCPP or **NC2P**—National church-planting processes focus on four initial components: a committed coordination or facilitation team, adequate information to clearly prioritize national needs for church planting, regular national gatherings of denominational and mission agency leaders to focus on the remaining task, and support systems to empower the harvest force in its task to disciple the nation.

SCP—Saturation church planting is viewed as an adequate number of churches who are able to fully disciple their cities and people groups. While discussion continues, this is generally seen as an approximate ratio of one church reaching out to every thousand unreached people. This ratio varies from smaller in rural areas (1:500) to higher in urban areas (1:1500). It may be of interest to note the ratio of mosques to population in Muslim-majority countries tends to be about one mosque for every four hundred people.

T4T—Training for Trainers is a disciple-making and church-planting movement popularized by Ying Kai and Steve Smith, which has resulted in 1.7 million baptisms and 150,000 church plants.[5]

---

4 https://joshuaproject.net/global/progress is helpful in the process of distinguishing priorities.

5 Steve Smith and Ying Kai, *T4T: A Discipleship Re-Revolution* (Monument, CO: WIGTake Resources, 2011).

Unreached People Groups—UPGs are people groups not yet containing strong indigenous church-planting movements that are able to disciple the people group to its fringes. When evangelicals comprise less than 2 percent of a given population, the church is often viewed as requiring help to reach a tipping point. Gratefully, the number of unengaged UPGs are decreasing as pioneer church-planting teams are deployed to serve them. By sheer numbers, however, 60 percent of the world is unreached, in the sense of remaining outside a relational, cultural connection with Christians who could introduce them to Jesus Christ. This graphic "big picture" may be helpful.[6]

Non-believers Living in "Unreached People Groups" (UPGs)

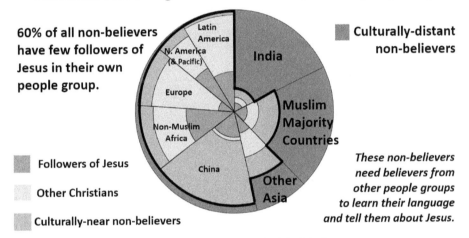

60% of all non-believers have few followers of Jesus in their own people group.

Culturally-distant non-believers

These non-believers need believers from other people groups to learn their language and tell them about Jesus.

Followers of Jesus

Other Christians

Culturally-near non-believers

Figure 1: "Big Picture" of Global Task

6 An excellent overview in animated video based on research by Rebecca D. Lewis and Chris Maynard prepared for students attending InterVarsity Urbana Student Missions Conference in 2018 can be viewed at https://www.youtube.com/watch?v=SVmTU13rgo8. Used by permission.

PART 1

A View from the Top

"Attempt great things for God, and expect great things from God."
—William Carey

The world will tell you to "follow your passion." I'm a fan of passion. For one thing, it gets many things done. Passion alone, however, is not enough.

We need godly passion that is born of a deep inner conviction that God has called you, and often comes with an anointing of his Holy Spirit. This is the kind of passion that lasts beyond whims and hardships. It inspires us to keep learning, to build, to adjust, to keep our eyes on the prize and our hearts full of God's glory, returning continually to abide in his presence.

A young intern from Syria, with wisdom beyond her years, once quipped in regard to a difficult group circumstance that required a cool and rational demeanor, "Keep fire in your belly and your head in the refrigerator."

Deep inner passion is important to launch. Lifelong learning is vital to arrive.

You have likely prayer-walked your building site, perhaps for months or years. You are nearer now to your time to build—or perhaps you have begun. Of course, we are not the first to build, so we are wise to learn from those who have gone before. The chapters in this section look back, drawing practical lessons from recent mission history applicable to your local setting.

The section concludes with a review of lessons learned that can be applied to a national church-planting process in your country.

If you can comfortably double-task as you read, you may want to keep one eye on the building site where you want to serve your nation—the uniqueness and challenges of its terrain—and one eye on practical principles and learnings that may prove valuable as you prepare to lay foundations and look up from there.

Learning to cooperate as the body of Christ to disciple nations is a process akin to the now proverbial building an airplane on the runway. There is much we know. There are successful models to guide us. Even so, it is natural, as we reflect on models that leave us with lessons to incorporate, that there will also be new questions raised, the learnings of others to consider, wins to celebrate, sins to confess, mistakes to compensate for, and always to be open to make necessary adjustments and adaptations.

CHAPTER 1

The Big Idea: Discipling Your Nation

"A goal should scare you a little, and excite you a lot."
—Joe Vitale

WHEN I WAS in my late teens I began reading the New Testament for the first time. Before I'd even finished the Gospels, I said to my brother Jack, "If this is true, then the gospel is the most important thing on earth, and I have to give my whole life to it." Soon after that I became convinced that Christ is not only the truth for me personally, but that he is also the hope of the nations. Soon afterwards I committed my life to the Lordship of Christ and knew the joy of the assurance of his salvation and eternal presence. Several years into a church plant in western Canada, during a routine morning "quiet time," I sensed the Lord direct my thoughts to means of mobilizing others to a higher priority for church planting, the embryo of a national church planting strategy. A few years later Carol and I joined a mission, Outreach Canada, to pursue national church planting strategies full time, first in Canada, then Europe, then through the Global Church Planting Network.

Today I'm just as caught up with the truth and visionary aspects of the gospel as I have ever been, reveling in how the Lord revealed his heart and mission purpose from the earliest passages of Scripture. In Genesis 3:15, the *protoevangelium* ("first good news"), the Lord foretold, almost immediately after the Fall, his promise and plan for redemption through the coming Savior. The *missio Dei*, mission of God, was introduced to Abraham in his call out of Ur of the Chaldeans to form a new nation for God's redemptive purpose, through whom "all the families of the earth will be blessed" (Gen 12:3 NASB). God's purposes from this point on were to prepare Israel to obey its calling to reflect God's holy character and make known his redemptive covenant to all the nations (Ps 66:1–4).

The New Testament celebrates not only Jesus the Messiah, who opened the way and invited every person into the kingdom of God, but also the empowerment of the Holy Spirit, which enables the church to fulfill its mandate to make disciples of all *ethne*, peoples, or families, of the earth.

Ultimately our mission is rooted in the Trinity who is the source of all that is, was and will be. The God the Father who loved us from before the foundation of the world, God the Son who gave himself as perfect sacrifice for people utterly lost and unable to redeem themselves, and God the Holy Spirit who empowers the redeemed for the mission of the Kingdom of God into all the world, is glorious community. God's *ekkelesia* reflects that community, holiness and mission.[7] Mission therefore is done in community, holiness and with the purpose of God's comprehensive goal always in view. Further, the Trinity is social within itself, concerned for relationship, just, loving and righteous. Our God is a sending God who desires the very glory of heaven to transform human experience and culture on earth. In all these ways the church is shaped and called to reflect the Trinity in the world.[8]

The post-Constantinian church, like Israel in the Old Testament, was slow to grasp its central call to disciple the nations.[9] The short version is that while by end of the sixth century 21 percent of the world population had identified with Christ by the end of the sixth century, global mission did not sustain advance beyond 21 percent for an agonizingly long twelve centuries.[10]

We would rather not remember that during these centuries the church not only suffered seasons of loss of internal focus, but also extensive, long-term external setbacks at the hands of Islamic and Mongolian expansion. Mongolian expansion ended as the devastating bubonic plague entered Europe from the east, decimating the Christian population by a hard-to-fathom one third. The following century, Muslim expansion took the lives of an estimated five million Christians.

---

7 Ed Silvoso, *Ekklesia: Rediscovering God's Instrument for Global Transformation* (Bloomington, MN: Chosen Books, 2017).

8 For a more complete missiology of church planting see Charles Van Engen, "Why Multiply Healthy Churches? Biblical and Missiological Foundations," in *Planting Healthy Churches*, eds. Gary Teja and John Wagenveld (Sauk Village, IL: Multiplication Network Ministries, 2015)

9 See "Constantinian" in the glossary.

10 For details drawn from Patrick Johnstone's *Future of the Global Church* see my blog entry of January 5, 2017 at www.murraymoerman.com/blog/2017.asp.

The global church "holding its own" under such circumstances may rightly, at least in part, ameliorate our disappointment. Yet it must also be noted that a critique of the Reformation reveals disappointment as well. The most commonly accepted year of the birth of the Reformation is 1517, when Martin Luther nailed his ninety-five theses to the Castle Church door. Preoccupied as the Roman Catholic Church was with doctrinal correction, and as later Protestants were embroiled in controversy, only about two hundred Protestant missionaries were sent out during the two hundred years after 1517.

The reawakening of earlier mission impulse didn't take place until the last part of the 1700s. The reawakening of God's global purpose was heralded by the Moravian refugee prayer movement, initiated in 1727, which sent out, in its first sixty-five years, three hundred missionaries. On average, one out of every twelve of their small number became cross-cultural missionaries.

Inspirational among them were the young men who sold themselves into slavery to reach three thousand Africans sequestered by an atheist slaveholder in the Caribbean. Their cry from the ship carrying them away, "May the Lamb that was slain receive the reward of His suffering," helped propel the community to send three thousand missionaries during its round-the-clock "prayer watch" which continued for one hundred years.

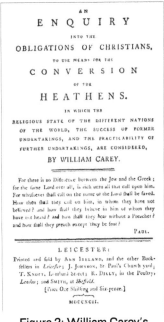

The ripple effect has not yet ended. John Wesley (1703–91) was greatly affected by encounters he had with those he called "the Germans."[11] William Carey likewise drew from their fire, challenging the English: "See what the Moravians have done! Can we not follow their example, and in obedience to our heavenly Master go out into the world and preach the Gospel?"

Carey's *Enquiry into the Obligations of Christians,*[12] published in 1792, proposed that the world be broken into continents and nations, estimating the size, population, and b religious majority of each, and where workers of which he was aware, from Europe, had been.

Figure 2: William Carey's
Enquiry into the Obligations
of Christians

---

11 John Wesley's encounter with Moravians is reported in *The Guardian* and in *Christian History* magazine. See Appendix 7 for links.

12 Full title: *An Enquiry into the Obligations of Christians to use Means for the Conversion of the Heathen, in which the Religious State of the Different Nations of the World, the Success of Former Undertakings, and the Practicability of Further Undertakings, are Considered.* Available from www.gcpn.info/home/regions/national-initiatives.

William Carey called for Christians to go to each nation—near or far, hostile or friendly—arguing that all nations were now within reach of committed believers. He challenged Christians to put the plight of those without Christ before their own comfort and ease. He argued that the risk of dying was limited, local food was available, and languages could be learned. For the support of qualified workers, Carey suggested the formation of societies, such as his Baptist Missionary Society that sent him to India.

Many such societies were subsequently formed, and thousands of gospel workers were sent, largely from Northern and Western Europe. Initially mission efforts went to the coastlands accessible by ship (1800–1910). The next era focused on more difficult to reach inland areas (1885–1980). The bewildering array of languages and people groups within nations sparked a third era, leading to growing specialization in mission strategy from 1935 through today.[13]

However, it was not until 1975 that the big idea of placing primary responsibility for discipling a nation fell not on *missionaries* from *outside* a nation, but on the *church*, unified in strategic mission purpose, *within* the nation. This "big idea"—linked with a systematic approach for doing so—emerged in the heart of James Montgomery while he was serving in the Philippines.

The story of the development of the "whole church, whole nation" vision and strategy is told in Montgomery's *DAWN 2000* and related writings.[14] The goal, unprecedented in mission history, of planting a church in every *barangay* (the smallest governmental administrative unit, generally home to about one thousand people) was put to church leaders of every denomination, and prayerfully accepted. In 1975, with five thousand Bible-oriented churches in the Philippines, fifty thousand *barangay* were anticipated by the year 2000. Therefore, forty-five thousand churches would need to be planted in twenty-five years to provide a church for every one thousand people/*barangay*.

When researchers reported finding just over fifty thousand churches in 2000, some might have concluded the mission of the church was complete. Some *barangays* were now served by more than one church, while others, particularly in the Muslim south, remained without Christian witness. Further, the population of the Philippines continued to grow, so the number of churches needed to disciple the country continued to grow also. Finally, as Jim Montgomery suggested early on, disciple-making and church planting is both necessary and *penultimate*, which is to say "a step before" the completion of the Great Commission. The leaven of

---

13 Ralph Winter, "Three Mission Eras," in *Perspectives on the World Christian Movement*, 4th ed., eds. Ralph D. Winter and Steven C. Hawthorne (Pasadena, CA: William Carey Library, 2009), 263; and www.missionfrontiers.org/issue/article/four-men-three-eras.

14 Many of Jim Montgomery's writings are available at www.gcpn.info/home/regions/nation-al-initiatives.

the gospel has yet to further penetrate structures and institutions to a depth that brings social and cultural betterment.

Readers may be familiar with the subsequent development of Dawn Ministries as a support organization for "whole nation" projects initiated in various parts of the world. A major review of this story has been undertaken by Raphaël Anzenberger, an NC2P leader based in France.[15] Each national experience has brought the thoughtful observer additional learnings, many of them about partnership and movement leadership. Many focused disciple-making movements are needed to engage thousands in each social segment and cultural space who don't know Christ.

But the "big idea" remains and provides the foundation for this book—the vision of mobilizing the "whole church" to disciple the "whole nation" by placing a transformative church inhabited by the risen Christ within reach of every person. "Within reach" does not mean that every person outside of Christ can reach a given church, but that a disciple-making community can and is seeking to reach every lost person.

This book is not for the faint-hearted. Rather it is for those willing to "put their shoulder to the wheel" to mobilize the whole church for a national church-planting process, or disciple-making movements contributing to that end. The book's focus is to provide practitioners a learning community and timeless resource in their long obedience in the same direction of bringing transformation to a nation.

Next Steps

- Have you ever considered a "whole church" to "whole nation" approach before?
- What might this approach look like in your context?
- What would the challenges be to implement this big idea?
- Which of these items do you need to lift up to the Lord in prayer?
- What will your next steps be?
- Are there teammates or others you need to talk to about these action steps?

---

15 See Raphael Anzenberger, "Whole-Nation Saturation Church Planting Towards A New Dawn?, PhD Dissertation, 2020.

CHAPTER 2

Disciple-Making and Church-Planting: Insights to Build On

"Therefore every scribe who has become a disciple of the kingdom of heaven is like a head of a household, who brings out of his treasure things new and old."
—Jesus (Matt 13:52 NASB)

YOU MAY IDENTIFY with my problem. I like my own ideas best. Yet we learn best in a wider community that shares common kingdom goals. Since I got involved in ministry and missions, many practical insights have been gained upon which we may profitably build.

Interestingly, in reviewing these insights we may find that although we have become certain of some, upon reflection we realize they could present a challenge to our assumed paradigm or to our personal comfort or the comfort of our friends. Here is an example of such an insight:

Smaller Churches Make Disciples and Reproduce Better Than Larger Churches

Christian Schwarz, in challenging the American church-growth movement, which he viewed as too technique-oriented and/or too difficult to implement in Europe, produced his wildly successful Natural Church Development in 1996.

In comparing smaller churches of under 50 persons with larger churches of over 2,500 persons, Schwarz uncovered a staggering difference. Per capita, smaller churches are 1,600 percent more effective in disciple-making leading to baptism than are churches of over 2,500 persons.[16]

---

16 Christian Schwarz. *Natural Church Development: A Guide to Eight Essential Qualities of Healthy Churches* (St. Charles, IL: ChurchSmart Resources, 1996), 46-48.

This vital insight, unfortunately in my opinion, was not further developed in the book (perhaps because megachurches are so widely honored in Christian culture). Yet, had the potential of smaller churches for world mission advance been highlighted, micro churches may have been widely celebrated earlier for the contribution they add to world evangelization.

Growth Performance: Global Survey of Churches

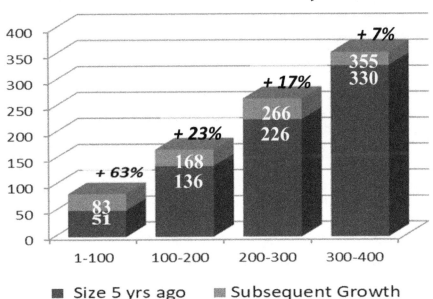

Figure 3: Growth Performance: Global Survey of Churches
by Christian Schwarz (used with permission)

Consider the example of a lay-led Mexican church that never exceeded seventy participants. When it approached this number, thirty-five participants formed another church, and each half was encouraged to win disciples to Christ until it grew again to seventy persons. The resulting network remained low-budget, bi-vocational, and reproductive. Had a well-meaning friend welcomed the network into an organization with higher standards, its growth likely would have stalled.

Another example involves a larger church with one thousand participants. Recognizing the importance of Schwarz's insight, the leaders took action—not in their own interests but in the interests of the kingdom. The church ceased its march toward megachurch status, divided into ten smaller churches of one hundred, and encouraged each of these smaller churches to grow and plant new churches often.

The point of these illustrations is not to undervalue megachurches or the tremendous capacity they have for social impact. I want, rather, to appreciate the value of small churches, including house churches, for their great potential for discipling a nation. In doing so, to the surprise of some, house-church networks have more significant social ministry than expected.[17]

Addition, However Rapid, Is Not Multiplication

Early on as a church planter, I developed the conviction that every local church should aim to plant at least two new churches—one to replace itself, because no church lives forever,[18] and another to extend the kingdom into a new community or people group. If a church does so, it is likely to continue birthing a third and then a fourth daughter church. This must be done quickly, while the mother church is still young and growing. Older churches that have stabilized in growth and begun to decline, like older people, are at first less likely to birth new churches, and then unable to do so.

After I finished seminary, my wife and I initiated a church plant, New Life Community Church (RCA), in Burnaby, Canada. As the new church grew, we experimented with planting daughter churches in a satellite model. We were having both a Sunday morning and Saturday evening service, each averaging four hundred worshipers. We then encouraged a member of the leadership group to lead a church plant, inviting as much of the congregation as desired to join them. Eventually we repeated that process four times. It usually took the mother church about two years to grow back to the size and leadership strength as before. One plant failed due to competing visions in its leadership team, two others were blessed to join other denominations, and the fourth became an independent international student church on a local university campus. The daughter churches were welcome to avail themselves of staff support, ministry training opportunities, and mother church programs for as long as they wished, and to wean themselves to relative autonomy as they deemed best.

Although this process added lost sheep to the kingdom, addition is not multiplication. Neil Cole strongly recommends avoiding careless language.[19] Rapid addition is not multiplication. Planting multiple daughter churches is not multiplication. During my time at New Life Community Church none of our

---

17 For instance, see the PPT slide (2018 GACX Forum) on social impact of house churches in an Asian context: http://www.murraymoerman.com/mm/downloads/GACX2018Forum-study-of-social-impact-of-housechurches.jpg.

18 The average congregation is active about the same number of years as the average human lifespan. This is not unnatural, but highlights the vital importance of birthing new disciple-making communities (aka daughter churches) while the mother is still young and vigorous.

19 Neil Cole, *Church 3.0: Upgrades for the Future of the Church* (San Francisco: Jossey-Bass, 2010), chap. 4. Cole's thinking is incisive and challenging. I highly recommend reading the entire chapter.

daughter churches planted daughter churches. We had added, but had not multiplied. A centralized organization that sends out many church planters is adding, not multiplying.

Friends in Switzerland use the phrase "Every 5" to remind and encourage every church to plant a church every five years and every disciple to disciple a new disciple, who in turn will reproduce every five years. In some countries this rate may seem challenging.

> Implement a planting model that aims, from the beginning, to produce multiplication.

Some more harvest-ready countries may find it realistic to aim higher. The point is less the rate than the aim to multiply.

To multiply, a disciple must enable a new disciple to depend on the Lord of the harvest to bring a third-generation disciple into the kingdom, who in turn is trained and brings a fourth-generation disciple into the kingdom. To multiply, a church must enable a new church to depend on the Lord of the harvest to bring a third-generation church into being, which in turn is trained and brings a fourth-generation church into the harvest field. We cannot, therefore, use an addition strategy to produce a multiplication result. Multiplication is a complete and radical departure from addition.

The application of this insight is vital to national church-planting processes. The natural form of growth in human populations is multiplication, as each generation produces a new generation. The church cannot keep up with multiplication by addition, and certainly cannot make gains on its God-given calling to disciple nations by addition.

The first step is to determine whether our planting strategy is based on addition or multiplication. The second step is to study models in which disciple-making and church planting are indeed multiplying to a minimum of four generations—and then apply them. May we have a holy dissatisfaction with addition! Exponential (https://exponential.org) may be the largest Western organization committed to nurturing holy dissatisfaction along with multiplication training—essentially replacing planting churches with planting networks of reproducing churches.

Like Reproduces Like

Because "like produces like," a church that is birthed by addition is likely, if it plants at all, to do so by addition. If a denomination or congregation is highly dependent on professional clergy, the church it plants is likely to be highly dependent on professional clergy. If a church that assumes disciple-making is done by those specifically called to this role plants a church, its daughter church is likely to reproduce a like view of disciple-making. If a church behaves as a haven of support

Ensure you
demonstrate the
characteristics you
want to multiply.

for its members in the context of a city with which it has minimal contact and on which it makes minimal impact, and that church plants, its daughter church is likely to produce a similar priority for congregational care isolated from the larger community.

The bad news *and* the good news are that like reproduces like. This is typically true of our character, family culture, the churches we plant, and the movements we seek to initiate.

This means a leader should know quite precisely what he or she wants to reproduce in a disciple-making or church-planting process and hold that vision firmly in mind from the outset.

It's clear that Jesus did. His engagement with twelve men, perhaps the most diverse twelve men one could imagine, with the purpose of forming them not only to be "fishers of men" but also to form within them the very image of Christ. Jesus was unrelentingly purposeful.

As Jesus sent the twelve (Luke 9), it appears the seventy-two added to them (Luke 10) were both similar to the twelve in ministry focus and very possibly people living out ministry modeled to them by the twelve.

The best way to build a multiplication DNA is to plant a new church with that DNA clearly defined in heart, ministry lifestyle, and—likely also—on paper.

Let me suggest a foundational challenge as you set out. Think long and hard about the difference between addition and multiplication and choose a multiplication model from the outset. List the elements you've seen in unhealthy non-multiplying churches that you do not want to reproduce and the elements you've seen in healthy multiplying churches that you do want to reproduce. Seeing both lists in writing will bring benefits that more than compensate for the time it takes to clarify your thinking. Do so before you start, because like reproduces like. Start off on the right foot.

Disciple-Making Precedes Church Planting

The purpose of church planting is to make disciples. Yet, as many rightly note, Jesus called his disciples, as first priority, to make disciples (Matt 28). He does not, in this passage, call us to plant churches. Churches were subsequently formed to strengthen and encourage disciples.

In the process of making disciples, Jesus began by teaching his disciples to seek out persons of peace (Matt 10; Luke 10). Persons of peace who responded to the good news of the kingdom in turn invited their *oikos* to form with them the nucleus of an embryonic community of faith. Like Jesus first went to the people of

Israel, Paul first visited Jewish synagogues, hoping they would receive Jesus as Messiah (Acts 13–14), but he in fact found more fruit among the Gentiles, where new disciples were eventually formed into churches. In most examples in Acts, this pattern of making new disciples first, and planting new churches second, is repeated.

> First, make disciples who will make disciples, then plant the church you want to multiply.

Making disciples first and forming churches afterward is not only the common biblical pattern but is logical since the primary purpose of the church is to gather, nurture, and train new disciples in their life and work in the kingdom.

Some suggest church planting and disciple-making can be seen as a "Which comes first, the chicken or the egg?" question. Yet it must be acknowledged, sadly, that churches as groups energized by a worship band can be planted without making reproducing disciples.

When we make disciples, however, a disciple-making community (aka church) is virtually inevitable. In this sense, church planting can be viewed as an "afterthought" to disciple-making (as first suggested to me by Kirk Anderson, a missionary in Balkan Europe).

Churches formed primarily for established believers, in and of themselves, do not actually advance Christ's final mandate. Making new disciples is the only direct obedience to the direct command of our risen Lord.

It is important to distinguish disciple-making from discipleship. Discipleship normally focuses on strengthening believers in their devotion to Christ, worship, spiritual disciplines, community engagement, and service. Disciple-making responds specifically to the command of Christ to make disciples of those who are not yet disciples and train them to make disciples in turn unto multiple spiritual generations. Maturing disciples of Christ multiply other disciples.

The church is increasingly recognizing this priority. As a result, disciple-making movements are emerging in a growing number of nations. In a Muslim-majority Asian nation a colleague wrestled with this challenge and found a way, beginning with training by David Watson, which could be summarized with this figure 4:

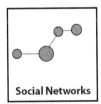
Social Networks

Seven Questions

Lay Leaders

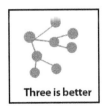
Three is better

Figure 4: Disciple-Making Movements

Contacts are sought within one's social networks. Group conversation around felt-need topics provide opportunity to reflect on Scripture. As Scripture comes to be valued, seven questions are introduced to deepen a sense of community and begin to bring change to lives in that small group. These are:

Questions:	Purpose:
1. What are you thankful for?	(Q. 1–2) Deepen community (preparing to become a worshiping and praying community).
2. What challenge are you experiencing? Read a relevant passage. Ask one or more persons to retell it in their own words.	
3. What do you learn about God from this passage?	(Q. 3–5) Learn by discovery rather than from a "teacher." (The Holy Spirit is teacher through Scripture.)
4. What do you learn about Jesus from this passage? (If the passage is OT, this question may not be asked.)	
5. What do you learn about people or yourself in this passage?	
6. What will you do/apply from what you learned in this passage, this week? ("Can you be more specific?")	(Q. 6) Become a disciple, i.e., a doer of the Word (immediately apply without delay).
7. With whom will you share what you learned in this passage, this week?	(Q. 7) Become a disciple-maker. Share immediately. Group participants share with others what they are learning/ experiencing from God. Those who show interest are invited to host similar group conversations.

Discovery groups are lay-led. Formal training is not required, but group leaders are mentored. As other groups are formed, they are mentored, together with other lay group facilitators, in a leaders' group. Group members are encouraged to invite those they share with to form their own groups. Each group tries to birth three groups in the next generation (see www.FocusOnFruit.org).

Other disciple-making models are available, some of which appear in footnote 35 and the recommended reading list at the end of this book. More continue to be developed and refined.[20] Readers can also search the Internet for tools and examples. My suggestion, however, is to choose a model that has demonstrated fruitfulness and learn from it. This is generally preferable to selecting a theoretical model or selecting components from multiple models.

---

20 The version Carol and I personally train with and use is a slight adaptation built on the insights of others www.murraymoerman.com/2mission/disciple/7questions.asp.

Obedience Completes Knowledge

The lordship of Christ has suffered an unintended reverse in some evangelical circles, due to an aversion to legalism, or more accurately, a misunderstanding of legalism. While rightly emphasizing themes of faith and grace, obedience has fallen under the suspicion of being linked to the view that obedience brings salvation—i.e., legalism. Hopefully we need not reiterate the Reformation theme that obedience alone does not result in salvation. At the same time, we must affirm unequivocally that full and costly obedience is clearly required by Christ of those responding to the gospel (Mark 8:34ff).

In this, knowledge is no substitute. George Patterson shares his surprise as a young missionary in Honduras at a discovery regarding graduates from the Bible institute in which he taught. Some of his students clearly understood the doctrinal component they had been taught about the Lord's Supper. Yet for unknown reasons they did not invite believers to the Lord's Table in the congregations they planted. This gap led Patterson to highlight the importance of obedience among his students—not as a means of salvation, but as an expression of it—in what he called "The 7 Commands of Christ."[21] The church-planting process then began to grow rapidly, as obedience took its rightful place in the Christian life.

This call to obedience is certainly not unique to Patterson, but it became a needed corrective to the view that right knowledge of doctrine is adequate to please God. This view is still found in some evangelical circles eager to avoid the dangers of legalism.

Disciple-making movements painfully birthed in North India by David Watson enlarged the emphasis on the seven commands of Christ to all the Scriptures with application questions like "How will you live differently because of what you have learned in this passage?" and "With whom will you share what you have learned?" The result, even in previously unresponsive areas, was growth so great that the missionary's supervisors at first doubted written reports. David Garrison has since documented the broad importance of practical obedience for church-planting movements in his celebrated study by that name.[22]

The importance of obedience completing knowledge should not be a surprise. Jesus made clear his disappointment with the religious leaders of his day who held tightly to precise interpretations of Scripture while ignoring obedience to its basic tenets (Matt 23). Likewise, giving the correct answer to the Father is no substitute for doing his will (Matt 21:28ff). Does this take us to legalism? No, it takes us to kingdom fruitfulness.

---

21 https://vimeo.com/256747496. Obedience to Christ is more multifaceted, of course, but these seven biblical practices help set new believers in the right direction.

22 David Garrison, *Church Planting Movements* (Richmond, VA: International Mission Board, 1999).

> Find a way, within your ecclesiology, to encourage house churches to mature and multiply in their most vital form.

House Churches Function as Real Churches

This affirmation of house churches may draw pushback from some circles. My purpose, however, is less to make a theological or ecclesiological statement, though good arguments can be made, than to make an observation of practical fact—i.e., house churches, though less visible, exist everywhere and undeniably advance the gospel and function in many ways as they have from New Testament days.

In response, some denominations have redefined their ecclesiology to include house churches, particularly those being planted to advance the kingdom. An increasingly common definition of the church is "twelve believers gathering regularly for exposure to the Word of God, worship, fellowship in Christ, and his mission to the world." A discussion of leadership and sacraments, or ordinances, may follow.

Other traditions may not consider house groups to be churches, but call them "Christian communities" or the like—valuing them highly, but not engaging in questions of sacrament or ordination at this level.

In many parts of the world, there is no controversy or discussion in relation to ecclesiology. House churches are simply normal and are celebrated and resourced as contributors to frontline kingdom growth. House churches are naturally flexible structures in settings of persecution. House churches likewise make sense in settings where larger institutions are no longer widely trusted. In fact, many see house churches as a precursor, in some ways, of disciple-making movements (DMMs) and the new paradigm of the post-Constantinian church.[23]

House churches are also responding to urbanization. In challenging urban economics, larger buildings are becoming too expensive to multiply with any sense of "movement." In many ways it makes more sense to aim at a house-church network in every high-density apartment block. We must adjust creatively or miss large swaths of urban people.

Christward Movements Outside of the Organized Church

Interestingly, and somewhat controversially for parts of the traditional church, Christward movements are also developing outside the traditional church. By Christward, I mean movements toward Christ, even if not yet toward the organized church.

---

23 See "Constantinian" in the glossary.

In a Western nation I met a middle-aged man who identified himself as Muslim. He was living alone, but full of joy. I asked him about his story. He told me that after becoming a Christ follower, he was in hiding from his wife and sons who were seeking to kill him. I asked, "Are you part of a Christian community?" He replied, "No, I'm not a Christian."

Confused, I asked him to explain. He said, "I love Jesus. He loves me and gave his life for me. I'm forgiven and a new man. If my family finds me and kills me, I will go to heaven; I will give my life for Jesus because he gave his life for me. But I will always be Muslim." By *Muslim*, he meant "submitted to God"; and he believed himself to be more submitted to God now that he was following Christ than when he followed Islam.

Some view a person like this as in transition from his old faith to his new faith. That may be so. God knows the human heart. Yet this man, like many from his background, is happy to take the name of Christ but not to identify as a Christian. In many cases, this is to remain culturally Muslim or to avoid being tainted by Western values—or both.

Most Muslims who turn to Christ do not remain socially isolated for long. In studies of Christward movements outside the Constantinian church, even after several spiritual generations, Christ followers are typically orthodox in the essentials. Here are examples of the questions that were asked: Who is Jesus? What is the Bible? How are we saved? Responses were predominantly clear, straightforward, and orthodox.

The same questions were then asked of youth group members in a large evangelical church in the United States. Teen megachurch adherents were far less certain, clear, or orthodox. Linear studies in both cultures remain to be conducted.

There is likewise a movement to Christ in Hindu culture, whereby people come to acknowledge the deity of Christ and even the reality of the Trinity, and then begin to ignore the thirty-three million gods (demons) of Hinduism. Such people who recognize Christ as above the Hindu pantheon may not necessarily engage with the formal church, although they may freely discuss their faith and confidence in Christ with others. Perhaps the question is more one of ecclesiology (church) than of soteriology (salvation).

In both examples, Muslim and Hindu, those involved in such movements have access to and familiarity with the Bible. While confusing in some circles and controversial in others, such movement toward Christ outside of traditional avenues remains an opportunity and perhaps even a sign of the urgency of the Living God to call the unreached to himself in Christ.

Some point to what they see as a parallel in Western culture. Many Westerners are disconnected from the church, or touch it only at weddings and funerals, yet

> Keep clearly in view the end result of the disciples you want to make and the churches you want to plant.

claim to follow Jesus. There is a difference, however. In the West, such people tend to be leaving the church. In Islam and Hinduism, they are in a process away from their roots. May God place his people nearby to love them and assist them into the kingdom.

Keep the End in Mind

A final, most important reality to be refreshed as we set out is the transformational power of keeping the end in mind in planting churches to reach the lost.

Initially many church planters have only a single end in mind: survival. Survival is a great first goal. Without it all other ends become moot. However, the Lord of the harvest has much more in mind for the disciple-making process involved in his call to disciple the *ethne*.

As we plant churches we can focus and pray from before we plant, not first on gathering a group but on making disciples. Our goal is disciples who are well equipped to make their own disciples of Christ unto multiple spiritual generations. These disciples will hold deeply in their hearts from the beginning the purposeful transformation of micro and macro communities into kingdom culture impacting the world for good.

Is that too much to keep in view before getting underway? No. Only by doing so can we be assured we are aiming in the right direction and will be satisfied when we arrive.

Next Steps

- What insights in this chapter challenge you to change patterns of behavior in ministry?
- In what practical ways can you apply or adapt these insights into your context?
- Which of these items do you need to lift to the Lord in prayer?
- What will your next steps be?
- Are there teammates or others you need to talk to about these action steps?

NATIONAL IMPACT often begins locally or with a subset of the larger task. In fact, the principles involved in discipling a nation are in many ways the same as those engaging smaller units, and in the end each of the smaller units also needs to be engaged to disciple your nation. The important thing is to begin somewhere, and always with the end in view.

Lighthouses

The idea is simple—on your city block or floor of your high-rise, you can begin with prayer-walking, engaging your neighbors and acquaintances in conversation and offering prayer for personal needs.[24] You could begin with one high-rise apartment or six city blocks. As you pray, develop relationships, and watch God move graciously to invite people into his kingdom, you can invite those who respond to meet for prayer or Bible study. It's an ideal setting in which to begin a DMM process.

CHAPTER 3

Practical and Tactical Beginnings

"Great things are done by a series of small things brought together."—Vincent van Gogh

---

24 James H. Montgomery, *I'm Gonna Let It Shine: 10 Million Lighthouses to Go* (Pasadena, CA: William Carey Library, 2001).

Varying Covid-19 distancing regulations have arisen between the writing and publication of this book affecting social relationships. While regulations remain in effect, adaptations in social engagement may require creativity, yet the crisis has also made people in every nation more open to discuss, from a distance, deeper questions of faith and meaning. In this sense the pandemic has made the "soil" of human hearts more responsive to gospel "seed" (Mark 4).

Connecting Christians who see the value of this to saturate their neighborhoods also with lighthouses could be a next step. On each set of city blocks and in each high-rise apartment building, you could pray for and find Christians who will join you in praying for their neighbors. From time to time, you could gather those Christians who agree for encouragement and prayer. The boundaries of your calling could be a few blocks or a square kilometer. The principle is entirely scalable.

Or you could gather a team and go up a step by inviting members of your church and other churches in your city to "adopt" a city block, floor of an apartment, or an entire high-rise apartment building. You could map the adopted (and unadopted) city blocks and apartment buildings. Ask the Lord to connect your team with Christians living in unadopted blocks or apartment buildings to fill gaps in this local model of discipling your entire city. As gaps are filled and people are coming to Christ through incarnational relationships with disciples of Jesus, you can expand the geographic scope of your vision to nearby towns or cities. The principle is scalable. None of us is called to do it all.

A Key People Group

It may be that you feel called to serve a particular underserved people group in your neighborhood or city. These people may be migrants of a particular ethnicity or religious background. Often overlooked are those in prison, who are frequently responsive, and academics, local politicians, and bureaucrats—though often less responsive, are equally in need of Christ. Research may reveal an overlooked people group or subculture of another kind—for instance, those who are deaf, sight-impaired, or living with other physical or mental challenges.

One such church serves those with social anxieties and handicaps of other kinds in a "drive-in" setting, where participants stay in their cars to listen to a weekly gospel message of encouragement—sometimes gaining courage to come out of their vehicle as confidence that they are truly accepted and can be part of authentic spiritual community grows. The Internet provides many more such opportunities to engage persons living with specific handicaps.

As you focus on a needy key people group in your locale, these principles can be used to move from vision to mobilization:

- identifying the need through basic research,
- sharing the need with people who could help,
- praying together,
- forming a leadership team,
- setting goals and initial objectives,
- training and mobilizing the wider body of Christ,
- sharing fruitful models to encourage and give practical models to those working with you.

Often this may be in an area of personal release or background of struggle. For example, several years ago I met a pair of tattooed Russian men who looked like they lived in a gym. In reality, they were church planters focusing on those in the drug and alcohol communities who were decimated by their addictions. In each community, the movement they were a part of set up an expression of a drug and alcohol rehabilitation center. As participants came to Christ, their families were filled with wonder and became open to the power of the gospel, and a disciple-making community was formed. In every one of the three hundred churches planted, this link of life-transforming rehabilitation was central.

Whatever under served people group to which you may feel called, many of the principles of a national process may well apply on a smaller scale. The Lord of the harvest will clarify the right-sized scale and harvest focus of his calling for you.

City Reaching

To engage an entire city is another level of challenge, which, depending on the size of the city, may be approached best in small bites. Larger cities are composed of many suburbs and can be approached systematically, in unity with believers found in them. Excellent resource thinkers and practitioners can be drawn on. John Dawson was one of the first to write about the spiritual dynamics and practical strategies of collaborating to impact a city for Christ.[25] Ed Silvoso brings a warm and passionate South American ethos, steeped with compelling stories and deep biblical insights centered in the unity of the body of Christ.[26]

Many towns and cities already have goodwill and informal gatherings of church leaders to pray regularly and act together on occasion. Moving vision from smaller goals such as prayer-walking and joint worship to a broader and more challenging scope of discipling a city often needs only a warmhearted and administratively capable leader to engage in a long obedience in the same direction. You may be that leader. Ask the Lord if that is so.

State or Province

A national church-planting process will need state or province coordinators. If you serve in this way, you will be part of a national team and receive input and encouragement from them. You may also convene city coordinators if your national process works with such a network.

---

25 John Dawson, *Taking Our Cities for God* (Lake Mary, FL: Creation House, 1989).

26 Ed Silvoso, *That None Should Perish* (Ventura, CA: Regal Books, 1994).

If there is not yet a national process and you don't believe you are called to initiate it, you can begin with the same process outlined above for people groups, focusing on the geography and leaders of your state or province.

In the complexity of India, committed leaders are treating Uttar Pradesh as a nation for strategy purposes and, even so, dividing it into smaller parts to focus on one part at a time according to the current capacity of the partnership. Scalability is a vital strength of the DAWN strategy that can be too easily missed when we are tempted to be intimidated by large or complex populations.

If other state or province coordinators can be found, a national process may emerge. Whether this happens bottom-up or top-down is of no consequence. What matters is only that everyone gains equal opportunity to know Christ, whom to know is life eternal.

The point is this. There is no cultural or geographic setting in which mobilizing the whole church to disciple the whole nation (a people group or geographic focus) is inapplicable. There is no setting, challenging as yours may be, where the application of these principles is not worth your time, the best of your energies, and the strength of your life. Don't say that it can't be done, or that it can't be done here. It can. And you can lead or make a strategic contribution!

Next Steps
- Where do insights in this chapter challenge you to change patterns of behavior in ministry?
- What are practical ways you can apply or adapt these insights into your context?
- Which of these items do you need to lift to the Lord in prayer?
- What will your next steps be?
- Are there teammates or others you need to talk to about these action steps?

CHAPTER 4

Accelerants

IT HAS BEEN NOTED that the modern mission movement did not rise from the Reformation. Rather it arose from evangelical movements that grew out of the freedoms birthed by the Reformation, aided by Catholic efforts in some ways. In consequence, the church grew to about 33 percent of the global population by 1900. However, we haven't been able to break free from this percentage for more than a century.

The reasons for this "macro stall" include the secularization of the West, the persecution by Marxism and Islam, the renewal of nominal Christians to active disciples (good news), which does not yet increase the percentage of Christians globally, and some mission efforts in areas where "low-hanging fruit" (receptive populations) have now been harvested, requiring a move to more-challenging environments.

The time to seek out and implement insights that have shown more likely to increase the rate of church planting in the past, and to abandon those that have been shown unproductive or even counterproductive, is now. The strategy points above and accelerants that follow may be added to your own list.

Our vital stewardship is to apply what we learn from history and experience and not be content to repeat past patterns without reflection. My conviction is that we are responsible to use all means, which are not counter to the teaching of Jesus, to accelerate disciple-making and church planting. The "accelerants" which follow will not be new to some readers. For many the challenge will simply be engagement and application.

In this context, it is important to point out the Global Alliance for Church Multiplication (www.GACX.io) distinguishes helpfully between implementers and accelerators. Implementers are frontline disciple-makers and church planters. Accelerators are those who train, support, and pray for frontline disciple-makers and church planters. Both, of course, are important, but in right balance, because the kingdom can be advanced by frontline disciple-makers and church planters, but not by accelerators alone. Jesus, we remember, trained only implementers.

For this reason, I suggest that organizations who view their role as accelerators to add to their ministry direct frontline disciple-making and church planting. Even if difficult organizationally, members of an accelerator organization can learn how to make disciples personally by using a training tool like Zúme Training (https://zume.training) or by joining a church-planting team. It is vital that the link between accelerators and implementers remain close and personal.

Understand and Implement Church-Planting Movements

Church-planting movements (CPMs) are recognized more and more widely to be both simpler than conventional planting models and, for that reason, to multiply more easily. The fact that the West is used to more complex structures and practices than CPMs require hasn't yet been widely overcome. The need to do so is increasingly urgent.

Before church-planting movements came into our vocabulary, George Patterson, a mission worker in Honduras, began teaching obedience to seven of the basic commands of Jesus. These commands included repentance, baptism, sharing in the Lord's Supper, love, giving, prayer, and making other disciples. Those who obeyed became leaders in the simple churches that were formed. New churches were formed as new disciples obeying Jesus' basic commands were identified.[27]

As such models multiplied, David Garrison, who served in the International Mission Board, began in the 1990s to research cases of disciple-making CPMs emerging in the IMB's work. A seminal summary booklet produced "aha's" around the world.

---

27 George Patterson, "The Spontaneous Multiplication of Churches," in *Perspectives on the World Christian Movement: A Reader*, ed. Ralph D. Winter and Stephen C. Hawthorne (Pasadena, CA: William Carey Library, 1981, 1992).

Church planters resonated with the goal implied in Garrison's definition of a CPM: "A rapid and multiplicative increase of indigenous churches planting churches within a given people group or population segment."[28]

It is important to note four key concepts:

Rapid—CPMs plant new churches more quickly than the conventional expectation.

Multiplicative—The goal is no longer addition but multiplication.

Indigenous—New disciples and churches are formed within the local culture and do not depend on outside resources to multiply.

Churches planting churches—Ordinary disciples take the initiative to make disciples and start new churches, without waiting for professional clergy for this foundational work.

Garrison also found the following ten components common to all the church-planting movements he studied. The first time you read them, it's hard not to nod in agreement, murmuring, "Yes, of course. How could we have thought otherwise?"

Prayer—CPMs are undergirded and moved forward in a culture of prayer—urgent, frequent, individual and corporate, passionate, vital prayer.

Abundant gospel sowing—CPMs grow as believers share Christ constantly and by all possible means, including personal testimony, mass media, seeking persons of peace, etc.—giving people around them an opportunity, real and personal, to know Christ.

Intentional church planting—Church planting is planned and purposeful, normally several generations in advance.

Scriptural authority—The Bible is available in the heart language of the people and believers see and use it as the primary authority in their daily lives.

Local leadership—Local leaders, rather than well-intentioned outsiders, take responsibility and give direction to the movement.

Lay leadership—Believers take personal initiative and leadership in the movement. Lay leaders do not wait for professional clergy to do what God has called them as lay leaders to do personally.

Cell or house churches—Small, simple, easily led, and reproducible churches meet in homes or storefronts in low-budget alternatives to dedicated buildings.

Churches planting churches—Local churches take the initiative in planting daughter churches rather than looking to denominations or other organizations. Local churches believe reproduction is natural and that they do not need outside resources to obey Christ's command to make disciples.

---

28 David Garrison, *Church Planting Movements: How God Is Redeeming a Lost World* (Monument, CO: WIGTake Resources, 2004).

> Make a specific plan to start and stop each practice which needs to start or be stopped.

Rapid reproduction—Christians have a sense of urgency to reach their lost neighbors and plant churches as often as possible to make more disciples.

Healthy churches—Quantity and quality are viewed as mutually exclusive. Each church is responsible for healthy worship, evangelism, discipleship, ministry to others, and fellowship.

On the other hand, Garrison's study found obstacles that impede the beginning of a CPM or slow and eventually stop a CPM in progress. However well intentioned, the following common practices or expectations are counterproductive to growth:

- Place non-biblical requirements on new churches. These expectations may include the purchase of land and buildings, paid staff, legal documents, minimum number of believers, etc.
- Require new churches to abandon local culture and subculture in areas unrelated to basic morality (e.g., Ten Commandments).
- Justify the worldliness, immorality, or bad behavior of nominal Christians in the community.
- Use models (expensive buildings and labor-intensive programs) that require outside resources, staffing, or funding to maintain.
- Put extra-biblical requirements—theological school or extensive training programs—on leaders before they can do ministry.
- Require everything to take place in sequential order. This could, for example, not allow the disciple-making process to start before conversion to Christ.
- Plant sterile churches that do not expect or plan to plant daughter churches in the foreseeable future.
- Hold to a boilerplate strategy for church planting, avoiding flexibility to new opportunities outside of the box.

I'm sure you could add to this list. In fact, it's easier to add to such a list than to turn from familiar practices. As a friend and colleague from the Global South points out, conventional denominations will have the most difficulty with the paradigm shift. If this is true in parts of Africa, the challenges will be greater in the Northern and Western hemispheres where conventional ecclesiology is more deeply rooted.

More specifically, as British mission leader Martin Robinson says, "Particular attention needs to be paid in the West to means by which leaders can be recruited and trained fairly quickly. This is complex in a situation where the 'guild' operates to keep such leaders from being recognized in church structures." Yet every denomination must find ways to call out and affirm ordinary Christians to do extraordinary things in and for the kingdom. There can be no place for protectionism in Christ's kingdom.

As a friend serving in India points out, "When we see successful strategies resulting in new fellowships, we are unfolding and exposing God's plans and purposes for us in these times." Effective CPMs show God's ideas and means implemented. Nothing is more powerful than seeing the work of God before us.

Don't Exclude the Excluded Middle

Most people have had experiences they don't understand; in some cultures— largely secular—such experiences are ignored or spoken of only in private. Yet some of these experiences are direct responses to prayer and can be used powerfully to testify to the grace and power of the gospel.

Paul Hiebert was born to missionary parents in India, where he began reflecting on why Westerners who accept spiritual reality generally accept only a material world and a spiritual world, ignoring or denying invisible reality within our material world—such as angels, demons, and God's direct hand in our affairs. He called this omission from the biblical worldview the "excluded middle"; and with Fuller Theological Seminary colleague Charles Kraft, Hiebert sought to restore this aspect of the power of the gospel to the Western church.[29]

Testimonies abound for those with ears to hear and mouths to testify. During a visit to North India I heard testimonies of simple, and in some cases illiterate, workers sharing the gospel with "signs and wonders" following prayer for needs for healing and deliverance from demonic bondage. As in other parts of the world, these testimonies included resurrections from the dead.[30] Our world and our God is no different from that of the Scriptures.

A story from the Every Home for Christ (EHC) ministry demonstrates the depths of God's passion motivating the same kind of supernatural intervention in mission today with that in the book of Acts (e.g., chapter 10).

A worker was sharing gospel literature door to door in a Muslim city of about one million people. Some accepted his offer to learn about the gospel; others did not. At one home a young man looked at the literature and tore it up. He said, "Leave now—and don't ever return or I'll kill you." The worker left shaken, but remarkably continued on his route, with courage given from heaven, and then returned to his lodging.

The next morning a sharp rap took him to his door, where he was startled by the presence of the young man he had encountered the day before.

---

29 Charles H. Kraft, *Christianity with Power: Your Worldview and Your Experience of the Supernatural* (Eugene, OR: Wipf and Stock, 2005); and *Worldview for Christian Witness* (Pasadena, CA: William Carey Library, 2008).

30 These resurrections, or resuscitations, as some prefer to call them, are different from Jesus' resurrection in that he was raised by the Father and lives forever, while resuscitation miracles today, and in his day, are temporary in that those who receive them still die before the final resurrection. This, however, does not reduce the glory of God's power bringing about the healing as pointer and testimony to the gospel.

Ask God to move in powerful ways that are outside your insight and control.

In a wave of fear, the worker wondered if he had been followed by the man who wished him ill. However, the young man recounted his experience of the past night. As he slept, he was awakened by a hand on his shoulder, shaking him sharply. Since he was alone, he jumped up to defend himself, thinking an intruder wished him harm. But he saw no one. He heard, rather, a voice: "You have torn up the truth. Why have you rejected my gift of salvation?"

He responded, "I didn't know. What shall I do?"

The voice said: "Go to the man who offered you the literature and read it."

"I don't know where he is," countered the young man. The voice then told him the worker's address, and the young man made his way to the worker's home as soon as it was light. He turned to Christ and was discipled by the worker, and eventually did some similar gospel proclamation himself.[31]

The God who gave the young man the EHC worker's address is the same God who gave Cornelius Peter's address in Acts 10. God's purposes and power have not changed.

It's hard to imagine church planting without some sort of engagement with the "excluded middle." Elijah Khoza, a former witch doctor from Zululand, South Africa, once said, "Every new church robs Satan of turf. Every new fellowship of believers takes away his power." No wonder the one who resisted Jesus (Matthew 4), resists us also. For this we must be prepared.

As a young church planter, late one afternoon I received a mysterious phone call. I heard only one word, weakly uttered: "Help." Then the phone on the other end clattered down. I thought I recognized the voice, that of a young single mother who had recently started attending our church plant. I drove to her home and found the front door ajar. So I stepped in—and was immediately overwhelmed with a powerful sense of the presence of evil. I didn't have the courage to proceed alone, so I backed out.

I remembered that the young woman had mentioned a neighbor across the street who was a Christian. I went to the door of the house that I hoped she meant and knocked. I asked the woman who came to the door if she was a Christian, and she responded positively. I followed up with, "Are you the kind of Christian who believes in the power of the blood of Christ?" Again she responded positively, so I asked her to join me in ministering to the young mother who had called for help.

Reentering the door, now with prayer support, the sense of evil remained strong. I began praying aloud for the young woman who lay crumpled on

---

31 Dick Eastman, *Beyond Imagination: A Simple Plan to Save the World* (Ada, MI: Chosen Books, 1997), 191.

the floor near the phone. My prayer partner began to sing a worship song. After a few moments, the young woman rose and glared at me with fire in her eyes, demanding, "Stop praying! She'll get worse." It was clear that the demand in the third person did not come from the woman, but from an evil being, so I countered, "She will not get worse! In the name of Jesus Christ, I command you to leave her!"

After a few moments of continued prayer and spiritual warfare, the young woman returned to the floor, speaking like a young child. After an additional few minutes she sounded like a teen, and then like herself. The demon never returned, and the young woman became a testimony to the power of the gospel and a long-term intercessor in the church.

On another occasion, a young man who had sustained head injuries in a motorcycle accident two years earlier "dropped in" to a prayer meeting in which he was just interested in seeing a girl. I didn't know him, but engaged him in conversation, learning that he had many surgeries, treatments, and medications—without effect. His pain was constant, resulting also in poor sleep. When I offered to pray for him, he received group prayer without enthusiasm, walking out shortly afterward with slumped shoulders.

The next morning the young man saw me in traffic and motioned me to pull over. He was ecstatic, having no pain for the first time in two years and having slept soundly the whole night for the first time in memory. The pain never returned. In this case the young man didn't engage in our church community. The Lord seemingly heals with no motive greater than love.

Many readers will have similar or greater examples of the power of the risen Christ manifesting his kingdom among us. Abundant examples are available in many cultures, East and West, North and South. As in the Bible, such remarkable occurrences, amazingly, do not always result in faith or subsequently following Christ. Very frequently, however, they do, because they place people in connection with the Living God who is the author of salvation. It is wise, therefore, to look at the world, including the realm of the "excluded middle," with the same eyes with which we engage the Scriptures.

It is my conviction that we can expect God to act on behalf of those he seeks to deliver from the slavery of Satan, just as he delivered his people from slavery in Egypt. We can ask for Christ's intervention to counter the works of the devil (1 John 3:8), and we can expect hearts to be turned to the grace and power of the gospel. God's kingdom is expanded both among those who are drawn for the first time to the lordship of Christ and his salvation, as well as among believers who frequently enter more deeply into the awe of our God in worship and thanksgiving.

Prayer

Some will argue that prayer does not always lead to acceleration of disciple-making and church planting. And they would be right. The interaction of prayer and the purposes of God remains partially cloaked in ministry. However, no disciple-making or church-planting movement bringing many into the kingdom takes place without sustained prayer and spiritual warfare.

Many are aware of the national impact of a church that takes prayer as its' primary calling. Many first-time participants have been overwhelmed by the passion of prayer for the harvest in a South Korean stadium. Seldom has the gospel grown more rapidly in a nation than in South Korea in the twentieth century. The church in Indonesia is likewise passionate about sustained corporate prayer, with 24-7 prayer towers dotting the nation and the gospel advancing remarkably in its majority-Muslim environment.

David Garrison found a clear connection between prayer and church-planting movements.[32] T4T (Training for Trainers) and DMM cultures commonly manifest personal prayer that consistently exceeds an hour daily, and often two hours or more.

Do you know how much you pray? Is the question important enough to you to keep track for a month? It's not about guilt. It's about yearning for the harvest. It's about the worthiness of God's glory to be revealed in the nations.

A devoted team in a majority-Muslim nation has seen over five hundred thousand people turn to follow Isa al-Masih (Jesus), as small groups consistently pray for family and friends with whom they share the good news. Prayer is not the only thing the small groups do, but it is the consistent thing. From two weeks to three months before taking next steps in kingdom advance, workers expanding the edges of the movement frequently prayer-walk the area, asking the Lord of the harvest for fruit.

Although rightly restoring recognition of the authority of Scripture to the church, the Reformation, sadly, did not place equal value on prayer. As a result, perhaps, much church culture does not place as high a value on prayer as on exposition of the Word.

The 24-7 prayer movement provides a primary Western exception. And there are others. Books on prayer abound. If you are committed to prayer in principle but wrestle in practice, let me suggest reading just a few paragraphs from a classic book on prayer each day. Then ask the Lord how he wants you to pray and respond.[33] A bolder, if less sympathetic, approach is espoused by Korean prayer leader Grace Cho: "Open mouth. *Pray.*"

---

32 Garrison, *Church Planting Movements*, 33.

33 If uncertain where to start, consider the classics listed in the link in Appendix 7.

See and Aim for the Fourth Spiritual Generation Before You Start

We've recognized how good it is to see people and new disciple-making communities added to the kingdom. Addition is good, but multiplication is even more wonderful!

> Build into the first generation what will be needed by the fourth generation to multiply further.

A key question, then, is how we can keep a discipling-making or church-planting process continuing when we can no longer be involved. Many leaders, including myself, have seen a planting process continue while we've had opportunity for direct influence, only to stop when our leadership involvement ends. How can this be avoided?

The best way is to aim, from the beginning, for the fourth, yet unseen, spiritual generation. This is true whether we are making disciples who make disciples or planting churches that plant churches. Experience shows it takes at least four generations for the DNA involved in an ongoing chain of spiritual reproduction to continue should the initial impetus leaders no longer be present.

It may be that Paul had this in mind when speaking of himself relaying gospel truths to Timothy, who would relay it to faithful friends, who in turn would relay it on to others (2 Tim 2:2). A leader can often observe and influence the disciple-making or church-planting DNA for up to four generations. After that, if disciple-making DNA is healthy, the process is more likely to continue when the initial leader comes to the limits of his or her relational capacity.

This means, essentially, that we need to work backwards from that fourth spiritual generation before it exists, at least mentally. The question then is, "For a fourth-generation disciple or church plant to continue to reproduce when I'm no longer around, what do I need to model, teach, train, and evaluate now in the first generation?" Think long and hard about this, and continue to do so in every phase of the first generation.

One movement facilitator likes the image of dominoes. The first one needs a push. Those that follow represent people in the same social segment (*oikos* or other friends) also coming to fall in worship of the Savior. As multigenerational momentum is established, additional lines representing multiplication into new social networks continue the momentum. The domino image, familiar from the childhood of many, is a memory aid to the goal of mobilizing multiple streams from a single starting point through influencing key people in many social networks.[34]

---

34 See https://vimeo.com/channels/223181.

Figure 5: Dominoes (used with permission)

The key is to do now, in spiritual generations one and two, what will be needed in generations three and four to continue the process into generation five.

This involves, at minimum and from the beginning, principles and practices such as:

- Sustained prayer
- Ensuring every small group has a local leader and a local assistant leader
- Transition from leading a small group personally, to coaching others to lead the group within the first five sessions
- Aim to begin three groups birthed from each small group.
- Keep all ministry components so simple that new leaders, still in the harvest, will be able to engage early as commitment to Christ grows.
- Do not invite persons with potential interest into the group. Rather, begin the next generation group in the home of that open person. Multiplying new groups grows the kingdom more rapidly than enlarging existing groups.
- Aim to begin new groups not with an individual but with preexistent social networks (oikos)
- When you have five or more groups, cluster several small groups for local eldership oversight and occasional combined gatherings, but keep small groups the primary locus of pastoral care, Scripture-centered learning, and accountability.

Like rows of dominoes, our eyes are continually on forks in the road ahead where new branches of small groups can emerge. You can read more about the principles mentioned above at www.FocusOnFruit.org, where the book *Core Skills for Movement Leaders* is available. This team uses dominoes in video training for android phones on https://vimeo.com/channels/223181.

Other practitioners have developed similar tools and trainings. The following is a partial list:[35]

---

35 https://www.gcpn.info/resources/Comparing_CPM_factors_by_7_practitioners.pdf.

- Steve Addison—www.movements.net
- Robby Butler—www.missionfrontiers.org/pdfs/33-3.pdf
- David Garrison—www.churchplantingmovements.com
- Dwight Marable—www.missions.com
- Neill Mims & Bill Smith—http://www.missionfrontiers.org/pdfs/33-2.pdf
- Curtis Sergeant—www.gcpn.info/resources/Curtis_Sergeant_CPM.pdf
- David Watson—No single website; google for many pages on various sites.

Many new movement leaders are emerging. The "Disciple-Making" section of the reading list at the end of this book recommends further resources.

The best way to begin is by jumping in! An excellent way to do so practically is by benefiting from the wisdom and experience of friends like those who have developed the Zúme Project (https://zumeproject.com). *Zume* is the New Testament term for *leaven* (Luke 13:20–21). The advantage is that all resources are online, providing tools both for the personal spiritual disciplines foundational to disciple-making as well as for those who become disciples, enabling them to continue the disciple-making process. Start a group yourself and learn as you go. Just-in-time learning-while-doing is the core of Jesus' method.

The decision to jump in is vital, because understanding the concepts themselves is not essentially difficult. Implementation, however, does not naturally follow. Field experience shows that fruit comes only to pragmatic "doer-leaders."

Why the difficulty to implement cognitively simple concepts? For many in the established church, it is because of the paradigm shifts involved. For professionals, it is reinterpreting honor in the conventional system, which values leaders of large churches, and reframing finance that supports it, since movements normally finance mission rather than clergy. In fact, the movement is a lay movement.

Other paradigm shifts include the shift from assuming:

- the necessity of church buildings for a permanent Christian community
- the need to evangelize, before we disciple, a potential convert
- we should gather a crowd, rather than focusing on a small group of individuals—in depth (start slow to go far)
- we should focus on specially trained people, rather than very ordinary people still in the harvest
- the lost should be taught by educated people, rather than allowing even unsaved people to facilitate discovery conversations firmly centered in Scripture
- knowledge to be central, to focusing first on those willing to be obedient.[36]

---

36 Listen to audio commentary from David Watson on twenty "counter-intuitives" of small group multiplication strategy: http://www.murraymoerman.com/3downloads/cpm.asp.

Movements

When multiple streams of four-generation "dominoes" emerge, continuing to multiply into increasing numbers of streams, we can celebrate a movement! The fact is, traditional program-based, classroom-style church planting is good and should continue, but it has not kept up with world population growth. Figure 6 depicts this rate of world population growth by region. [37]

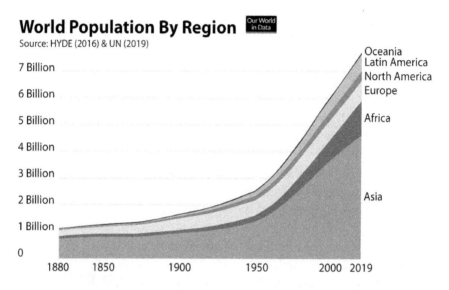

Figure 6: World Population by Region (used with permission)

As the world population curve has become steeper in our lifetime, traditional models of church planting, even in best-case scenarios, barely keep up and often do not. Only movements have shown the ability to introduce people to Christ at rates exceeding population growth.

A movement is commonly defined as one thousand persons who have come to Christ within multiple disciple-making streams and extending to four or more spiritual generations. When a disciple-making team has seen four streams of four generations and one hundred micro-churches, hope is high that with much prayer and careful coaching the movement can grow to many thousands of believers, as many movements have. Some have grown to a half-million disciples, normally composed of house churches gathering from time to time in larger clusters for public worship. Interestingly, where the primary focus shifts from nurturing and coaching small-group multiplication to gathering people into larger public groups, growth of the movement slows or even stops.

---

37 https://ourworldindata.org/world-population-growth.

To keep a movement growing, great care is required to diligently track emerging leaders and equip them to identify and train apprentice leaders, deal with pastoral needs, and function as a living, growing network. Many best practices continue to emerge on the anvil of field experience. Many of these aren't novel, but simply the application of practical spiritual disciplines—including prayer, Scripture, training, abundant seed-sowing, coaching, mentoring, leadership retreats, record-keeping (of groups, leaders, and finances)—to nurturing movement health and growth.

Movements do not presume the use of any single training tool. Disciple-making through multiple streams in multiple generations can emerge by applying the principles of CPM and DMM using the training tools of T4T, DBS, Zúme, 4 Fields, and others. The key is to focus on the underlying biblical principles of multiplying kingdom movements.[38] Central to these are the intention to make every follower of Christ a reproducing disciple rather than merely a convert.

A "Two Rail" Approach

Can commitment to a movement philosophy of ministry intersect fruitfully with the traditional church? Many have noted the dramatic contrast in approach between the conventional "temple church" model (as South American believers sometimes call it) and the CPM/DMM paradigm. Leaders on every continent have attempted to transition from a conventional Constantinian model to various forms of CPM, DMM, or other small-group multiplication models. Doing so has proven difficult. Inertia is strong. Sadly, some have even inadvertently damaged the church they sought to transition in the process.

Better is what some have called a "two rail" approach. The image of two rails comes from a set of train tracks, close but never merging.

One rail is the conventional church. It continues largely as it has. Its members may be aware of the "second rail" and perhaps have even been invited to participate. In high-security contexts it may be wise for the rank and file of the "above ground" church to be unaware of the "underground" rail for the purposes of plausible deniability. The leader of the conventional church, however, is aware of and deeply desirous for the success of the "second rail" church. In some cases, the conventional church leader even signs an agreement with workers initiating or coaching the "second rail" church, agreeing on separation principle. Occasionally, the conventional church leader will even claim responsibility for the small groups should one be discovered by government authorities, sacrificing the smaller "above ground" church for the larger "underground" church. In four case

---

38 Since movements have many proponents (and requisite critics) there is debate about best principles and practices. Overall, however, there is remarkable convergence. A recent (2020) multi-agency team outlines principles broadly: https://docs.google.com/document/d/1ps b6fbKIPAaik2QsyFpkdCgVtKzzHatjGZYp7B35VO8/edit. A great deal can also be learned by searching the Internet for "disciple making movement principles."

studies, the conventional church's second rail tended to grow to be four times the size of the "above ground" church in four years.

The second rail is typically a version of CPM/DMM or other small-group multiplication strategy. It will need to be led by someone other than the leader(s) of the "above ground" church to develop fully. It is difficult for leaders to give their best to the vision of both models at once.[39]

Seminaries may also choose to train for conventional church leadership or for underground church leadership, or develop separate training rails for their students. In one Muslim-majority nation a small seminary began training second rail students several years ago. All those students have now seen third spiritual-generation believers. Other students have chosen to "switch rails," with 40 percent of active students now using a CPM/DMM model. In a recent quarter the total number of new believers reached four thousand (all Muslims), and this quarter the number reached seven thousand. A more established seminary in the same nation has found it difficult to train students for ministry in both rails at the same time. As a result of not separating the rails more clearly, less fruit has developed.

Benefit Fully from the Power and Encouragement of Mentoring

Research has shown that coaching benefits us all, helping us do what we intend to do. Ed Stetzer is widely quoted as saying, "Church planters who met with a mentor/coach weekly led churches that were more than twice the size of churches whose planters did not have a coach."[40]

Some cultures find the concept of coaching too impersonal or performance-oriented, preferring the more relational and familial concept of uncle. The helping role of a mentor may be more widely acceptable.

If our intention is to follow the calling of God on our lives, it is worth doing so to the best of our ability and with all the strength God gives us (Col 1:29), and a mentor can help. There are few highly effective leaders who do not benefit significantly from the insights, questions, and perspective of a mentor or coach on an ongoing basis. Some even have several—one helping with work or ministry, another to help more personally with emotional health, keeping marriage and family life balanced, and progress to deeper spiritual formation to end well.

Looking back, I've had at least three mentors, the first being a kind-hearted college professor who took it upon himself to invest in me through my four years at that school. He remained a friend until his death, as did his wife after his death.

In my early years as a church planter, a semiretired businessman, who was also committed to the success of the church, invited me to his home weekly.

---

39 Roy Moran attempted to do both. *Spent Matches: Igniting the Signal Fire for the Spiritually Dissatisfied* (Nashville: Thomas Nelson, 2015).

40 www.citytocitymiami.com/church-planter-coaching.

He would ask about the issues I was facing, my plans to resolve the problem, and how I intended to go about the needed changes. He certainly wasn't uncomfortable questioning me to make sure I had thought and prayed each matter through. He critiqued my preaching and prayed for me without fail. He wanted me to be the best I could be in the Lord's strength. The church wouldn't have come to the level of success and maturity we experienced without him.

How are you benefiting from your mentor or coach? Who are you investing in for the kingdom?

In a later stage of ministry, the man I had reported to organizationally for years became a friend in the process; and after our organizational roles changed, we remained friends and prayer partners as he continued to mentor me. He was trained and gifted in such a way that he could have charged for his services. While in fact many leaders do pay to benefit from another person's wisdom and experience, which is a legitimate service, mentors often give from their hearts.

Mentors in different stages of life and ministry provide a variety of gifts, and leaders who are serious about following the Lord shouldn't be without a mentor for long.

Encourage Movements to Disciple People Groups to Their Fringes

Who is best equipped to disciple the people group of which they are a part? The answer would appear to be a truism: those who are already part of the people group and do not leave it when they become followers of Christ.

Yet missionaries in many settings continue to invite new believers from the people group in which they are working to become part of a church composed of the people group of the missionary. This practice causes the new believer to be viewed with suspicion by their people group of origin and the gospel to be viewed as a foreign entity.

Donald McGavran was a missionary in India when he argued that it is far better to encourage new believers to stay in their family, tribe, or people group and be an indigenous witness to the resurrection of Christ from within. There they should form a church as a "homogeneous" group rather than leave their social circle to join the church of the missionary. They can disciple their own people group to Christ more effectively than can the missionary from a different people group. The task of the missionary rather is to identify new people groups and equip new believers in them to disciple their own people group to its fringes. The missionary is primarily a resource person as coach and support person.[41]

---

41 Donald A. McGavran, *Bridges of God: A Study in the Strategy of Missions* (Eugene, OR: Wipf and Stock, 2005), which has been condensed into an article in *Perspectives on the World Christian Movement*, 335.

Identify unreached and least-reached people groups in your nation to disciple them to their fringes.

During Lausanne '74, Dr. Ralph Winter called the global missions community to give priority to the large number of people groups remaining unengaged with the gospel, focusing particularly on that part of the world which came to be known as the 10-40 Window. This has brought great advances in recent decades, as prayer and church-planting efforts have become more sharply focused, although this remains a needed activity.

It is likely that your country has "unreached" people groups (less than 2 percent evangelical), or even "unengaged" people groups (no churches or planting underway), and certainly many "least-reached" people groups (less than 5 percent evangelical).[42] It is vital that disciple-making movements within a national church-planting process give priority effort to those with the least access to the gospel.

We need to recognize, however, that these categories must not become either/ or thinking. Using France as an example, there are several unreached people groups in France and in most nations of the Francophone, yet most of the traditional indigenous French population remains unengaged with the gospel. Where should the focus of the national church-planting process be in that nation? The answer is both, because this is a polarity to be managed rather than a decision to be made. Within a national church-planting process, people and organizations with unwavering commitment to establish disciple-making communities within comparatively smaller unreached people groups—for example, Muslims— must be found. At the same time, the Lord of the harvest passionately loves the traditional indigenous French population who are in the majority. Who does he love most? Need I ask?

As the gospel is established in each people group in our nation, it is wise to encourage followers of Christ within that people group to disciple its members to the fringes. If believers in each people group do so, the task to which we've been called will be completed more quickly in our nation than if we ignore people group realities.

Some counter that the vision of Christ's kingdom as depicted in Revelation 5:9 praises God that he has purchased by Christ's blood those from "every tribe and

---

42 These terms were first proposed by Ralph Winter. See Ralph D. Winter, and Bruce A Koch. "Finishing the Task" in *Perspectives on the World Christian Movement*, 4th ed. (Pasadena, CA: William Carey Library, 2009), 539. Definitions of these important terms will likely continue to be discussed. Refinement and current standards are available from https://joshuaproject. net/global/progress. For an excellent article on the history of these important terms, see Dave Datema, "Defining 'Unreached': A Short History," *International Journal of Frontier Missiology*, 33:2 (Summer 2016), https://www.ijfm.org/PDFs_IJFM/33_2_PDFs/IJFM_33_2-Datema.pdf.

language and people and nation" (NIV) to worship in glory. This is wonderfully true and the ultimate end toward which, by God's grace, we move with certainty. In anticipation and foretaste of that glorious day, many multiethnic churches have been formed globally. May their tribe increase! Unfortunately, some proponents of multiethnic churches charge that churches not exhibiting this diversity are racist. This is unhelpful for two reasons. First, it is often not true. If true, of course, those churches must repent. Second, it makes multiethnic churches a standard, which in fact then becomes a barrier to many who are not yet in Christ. Far better to allow such people to come to Christ within their own people group, then at a later point to become part of a multiethnic church as they come to believe this to be God's calling.

In summary, the gospel moves most effectively along people group lines. At the same time, and without either/or thinking, we must cross people group lines at every point necessary to begin a church-planting movement within a people group lacking adequate Christward movements.

Social Media as a Means of Multiplying Virtual Disciple-Making Communities

There is little debate about the power of social media to speed ideas—both those which are true and helpful and those which are false and unhelpful—across their nation and around the world. You may have noticed, for instance, in response to "Thank you," how quickly "You're welcome" became "No problem" in many cultures. While many prefer the more gracious "You're welcome," there is little doubt that the change could have been made as broadly and quickly without social media.

Prior to COVID-19 there was, however, debate in the Christian community about whether "virtual churches" formed in this dynamic environment were real churches. No more! Almost every congregation with the means to do so has gone virtual with many celebrating wider participation as people anywhere in the world are able to join in. Particularly small congregations report growth as those who had moved to other communities reengaged. More significantly, Muslims and those of other faith communities who would not have visited a church publicly, were able to "sit in" and experience Christian worship, teaching, and community in the congregation of their choice, while retaining anonymity. I suspect when COVID-19 is over most congregations will retain a virtual ministry in addition to returning to physical gatherings.

Prior to COVID-19, an expat worker friend developed a simple website seeking to engage adherents of a specific religious group. Online mentoring of adherents of the religious group resulted in new disciples, additional ideas and resources were added to the site, and intercessors from abroad added sustained, concerted prayer. Within a few years, the number of people in the religious group exploring and enquiring about Christ increased to the point that the server had to be upgraded several times at the request of the Internet service provider.

Others are training small groups for disciple-making,[43] apologetics, online evangelism, resourcing chat rooms, and providing global access to gospel material. Don't miss "Media to Movement" resources such as Kingdom Training for virtual ministry.

While the verdict may still be out whether those coming to Christ by means of the Internet will grow, mature, and become part of face-to-face disciple-making communities, efforts must continue. Your national church-planting process should encourage social media savvy friends, and now, in light of COVID-19, every congregation and ministry should connect and strengthen efforts in your nation toward a tipping point to Christ.

Conclusion

Each of these accelerants make significant contributions to kingdom growth and are to be celebrated as such. Heaven cheers us on! Each stream and applied insight also contributes to the day when individuals in every social network in the nation will have encountered our glorious King of kings and Lord of lords.

As we progress in making and multiplying disciples, there comes a time to overview the nation as a comprehensive whole. What has been the net effect of efforts within it to reproduce disciple-making communities? What gaps remain? How can these gaps collaboratively, and perhaps more strategically, be filled so that all ethnic, geographic, and cultural spaces are engaged with the good news of Jesus Christ? Is it possible to even try?

National processes to mobilize the "whole church" to disciple the "whole nation" are challenging to facilitate. My friend and colleague, Russ Mitchell, recently surveyed over one hundred leaders with recent or current experience in this process, correlating responses with the degree of success they experienced. The next chapter, written by Russ, shares valuable insights that he discovered in the process.

Next Steps
- Reflect on a key point in this chapter that stood out to you.
- What are some practical ways that you can apply or adapt this point or other insights into your context?
- Which of these points do you need to lift up to the Lord in prayer?
- What will your next steps be?
- Are there teammates or others you need to talk to about these action steps?

---

43 See https://zumeproject.com.

CHAPTER 5

A Study in Nationwide Disciple-Making Processes

By Russ Mitchell

HISTORY SHOWS that not all saturation church-planting or disciple-making processes produce equal fruit. What makes the difference? If we have limited resources, which emphases are most fruitful?

These are some of the questions posed at the beginning of the 2017 National Church Planting Processes Survey. This study aimed at assessing the effectiveness of the whole-nation disciple-making process, sometimes referred to as saturation church planting, or DAWN initiatives. Seven significant insights emerged from the analysis of participant responses: insights that, when acted upon, can guide the development of effective nationwide disciple-making processes.[44]

The Background of this Study

DAWN is an acronym for "Disciple A Whole Nation." Most readers will associate this phrase with Matthew 28:19–20, the Great Commission. In a nutshell, "DAWN aims at mobilizing the whole body of Christ in whole countries in a determined effort to complete the Great Commission in that country by

"Numbers have an important story to tell. They rely on you to give them a voice."
—Stephen Few

---

44 In two papers offered elsewhere, I further develop ways that insights from this research help advance national church-planting processes. The first was shared at a gathering of international church-planting catalysts in Berlin, Germany (February 2018), entitled "DAWN 2.0," which is available at http://ocresearch. info/sites/default/files/DAWN%202.0.pdf. Also see "The Vital Role of Church Leadership in Advancing a National Church Planting Process," presented at the eighth Lausanne International Researchers' Conference, in Nairobi, Kenya, May 2018. See Appendix 7 for a link to download this paper.

working toward the goal of providing an evangelical congregation for every village and neighborhood of every class, kind, and condition of people in the whole country."[45]

DAWN grew out of Jim Montgomery's missionary work in the Philippines with Overseas Crusades, now known as OC International or One Challenge—the same organization that I serve with today. In the 1970s, Montgomery played a key role in motivating and mobilizing Philippine church leaders to set a goal of establishing an evangelizing congregation in every small community of that country by the year 2000. It "dawned" on Montgomery that the best way to disciple the whole nation of the Philippines would be to establish a "witnessing cell of believers" in every population center in the country.[46] Projections estimated that this would require fifty thousand churches, quite an audacious goal when there were roughly five thousand evangelical churches in the country! But by 2000, the Philippines had more than fifty thousand evangelical churches, although not every small community had a witnessing church.

The DAWN vision, birthed in the Philippines, developed into a strategy for world evangelization. In 1985, Montgomery founded Dawn Ministries to promote national church-planting processes in other nations. Montgomery's book, *DAWN 2000: 7 Million Churches to Go*, published in 1989, was key in spreading the vision globally. DAWN became perhaps the most significant world evangelism strategy during the final decade of the twentieth century, as DAWN initiatives became a significant part of the AD2000 & Beyond Movement and were championed by the Lausanne Movement and the World Evangelical Association.

Although DAWN initiatives were launched in approximately 150 countries,[47] a scholarly review of the effectiveness of these initiatives on a global scale has yet to surface. So, beginning in June 2017, at the invitation of Murray Moerman, who has written this book to commemorate the thirtieth anniversary of the publication of *DAWN 2000*, I began this first of its kind multinational study on the effectiveness of whole-nation church-planting initiatives.

The 2017 National Church-Planting Process Survey

A twenty-one-question online survey was created to gather data for this study.[48] A goal was set to have input from 100 persons with significant experience in

---

45 Jim Montgomery, *DAWN 2000: 7 Million Churches to Go* (Pasadena, CA: William Carey Library, 1989), 12.

46 Ibid., 52.

47 Steve Steele, "A Case Study in Cooperative Evangelism: The Dawn Model," a paper presented at the Billy Graham Round Table of Evangelism at Wheaton College, 2002, 1. On page 5 Steele mentions 155 countries. It is claimed that 80 percent of the world's population lived in countries where DAWN initiatives were active.

48 https://ocresearch.info/sites/default/files/DAWN%202.0.pdf, appendix 2.

advancing national church-planting projects—a goal that was exceeded, as 117 people participated in the survey, reporting on approximately sixty countries.

The first four survey questions gathered relevant information about the respondent's church-planting role and experience. The key question of this study asked, "What would you consider to be one or two of the most significant lessons (positive or negative) that you have discovered about facilitating a national church planting process?" Responses to this question provided numerous, rich insights.

The rest of the survey focused on the country where the respondent had the most significant experience. Participants were first asked to rate the effectiveness of the national church-planting process for the country of their *most significant experience*. Thirteen additional questions evaluated how well the DAWN strategy was implemented in the country of the respondent's *most significant involvement*. Twelve of the questions were based on the eight-point DAWN strategy elaborated in Montgomery's subsequent book, *Then the End Will Come*,[49] which he considers "the ideal DAWN strategy."[50] An additional question solicited information about parachurch organizations that may have made significant contributions to national church-planting processes.

I consider the following seven insights that emerged from the evaluation of survey responses to be the most significant. The first three followed from statistical analysis; the rest emerged from responses to the key question.

Seven Insights from the 2017 National Church-Planting Process Survey

1. The "ideal" DAWN strategy is effective.

This study's findings support the generalization that the better a country implements the "ideal" DAWN strategy, the greater the effectiveness of the national church-planting process.

Figure 7, on the next page, correlates each respondent's effectiveness score for the country of his or her most significant involvement with the average of the thirteen DAWN process variables studied. One hundred and ten cases are plotted here.[51] The dots represent the intersection of each respondent's evaluation of effectiveness of the national process on the Y axis, and the average score of all the DAWN process variables on the X axis.

---

49 Jim Montgomery, *Then the End Shall Come* (Pasadena, CA: William Carey Library, 1996), 63–73.

50 Montgomery, 63. This eight-point framework strategy provides a more workable theoretical basis for this survey than the "13 Steps to a Successful Growth Program" for denominations outlined in *DAWN 2000* (211–19) or the twelve "strategy ingredients" (170–71).

51 Although 117 persons participated in the survey, 3 did not complete the evaluation section of the survey. It was determined that 4 other participants also did not provide reliable data, either because directions were not followed or understood (English as a second language issues), or that outlier scores were not justifiable based on the explanation provided or tests for internal consistency.

"What would you consider to be one or two of the most significant lessons (positive or negative) that you've discovered about facilitating a national church planting process?"

The trend line indicates that the better a country implements the ideal DAWN strategy, the greater the effectiveness of the national church-planting process.

While the overall trend shows that the better the DAWN strategy is implemented, the greater the effectiveness of the nationwide church-planting process, the graph also shows outliers or exceptions to this generalization. This may raise questions for some: Is it necessary to implement all elements of the DAWN strategy? Are there shortcuts? Why did the strategy not seem to work in some cases?

Clearly there are no shortcuts. Further analysis shows that *every element of the DAWN strategy studied benefited the national process at some point.* No factor was shown to be extraneous. However, analysis also indicated that the elements of the ideal DAWN strategy do not make an equal contribution to overall effectiveness.

NCPP Outcomes and Process Compared

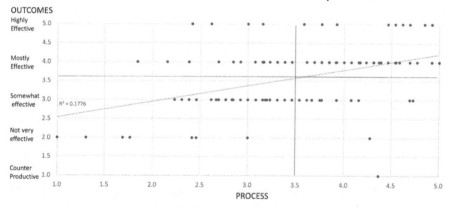

Figure 7: Plotting Effectiveness and Process Scores (used with permission)

It is useful to call to mind the Pareto, or "80–20 principle," which postulates that for many events 80 percent of the effects generally come from 20 percent of the causes. This implies that only two or three of the thirteen elements studied may be responsible for 80 percent of the results. Indeed, this was found to be so, as only two elements of the ideal DAWN strategy have a statistically significant relationship to an effective national church-planting process: "national leaders" and "seminars and consultations." These two elements largely account for the difference between higher and lower performing countries. The following points focus on these two significant factors.

2. "National leaders" is the most significant factor for developing a whole-nation church-planting process.

National leadership is *the most statistically significant factor contributing to the effectiveness of a national church-planting process*—making twice the contribution to the effectiveness of the nationwide process as the second-most identified, "seminars and consultations." When comparing more effective national processes with those that are less effective, national leaders was the highest-rated factor in the more effective group.

Upon analyzing the responses of survey participants to the key question, it was surprising to find that the predominate theme pertained to *leadership*. This was the most frequently mentioned positive factor, as well as the most frequently identified negative factor that hinders church planting.

It appears that developing visionary, competent, courageous leadership with Christlike character is the most significant factor contributing to an effective national process. On the other hand, survey participants pointed out that poor leadership—at national, denominational, or local levels—presents a significant hinderance to effective disciple-making.

Multiple field workers mentioned "buy-in" by church leadership as a key factor for advancing a national church-planting process. This is consistent with what evangelical leaders have pointed out. Charles Spurgeon may have been first to assert the church to be the world's hope.[52] Yet as John Maxwell declares, "Everything rises and falls on leadership." When it comes to advancing a national church-planting process, national leadership is the key. *To advance a whole-nation disciple-making process, focus on developing church leadership.*

3. "Seminars and consultations" is the second-most significant factor contributing to an effective nationwide disciple-making process.

The second statistically significant element of the ideal DAWN strategy is seminars and consultations. Seminars and consultations provide more than just instruction. In Montgomery's thought, the aim of these events is to motivate, train, and mobilize denominational leaders, organizational leaders, local pastors, and Christian workers to develop and implement their own church-planting action plans.

Several survey participants expressed that seminars and consultations should not just be national events, but ought to be held in different regions of a country, and preferably at the local level. Countries with an effective national process did a better job at holding seminars and consultations throughout the country over an extended period.

---

52 www.ccel.org/ccel/spurgeon/sermons51.xxxvii.html.

Focusing attention upon these two critical factors, without omitting the other elements of the ideal DAWN strategy, leads to a more effective nationwide disciple-making process.[53]

4. Relationships are foundational to a fruitful national process.

Now we turn to the insights gleaned from responses to the open-ended key question, "What would you consider to be one or two of the most significant lessons (positive or negative) that you have discovered about facilitating a national church planting process?" Under point two, it was already reported that leadership was the most frequently mentioned theme. The second-most frequent theme pertains to *relationships*, which are viewed as foundational. Specifically mentioned were relationships between expatriate workers and national leaders, as well as relationships between denominational leaders and local pastors. Also, broader relational concepts such as unity, networking, partnerships, and teamwork fit here, as do mentoring and coaching. Several participants spoke at length about the value that coaching and mentoring bring to the process, especially for developing leaders and training church planters.

Good relationships are foundational to a fruitful national process. As my friend Ron Anderson, Lausanne Catalyst for Church Planting, says "It is relationships that propel church planting." Those advancing national church-planting processes will devote significant time to *developing healthy networks of relationships*. This could well be the first step to developing a national process.

5. Refine the process.

Several themes that surfaced in analyzing the open-ended key question—contextualization, fruitful practices, systems, disciple-making, and multiplication—group nicely under the broader theme of "refinements." We do well to consider the ideal DAWN strategy as a broad framework, wherein local practitioners are encouraged to refine and adapt the disciple-making process for their ministry context. Montgomery himself expected that field workers would contextualize the disciple-making process in each context, be it a local, regional, people group, or national basis. Flexibility in methodology need not compromise vision. Therefore, it would be improper to uncritically view or implement DAWN as a "one size fits all" or "standard solution strategy."[54]

Our survey shows that practitioners continue to contextualize and refine the disciple-making process. Several respondents pointed out that best practices may change over time, as the society and culture change. Christian leadership

---

53 Further statistical analysis shows that all thirteen variables in the study benefit the national process at some point. No factor was shown to be extraneous or needless.

54 See Edward Dayton and David Fraser's chapter on "Strategy" in *Perspectives on the World Christian Movement*, 569–72.

consultant Bobb Biehl reminds us, "Never recreate the wheel—but never stop refining the tire."[55] Likewise, never stop refining the whole-nation disciple-making process.

Consider the ideal DAWN strategy as a broad framework wherein local practitioners are encouraged to refine and adapt the disciple-making process for their ministry context.

6. *Think critically about what it is going to take to disciple the whole nation.*

Goals are essential to the ideal DAWN strategy. Normally these are thought of as numerical goals for church planting at a national, denominational, or organizational level. However, other goals have been included—for example, the mobilization of cross-cultural workers.

Survey responses show practitioners continue to wrestle with "What's it going to take?" to disciple a whole nation. Some participants in this study indicated uneasiness with merely championing a national goal for church planting. Several pointed out that in the countries where the numerical church planting goal was met—for example the Philippines—the more challenging church-planting goal of *saturation* was not met, as there are still many communities, neighborhoods, and ethnic groups without a witnessing church. Others observed that although more churches were started in their contexts, obedient disciples were not made. Still other participants expressed their disappointment that starting more churches did not result in significant kingdom impact in their communities or country.

Two participants who served with Dawn Ministries shared at length goals for a national process. They proposed that the harvest of souls alone through saturation church planting is insufficient. Churches also need to be healthy, and signs of kingdom transformation should be evident in communities and entire countries. Thus, a triad of goals was proposed for national processes: harvest, health, and holism.

These diverse comments point out that merely planting a particular number of churches in a country, while necessary, is not the end goal. Montgomery certainly understood that the national church-planting goal was not the end. He liked to use the term *penultimate* in describing DAWN national church-planting goals.

To the DAWN way of thinking, they will then have reached the penultimate measurable goal for the discipling of a whole nation and all its people groups. Everyone will be within easy access of a cell of believers who are incarnating—although imperfectly—the Lord Jesus Christ.[56]

---

55 Bobb Biehl, *Masterplanning* (Aylen Publishing, 1997), 152.

56 Montgomery, *DAWN 2000*, 52.

Everyone now has a church within easy access both in a practical as well as cultural sense where he or she can attend and be further trained in discipleship should he or she become a believer. The *penultimate* step for making a disciple of every "nation" in a country has been reached. In a nutshell, that is what DAWN is all about.[57]

So then, we ought to view church planting as necessary but insufficient to disciple a whole nation. Church planting alone will not adequately fulfill the Great Commission—but the Great Commission will not be fulfilled apart from church planting. Disciples will not be made, and communities will not be transformed, without establishing witnessing cells of believers within every segment of society. Church planting is an essential means to a discipled nation. Therefore, setting goals for church planting—or better, saturation—is entirely appropriate. So continue to think critically about "What's it going to take?" to disciple the whole nation and set appropriate goals.

Realizing that church planting is not the end goal prepares us for the long-term process of discipling the whole nation and leads to the final significant insight from this study.

7. Success requires a long obedience in the same direction.

One tenth of the survey's participants shared a lesson related to this theme: Developing a national church-planting process requires a long obedience in the same direction.[58] As the experience in the Philippines shows, discipling a whole nation is a long process. The initial objective involved in a process of over twenty-five years continues still today, with updated goals, now into its fourth decade.

A shortcoming of some national church-planting processes is that they viewed the task as a sprint rather than a marathon, and consequently failed to keep the momentum going. In some cases, the proposed national church-planting goal was met and the process stopped—even though the entire nation was not fully discipled. Others passed a milestone year—for example, the AD2000 & Beyond Movement—and the initiative ceased. The focus, the energy, and the collaboration were left to dissipate. It seems that Montgomery's counsel, "Make new plans," was forgotten.[59] So do not stop a national process until the task is finished. "One way to keep momentum going," writes journalist Michael Korda, "is to have constantly greater goals." The vision of a discipled nation certainly provides motivating goals that drive a long obedience in the same direction.

And let us not forget that Jesus himself framed the Great Commission in terms of a long obedience in the same direction. "Make disciples ... teach them

---

57 Montgomery, 13.

58 In the conclusion of "DAWN 2.0," I explain this theme in greater detail.

59 *DAWN 2000*, 219.

to obey … until the end of the age." So let's keep whole-nation disciple-making processes going until he comes again.

> Church planting is necessary but not sufficient to disciple a whole nation.

Turning Insights into Action

The end goal of the 2017 National Church Planting Process survey was not only to gather data but to turn this data into insights that ultimately shape what happens on the ground, leading to the development of effective nationwide church-planting processes. This section will focus on turning insights into action.

The role of expatriate workers

Most survey respondents (62 percent) had experience in two or more countries. This observation highlights the contribution of expatriate workers in developing a national church-planting process. Expatriate workers can be particularly helpful in the early stages of developing a national process. Several respondents elaborated on the role of the expatriate in doing so, highlighting the intricacies of being a cross-cultural change agent.

The importance of expatriate workers developing relationships with national leaders was a frequently mentioned lesson. It was pointed out that expatriate workers do well to serve alongside national workers in developing the national process. One respondent pointed to a number of skills that benefit expatriate workers: learning the cultural dance with national leaders, honoring, listening, faith, timing, and risking. Realistically, expatriate workers can bring important resources to the table: experience, know-how, a relational network, organizational support, and funding.

The key role of the initiation group

When sorting the average scores for each of the thirteen elements of the ideal DAWN strategy studied from the highest to the lowest, an interesting pattern was observed. I had a significant "aha" moment when I observed that the six highest scoring elements came chronologically early in developing a national church-planting process. I have chosen to group them together under the general heading of *initiation*.

I also observed that the lower-scoring elements came into play later, in the development of the national church-planting process. I have grouped these variables together under the general heading of *implementation*. Figure 8 shows the elements that are a part of both the initiation and implementation elements.

The Development of a
National Church Planting Process

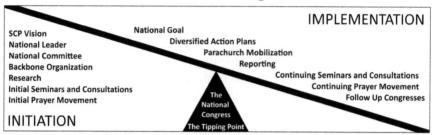

Figure 8: National Church-Planting Process (used with permission)

Further reflection on the developing process yielded these insights. The items in the *initiation* list can largely be accomplished by a devoted core group having adequate funding. The items in the *implementation* list require more buy-in from national leaders.

I have already been pointed out how important buy-in by church leadership is for advancing a national church-planting process. If the buy-in of national leaders is low, there won't be a strong prayer movement, widespread seminars and consultations, or a meaningful national goal. Parachurch organizations will not be mobilized. Diversified action plans (at denominational, organizational, and local church levels) will not be developed. There certainly won't be exciting developments to report, and little need for any follow-up national congresses, as these national gatherings are often called,[60]

Ideally, the tipping point for buy-in occurs at the national congress, but this is not always the case. The initiation group needs to intentionally work at building relationships with national leaders to achieve buy-in. Early adopters and innovators need to be encouraged leading up to the national congress. After the congress, the early, majority adopters need support, and late adopters need to be helped to get on board. Buy-in by national leaders is not an accident. It is intentionally developed. One person alone will not be able to achieve wide buy-in by national leaders. It will require a national-level team, and likely regional teams.

DAWN 2.0

This section presents a model that brings together both old and new elements that contribute to the development of a national church-planting process. We might also call this model DAWN 2.0. This model suggests how the various elements are incorporated into the national process over time (see Table 1).

---

60 *Congress*, though admittedly a Western term, seeks to highlight the vision that we gather not only to *confer* (conference), but in addition to *decide together* (congress).

The twelve elements belonging to the "ideal" DAWN strategy are listed in the top half of Table 1 and are labeled "DAWN 1.0 Elements." New elements that emerge from this study appear in the bottom half of the table and are labeled "DAWN 2.0 Elements." These new elements include the backbone organization; relationships; the importance of developing godly, competent national and local church leadership; training; coaching and mentoring; sharpened goals and action plans; refinements; and the role of expatriates in developing a national planting process in a new country.

Table 1 also brings into view the development of key elements over four phases, about which more will be said shortly.

	Elements	Phase 1	Phase 2	Phase 3	Phase 4
DAWN 1.0 Elements	National leaders work together to mobilize the whole Body of Christ to disciple the whole nation.	Initiate	Develop	Expand	Continue
	A saturation church planting vision drives the movement.	Initiate	Develop	Expand	Continue
	Research guides the process.	Initiate	Develop	Expand	Continue
	Key stakeholders gather for a national congress.	Identify Stakeholders	Develop Relationship	Gather at Congress	Continue Relationships
	A national SCP goal is set.	Cast Vision for a Goal	Clarify the Goal	Achieve "Buy-in"	Evaluate and Revise Goals
	Denominations and mission groups implement their own action plans.	Discover Current Action Plans	Evaluate Action Plans	Implement New Plans	Continue the Process
	The movement grows through on-going research, publications, seminars, and follow up gatherings.	Initiate	Develop	Expand	Continue Processes
	Effective prayer movements under-gird the process.	Initiate	Develop	Expand	Continue
DAWN 2.0 Elements	Relationships	Initiate	Develop	Expand	Continue
	Expatriate worker involvement	Expatriates Engage	Develop Partnerships	Local Leadership Empowered	Relationships Continued
	Local church leaders engaged	Initiate	Develop	Expand	Continue
	Workers trained	Initiate	Develop	Expand	Continue
	Leaders developed through coaching and mentoring	Initiate	Develop	Expand	Continue
	Backbone organization	Identify	Develop	Continue	Continue
	National church planting processes refined	Ongoing Learning and Adjustments			

Table 1: Elements Contributing to the Development of a National Church-Planting Process

The time frame envisioned for the process could span decades. We need to remember that facilitating a national process is a marathon, not a sprint! Perhaps the image of a relay race is appropriate, as leadership may well change, and the baton handed off before the race is finished.

One advantage of this overview of the National Church-Planting Process is it enables one to have all the elements in view from the beginning. As a national process develops, there will be critical moments to emphasize and develop particular elements. For example, although goals, prayer, and research become prominent in Phase 3, they are very much a part of the national process from the very beginning, as the next section will clarify.

Facilitating a national church-planting movement is more of an art than a science. A good illustration comes from comparing a jazz musician to a classical musician. Those involved in both schools of music point out that for jazz musicians, theory and practice are inseparable. Both must be integrated. Moreover, jazz musicians need to be skilled at playing by ear and following the lead musician.

By contrast, classical musicians do not necessarily need to understand music theory. Their task is to play the music as written by the composer. Recall the insight that it is necessary to contextualize and refine the national process. One standard solution most likely will not fit every context. So facilitating national processes is more like jazz. Practitioners need to understand the principles behind developing national church-planting processes and adapt them to their local context.

Facilitating a National Church-Planting Process

Some workers, pondering all that is involved in developing a national process, may become overwhelmed or perhaps think, "This will never work in my country." If this is the case, perhaps it would be useful to divide the development of a national church-planting process into four phases.

Phase 1: Lay the foundation

These initial steps can be implemented in any context and help to lay the foundation for a national church-planting process:

- Develop relationships that will open doors to assist leaders, local churches, ministry organizations, and eventually denominations to develop and implement their own action plans.
- Gather information about context—the "harvest force" and the "harvest field."
- Nurture a prayer movement.[61]
- Cast a vision for discipling the whole nation (saturation church planting).

Involving experienced practitioners from outside may accelerate the initiation of the process.

---

61 Paul Watson, one of the leading trainers in the field of disciple-making movements, observes "Every Disciple Making Movement is preceded by a Prayer Movement."

Phase 2: Build the people and structures that support a national church-planting process

As a core group of people catch the vision for discipling the whole nation, focus on the four key variables, which over the long run have proven fruitful in advancing an effective national process:

- Develop leaders through personal mentoring and coaching.
- Hold seminars and consultations for planning, strategy development, training, and coaching.
- Develop the relational network, structures, and systems that support the national process.
- Assist local churches, mission organizations, networks, and denominations to develop and implement their own action plans for church planting and disciple-making.

Phase 3: Launch the national church-planting process

As an ever-increasing number of leaders, workers, and institutions begin to pursue a national disciple-making vision, perhaps the moment is right to add these elements of the ideal DAWN strategy:

- Form a national committee with appropriate national leaders.
- Research the whole nation to learn more about the harvest force and the harvest field.
- Hold the first national congress. Discerning the right timing to do this is important.
- Set national goals.

Phase 4: Keep the national church-planting process moving forward

Give priority to:

- Holding follow-up gatherings at local, regional, and national levels.
- Refining your systems and contextualizing your church-planting process for greater fruitfulness.
- Reporting regularly on developments to keep people informed, encouraged, and focused.
- Establishing a permanent research process "owned" by the national church.
- Setting new goals and dreaming new dreams, following the leading of the Holy Spirit.

The four phases of the DAWN 2.0 model help break down the overall process into more manageable tasks.

Moving Toward AD 2050

After more than forty years of field experience, we can affirm the value of the DAWN strategy, and we certainly know more now about advancing whole-nation disciple-making processes than before. What might this mean for the future?

First, it would be a major accomplishment if a committed group of national leaders, actively advancing a whole-nation disciple-making process, existed in every country. Readers may be interested in assisting toward this global vision.[62]

Second, in our present context, whole-nation or saturation church-planting initiatives sometimes seem to take a back seat to church-planting movements or disciple-making movements. Few will deny that the breakthroughs CPMs and/or DMMs are having among some of the most resistant ethnic groups are wonderful developments—illustrated with stories of how God is giving the growth. However, CPMs and DMMs are not replacements for saturation church planting and whole-nation processes.

Disciple-making movements and whole-nation processes are complementary. In my judgment, whole-nation processes augment disciple-making movements in at least three ways:

First, DAWN provides a biblically based, whole-nation vision for saturation that involves the whole body of Christ. Second, the ideal DAWN strategy offers an effective, contextualizable framework to mobilize the entire body of Christ to work together toward discipling a whole nation. In this context, DMM is an exceptional high-value tool. Third, national processes capitalize upon the power of good information gained through research. Recall Montgomery's description of a whole-nation initiative:

> It is a DAWN project if … it is built on the premise that the most direct way to work at the discipling of a whole nation is to fill it with evangelical congregations so there is one within easy access both practically and culturally for every person of every class, kind and condition of mankind in that nation.[63]

To accomplish this goal, good information is needed to motivate leaders, mobilize prayer, establish relevant goals, shape strategy, solve problems, and provide insightful evaluation.[64]

These three elements—a whole-nation saturation vision, a whole-nation strategy, and research—are not always core to CPM/DMM DNA. On the other hand, CPMs/DMMs provide effective tactics for establishing "witnessing cells" in every segment of society.[65] In addition, some highly effective early CPM projects in Asia had clear saturation intent and effect.

The ideal DAWN strategy leaves the tactical questions of how to plant churches and make disciples up to the local leadership. So CPMs and DMMs are called forward to flourish within the whole-nation process. We might consider DAWN

---

62 If you would like to begin in your nation or assist to beginning such a process in other nations, please see Appendix 7.

63 Montgomery, *Then the End Shall Come*, 65.

64 This list of outcomes requiring good information largely follows the development of Nehemiah 1–5.

65 Montgomery, DAWN 2000, 50.

to be a macro strategy, while CPM/DMM fits better in the realm of tactics. DAWN provides the big picture of what needs to be done; CPM/DMM focuses on how to effectively establish witnessing cells of obedient believers. Thus the two approaches to disciple-making are complementary and mutually beneficial.

Twenty-first century church leaders who are shaping the disciple-making strategy of the church can only benefit by familiarizing themselves with the strengths of the ideal DAWN strategy and enriching themselves with the insights of field practitioners, as they continue to refine the process to best suit the realities of their ministry contexts. Otherwise, in AD 2050 people may be saying, "Thanks be to God for great DMM breakthroughs! But in this country there are still rural and urban areas, ethnic groups, and other segments of society that are less reached. Those who claim to know Jesus are not yet obeying all his commands. Society has yet to be transformed to reflect God's desire for justice, mercy, holiness, peace, and all the other blessings of his kingdom."

Combining what we have learned about whole-nation disciple-making processes and disciple-making movements is the surest way to make the greatest strides toward fulfilling the Great Commission in the next generation.

> Combining what we have learned about whole-nation disciple-making processes and disciple-making movements is the surest way to make the greatest strides toward fulfilling the Great Commission in the next generation.

Biography

While serving with OC International, Russ Mitchell enjoyed fifteen years of fruitful ministry in Romania, where he helped develop the national church-planting process and cross-cultural missions movement that continues today. His key contributions in research led to consultations with workers in Ukraine, Moldova, and Mongolia. For six years Russ was assistant director of the OC Global Research Team and presently serves as director of Training for One Challenge.

Next Steps

- Reflect on a key point that stood out to you in this chapter.
- What are some practical ways that you can apply or adapt these insights into your context?
- Which of these points or insights do you need to lift up to the Lord in prayer?
- What will your next steps be?
- Are there teammates or others you need to talk to about these action steps?

PART 2

Starting Where You Are

"Twenty years from now you will be more disappointed by the things you didn't do than by the ones you did do. So, throw off your bowlines. Sail away from the safe harbor. Catch the trade winds in your sails. Explore. Dream. Discover."

—Mark Twain

A common question raised by leaders whose hearts are stirred by the vision of national disciple-making and church-planting strategies is "How do I start where I am? What are the essential to-dos in getting underway and sustaining the process?"

Part 2 of this book aims at responding to these practical questions, particularly focusing on the first two years.

We begin in this stage, by faith, with progressive goals resulting in a national process. We build knowing that the discipling of people groups and nations remains foremost, from the day of Christ's ascension, in the eternal purpose of our risen Savior. We build knowing that the challenges of mobilizing the national church are great. We build knowing that cultures and contexts vary. We build knowing that we need ongoing personal, deep, lifelong learning that requires both humility and courage.

Like an iceberg, much of the initial work, especially in the heart of the leader, is done out of sight—deep under the waterline.

CHAPTER 6

Initiating a National Process

THE JOURNEY is likely to be a long one. For this reason, preparation is vital, and the most important preparation is personal. The first step (to be returned to often) typically takes place in private, and the next in public. This order is important because preparation of the heart is critical for facing public challenges. It was so in the missional life of our Lord Jesus and therefore in our calling to follow him.

Many have been often blessed, reoriented, and challenged by the spiritually powerful words of Henri Nouwen, shared in a commencement address.[66] He first urged communion with the Father, then authentic community with those with whom we are on mission, followed by our public engagement in the world so loved by God.

This chapter addresses readers in two contexts. One context may be that of a national serving in his or her own country. The other is an expat worker serving in a host nation. In each instance the chapter assumes a situation where a national process in not yet place (or in larger nations, several regional processes are not yet in place) or still embryonic. In each case the process is to be undertaken with humility and a servant heart.

"Start where you are. Use what you have. Do what you can."
—Arthur Ashe

---

66 An audio recording is available at www.murraymoerman.com/2mission/renewing/renewing_missional_communities.asp.

The national leader may find the chapter challenging but straightforward. The expat worker may not yet be viewed as a leader by national peers. Trust takes time, sometimes a long time. In the case of the expat worker, there are two options. He or she can look for a national leader to support in the process outlined in the chapter. The kind of leader to look for is discussed below. Or the expat worker can begin the process personally, humbly, boldly—praying that trust grows but willing also to hand off leadership to the person national leaders may choose later and willing to serve that person. The servant-leader role of an expat worker is discussed further in chapter 18. The general process involved for a national leader or expat worker, however, is similar.

In an ideal scenario, the first two years will generally be divided as follows. The first six months are preparatory, working largely alone or with a few teammates. The second six months will focus on seeking early adopters and establishing a mandate for wider engagement. The next twelve months take you through a national congress and countrywide engagement among the least-reached.

A. Privately, Before Public Engagement

When a substantive building project is undertaken the first months normally involve constructing foundations which may not be seen. Jesus prepared for public ministry in a private retreat (Luke 4). Likewise a focused season off-the-radar can prepare us well for public engagement.

1. Confirming God's calling in prayer

In Scripture and in experience, the calling of God is foundational to faithfulness in the difficult places. A review of the calling of Abraham, Moses, Jeremiah, and others is profoundly instructive. Genesis 12–13, Exodus 3–4, and Jeremiah 1 are well worth reading and reflecting upon in this context. We are not primarily volunteers. God's calling always precedes our response because we will need his call for strength on the journey. Other Scriptures overview the call of many who required deep inner work before engaging in the outward work to which they were called: Gideon (Judges 6), Isaiah (Isaiah 6), Mary (Luke 1), the twelve disciples (various passages), and Saul/Paul (Acts 9 and 26).

At three junctures in my own life—in planting a church, in leaving a salaried position to begin Church Planting Canada, and in leaving behind our five young adult children in order to serve overseas—the rock-solid certainty that Carol and I were called of God to do what we deeply knew would be difficult was vital to endurance, faithfulness, and fruitfulness to our abiding in Christ.

Sometimes I've had a sense of calling which I took to the Lord in prayer for confirmation. On other occasions, while I was praying I received what I believed to be a calling from God to participate in his answer to my prayer. From the testimony of Scripture, this is generally a private experience, only later to be shared and confirmed by friends.

2. *Finding friends who share your heart*

You may already have close friends who can pray with you, confirm your calling, and possibly even work alongside you in the months and years to come. Or you may yet need to find them.

In either case, you will need a team to pray, stand, and run with you for the duration. When Carol and I sensed we had heard the Lord call us away from a secure and successful pastoral role, we shared our sense of the future with a couple who had been part of the church we had planted. They affirmed the calling and committed finances to the season of transition, continuing as friends and supporters to this day.

Peter Wagner's *Prayer Shield* [67] had deeply influenced me, so we invited others to pray with us. This team has continued to meet monthly for over twenty years now—to share our hearts, needs, and plans, and to pray for us and national church-planting processes at home and abroad. But more about prayer support later.

3. *Initial research: gathering and distributing a basic overview*

The need for church planting in a nation may be evident. In others, it is less easy to see. Regardless of how obvious the least-reached in your nation may be geographically, ethnically, or by worldview, some basic research and mapping will help bring the picture into sharper focus.

Research engages the hearts and minds of Christian leaders in your nation. Initially it need not be comprehensive or perfect, since more can be done once a national process is underway.

Important categories on which to focus initially involve the distinction between harvest field (the unreached) and harvest force (devoted followers of Jesus). Try to gather some information in each category. In your search, don't overlook excellent international research agencies, some of which may have gathered information to benefit your quest. [68]

---

67 Peter Wagner, *Prayer Shield: How to Intercede for Pastors, Christian Leaders and Others on the Spiritual Frontlines* (Glendale, CA: Regal Books, 1992).

68 Sometimes you may be able to benefit from the work of an international research agency. See http://www.murraymoerman.com/mm/downloads/International ResearchAgencies.xlsx.

> Don't try to do too much in your initial research. The point is to start a conversation.

How many churches are there in your country? Look for a resource or an individual who may have already researched this question. The number doesn't need to be exact at this point, as it will continue to be refined. Divide the current population of your nation by the number of churches for a population-to-church ratio. Identify the highest and lowest ratios to compare provinces, states, or major cities. How many more churches need to be planted in each to provide a church for every one thousand people or for every two thousand people? Often a tentative goal may be more appropriate at the start than to focus too quickly on a final goal. We'll explore this further later in the book.

Identify the primary people groups (ethnicities, languages, religions) in your country and where they are concentrated. What percentage of these groups are engaged in a Christian community, and which of these communities are growing? Which groups may need the most encouragement or assistance?

Denominational records may reveal which denominations or organizations are planting most vigorously and whether groups are growing or declining. Explore the groups that are planting successfully. How do they train leaders? How are they making disciples? Are these disciples making more disciples? How do they engage the communities they are trying to each? Which groups are responding to the gospel?

However, don't try to do too much in your initial research. The point at this stage is to begin a national conversation that will lead to prayer, shared vision, a mandate—and, most importantly, vigorous engagement with the unreached.[69]

Information to stimulate an initial leadership conversation may already be partly available, in some nations, from government census data, ministry websites, or an umbrella group like the World Evangelical Alliance. Consult a recent edition of *Operation World* and, if possible, speak with those who assisted in compiling the information cited. This initial research is often a matter of "mining" information that is already available and drawing insights that have not yet been drawn.

Your nation may be one that discourages gathering the kind of information you are seeking, requiring you to start almost from the beginning. If so, this initial research may be comparatively less important

---

69 A sample of initial research to engage national leaders in Canada, prepared by Lorne Hunter, can be downloaded from this footnote number in Appendix 7

since the Christian community will already be deeply aware of their need. Your focus can then turn to the following steps. Some of these steps I recognize are more easily applicable in countries with lower levels of persecution and higher levels of religious freedom. Yet prayerfully sought adaptations can be made.

B. Gather Leaders and Invite Discussion

1. *Make initial contact*

Gathering leaders can be challenging, but a direct approach is best. In countries where security is not an issue, initial communication can be through the ~~post~~ mail to increase likelihood of being read, followed by an email or phone conversation as needed. While mail is costly it's worth it in this instance since leaders generally don't open emails from people they don't know. In this initial mailing to organizational leaders, you can include the results of the initial research with a cover letter inviting them to meet with you and other leaders to discuss how best to encourage the broader body of Christ to respond to the need.

You can then make a follow-up phone or Zoom call, or ideally a personal visit to discuss questions or concerns raised by your research, and to receive a preliminary response to the invitation to gather with other leaders. There is always something to learn, trust to build, and relationships to develop. Don't be discouraged if some leaders are too busy, respond skeptically, or don't want to engage with you. At this point you are looking for early adopters.

2. *Gather leaders*

National leaders (denominational and "pro-church"[70] organizations) can normally self-fund and should be encouraged to do so. Willingness to make an initial sacrifice surfaces a leader who already grasps the vision and is willing to engage the conversation.

In some settings, security considerations will require privacy and caution. In others, wider publicity may draw additional leaders and intercessors who can be invited to pray.

In planning your initial gathering, you may wish to allow for prayer, worship, community-building, a review of the initial research previously emailed or mailed to participants, and a restatement of your purpose for

---

70 "Pro-church" is a term suggested by John Wagenveld, founder of Multiplication Network Ministries, for sodalities often termed "mission agencies" or "parachurch organizations," to underscore the intention not to do the work of the church but to assist the church.

People who initially respond negatively are not necessarily against your vision. Be careful not to respond out of personal insecurity, but listen and learn.

coming together at this juncture. An approach you can adapt is posted on my website,[71] or you could develop your own model. Be creative—and bathed in prayer.

3. *Share the vision and invite discussion*

There will be questions and challenges. Some leaders who are already basically committed may offer challenging questions to see if you've thought the matter through, to test your character and leadership skills, or simply as an expression of their personality. Don't be intimidated, react defensively, or assume questions or resistance reflect a rejection of your vision. Rather, pray, reflect, be patient, and invite others to offer their input to the questions or challenges.

Take notes of the discussion. Initial questions raised may well arise in other contexts or be helpfully addressed in subsequent communications. There is always something to learn or reflect on in the questions or objections of those who give initial feedback. In many cases it simply reflects how people process their emotions or ideas that may cost them something.

I've learned this with some difficulty, and I still feel insecure when a respected leader challenges a strategy that I hold dear. It feels personal, but often it isn't. Listen, and don't respond too quickly. Let others in the group offer their thoughts also. The Holy Spirit will lead.

4. *Give time for prayer toward relational unity and reconciliation*

In some contexts, historical relational issues, whether public or under the surface, may cause resistance to a national process, even threatening to prevent it. One way to uncover and bring healing to issues, when possible, is to invite leaders to a prayer summit retreat or other relaxed setting to pray for personal needs, for unity in the body of Christ, and for its work in the nation. Sometimes this can take place ahead of time. Other times it is necessary to pause the process to ask the Lord to heal wounds in the body before advancing.

I was amazed in an early prayer summit that remarkable confession and reconciliation took place between traditional and charismatic denominations. One leader stood to confess, somewhat humorously, that leaders in his denomination advised young people not to date members of the denomination

---

71 A sample agenda can be found at www.murraymoerman.com/2mission/Agenda-for-discussion-of-initial-research-survey-Oct.96.pdf.

of another leader in the room! The other leader confessed the same was true in his denomination, seeking to shield young people from charismatic influence. The exchange led to deep public confession, repentance, and commitment not to let denominational distinctives prevent collaboration in a national church-planting initiative.

> Dig deep the spiritual foundations of prayer, unity, and, if necessary, repentance and reconciliation.

Even when a season of prayer and reconciliation precedes the discussion of the need for church planting or agreement to advance together, old wounds may reemerge at an unexpected moment. Don't attempt to make peace lightly, smooth things over, or press through anyway. The unity of the body of Christ is vital to the mission of the church (John 17). Leaders must model the reconciliation made possible through the gospel. This is vital because reconciliation is the very heart of the gospel and the center of the cross. This doesn't mean that leaders who refuse to be reconciled should be allowed to stop a national process, only that they should be offered an environment in which they are invited to pray, listen to the Lord, repent if he so speaks, and be reconciled for the sake of the gospel.

Culture influences how reconciliation will most effectively take place. In individualistic cultures, one person may be able to ask forgiveness on behalf of his or her group. In group-oriented cultures, the process may require additional time and consultation. For the sake of integrity, some leaders in France needed to return to their denomination to consult, pray, and ensure they had a broad mandate to accept an apology and be deeply reconciled. It is worth the process!

5. *Ask for a mandate to call the broader body of Christ together*

After presenting the need for church planting and giving opportunity for questions and discussion, briefly restate the need and vision and ask for a mandate to form a small team to work toward the shared vision.

If the process to this point has been open and relaxed, the group may easily give an informal mandate by consensus. In some situations, a formal vote may be needed to lend authority to the decision. In my experience, it is unwise to extend the process of seeking a mandate to move forward. You will often sense from the Holy Spirit when the decision point has come. If some leaders remain hesitant, you could suggest a time-limited mandate, with review—for example, in three years.

Small teams
with the "power
to add" are often
best to start.

Initially, the small team receiving a mandate from the larger group serves under its supervision and reports back from time to time. Its immediate focus, however, is on taking the necessary steps to draw in the broader body of Christ to discipling the nation. The smaller team can be called a coordinating, operational, or catalytic team. For the purpose of this chapter I'll use the term coordinating team.

6. *Form an initial team*

A mandate empowers the small coordinating team to move forward. The team can form immediately, while still part of the mandating group. Ask for volunteers or nominations from those gathered. Seek a balance of representation from respected organizations. Not every organization needs to be represented, however. I've found that top leaders in larger denominations and mission agencies generally don't have time to serve, and often an operational person will be a more effective contributor. It is important, however, that this person has the blessing of his or her top leader.

Size may not be critical in the initial formation of the coordinating team. In some cases, smaller is better, with the "power to add" to ensure the necessary spiritual gifts and capacities moving forward. When the larger group is satisfied with the advance team they've chosen, move to prayer—and receive it immediately and gratefully.

Even if a leader or segment of the body of Christ isn't ready to publicly support a mandate to move forward, that person or segment can humbly be asked to release those who do, even to bless them and pray for them. There are rare occasions in which a leader is personally supportive, but cannot, for political reasons, commit his or her organization. Sensitivity and patience gain much ground.

It is essential for the team to meet soon, even within twenty-four hours, to plan a meeting schedule and to begin deepening friendships. My suggestion is that the team aims to develop a culture of regularity—meeting perhaps monthly the first year and then quarterly after that. (Sub-team leaders can be brought in as needed. More about sub-teams in chapter 9.) There is excellent material available to resource this stage of developing a national team. A great place to start is a practical article

by Phil Butler: "Reflections on High Performance Ministry Networks."[72]
In the first ninety days you may wish to consider the following priorities:

- Identify personal strengths of team members and ask each person to work at tasks fitting his or her strengths. For example, one may have an interest in event planning, another in face-to-face relational connections with church-planting leaders, another in ensuring a good means of broad regular communication, and others in research, training, administration, or prayer mobilization.

- A size of seven to ten persons is ideal relationally, with each team member willing to recruit a separate sub-team if needed.

- Set team objectives for the first year. Some personalities and cultures are less inclined to set objectives. However, each team will need to clarify how to best mobilize the body of Christ to multiply disciple-making communities among the lost and least-reached.

C. Gather National Leaders as Broadly as Possible for an Initial Congress to Seek Broader Buy-in

A common objective for the next year is to gather a cross section of Christian leaders to consider the national need for church planting. This should include denominational and pro-church organization leaders, Bible school and seminary teachers, pastors, church planters, and others committed to disciple-making. The purpose of engaging them is twofold—refreshment of their personal commitment to Christ's calling to disciple the nation and beginning to seek a committed response from the organizations they lead.

The means to personal and organizational engagement is commonly sought by inviting a broad selection of leaders to what many have called a "congress." The term is rooted in the Latin *congressus,* used in the late Middle Ages to denote a wartime meeting. Today the term carries a sense of gathering to enact decisions. In my mind this is preferable to the term "conference," since conferring does not imply outcomes of decision, resolve, or action.

In Spain, Ron Anderson's team adopted the concept of "la Plaza" to discuss needs and make plans. This, I expect, will gain influence in Spanish culture. Whatever term you use, emphasize the need to make firm individual and organizational decisions to advance the gospel through disciple-making and church planting, in an environment where decisions are recognized to likely be costly. Whichever term you use, emphasize the need to make firm individual and organizational decisions to advance the gospel through disciple-making and church planting, in an environment where decisions are likely to be costly.

---

72 Available at www.GCPN.info\resources\High-Performance-MinistryNetworks-Phil-Butler.pdf.

Be clear about the kind of responses you will expect from those who will participate in the congress.

In many cultures, a year or more may be needed to plan well and ensure the availability of the leaders you seek. The preparation process should include three categories—preparation for the gathering, the event itself, and desired responses and outcomes.

1. Preparation

a.) Clarity on desired outcomes

Key to success is a clear vision of the purpose of the gathering, which is achieving the desired responses and outcomes from those with the ability to broadly influence the body of Christ toward discipling the nation. It may be helpful to have a brainstorming session on how to best achieve these desired outcomes during the upcoming congress early in your planning process. Keep the congress planning team small and focused, perhaps seven to ten people.

Program planning can then be built around this primary purpose and desired responses. What kind of activities, case studies, or speakers will you seek? How much "white space" will be left open in the program schedule to leave time for networking and informal meetings? What should be in the registration packet? Many of these questions will be answered in the context of the desired responses you envision from participants.

Keep in mind your purpose of mobilizing an ongoing national saturation church-planting process. How will this purpose be accomplished? Aim to be specific. The following is a sample list generated by a focus group planning for an SCP process, which you might find helpful:

What are the purposes of upcoming national SCP gatherings?
- to mobilize a national SCP process
- to challenge leaders with current information on the nation's harvest field and harvest force
- to mobilize prayer
- to call to decision regarding action and goals, personally and organizationally
- to provide space to plan details of personal and organizational responses
- to provide an environment in which participants can be equipped, at least in part, toward implementation of their goals via:

- learning opportunities, tools, and resources
- new partnerships of cooperation and collaboration
- the inspiration of case studies and models
- ample networking space to develop relationships and learn in community

Invite to the congress primarily teams who already work together, ideally from every denomination and mission agency.

b.) **Invitations**

Take time to develop your invitation list and to seek recommendations of others who should be invited. In restricted cultures great caution may be needed, but it remains important to invite as widely as possible, based on the recommendations of leaders you trust.

A primary way of overcoming trust issues is to invite teams who normally work together to come to the congress. As they share a common experience, they can set goals together and move forward in implementation for multigenerational disciple-making and church planting. Teams who already work together in restricted cultures also reduce the likelihood of infiltration.

Sometimes denominational distinctives arise in the conversation about invitations. In one case, the wisdom of inviting a "Jesus only" (non-trinitarian) group was questioned; in another, a liberal denomination or one of the historic traditions.

While each team must answer this question in its context, you may wish to reflect on these considerations. Frequently it is helpful to adopt an existing broadly endorsed creed—either ancient, as the Apostles' Creed, or more recent, such as The Lausanne Covenant[73]— rather than writing a new statement. We are often pleasantly surprised how widely a solid, biblically orthodox creed is endorsed among leaders outside our own tradition. In the end we should not put ourselves in a place to judge doctrinal integrity. A person's statement should be accepted at face value. In one setting, a national leader was struggling with whether he wanted to encourage the multiplication of churches within a certain stream. In the end he asked the leader of that organization a decisive question, "Do you serve the risen Christ?" and accepted that leader's simple positive answer. I recognize that high-security settings require more than doctrinal agreement. In such settings, invitations may need to be limited to those recommended by a trusted friend.

---

73 www.lausanne.org/content/covenant/lausanne-covenant.

Gather further research, case studies, maps, and other materials that issue a prophetic challenge to the church in the nation.

Some invitation teams may consider whether a group exhibits openness to change. At the same time, I've seen involvement in a national process stimulate wonderful change in groups which I had thought to be most resistant to change. An additional question involves the nature and health of the churches that are being started. You may choose to first engage groups modeling disciple-making and planting the kinds of churches most effectively reaching and impacting their culture. By involvement in a national process such groups can both increase rates of multiplication and model Biblical DNA for more nominal churches.

c.) **Further research**

You may have time to gather additional research before the congress and format it in a way that is both clear and compelling to those concerned to obey Jesus' call to disciple all *ethne*. For example, you may attempt to gather historical data to see more clearly growth trends among national denominations or movements. If data can be found, you may be able to compare growth rates between organizations in the last five years, ten years, etc., to see if growth is increasing or decreasing. Many times this information will be new to the denominations or organizations themselves, as they are preoccupied with the challenges of daily life and ministry.

Not all, of course, will respond positively to new information. Some may ignore or even deny it as a threat to prestige. Don't take this personally. Sometimes more fruitful responses emerge over time after additional thought and prayer.

Among organizations that are growing, it can be helpful to discover how they have been overcoming challenges others have found more difficult. Case studies developed can present key findings in the form of practical, transferable concepts that can be implemented by others.

There are multiple benefits to helping denominations and planting organizations understand themselves. New insight can bring fresh motivation. Seeing other denominations making disciples, planting, and growing effectively can awaken a desire to learn, change, and make positive adjustments. To use a fishing analogy, if some fishermen are drawing fish from a lake, other fishermen cannot doubt there are hungry fish in the lake.

Charts, graphs, and simple color-coded maps showing priority needs of least-reached peoples by language, worldview or religion, geography, or other information will help move leaders to strategic commitments to plant among those who have had the least opportunity to meet and follow Jesus.

Research and other material can be bound into a booklet distributed during the congress, providing opportunity for reflection in the days following, as priorities are reassessed and decisions made are revisited. An introductory article by a nationally respected leader highlighting portions of the content and challenging readers to appropriate response may be part of the "prophetic message"[74] of the booklet.

d.) **Setting accurate expectations**

It is important to set accurate expectations for those who register for the gathering. While inspiration is a likely outcome of the event, it is not the paramount purpose of the event. Big-name plenary speakers draw crowds, but don't always bring lasting change. For this reason, I suggest limiting program space for plenary speakers in favor of prayer, working groups, goal-setting, and planning.

It is important to clarify in the invitation that the primary purpose for gathering is to begin a process, not to hold an event. Priorities will be praying, working with your own team to set goals and plan as the Lord leads, and developing new relationships with leaders from other streams of the body of Christ who will cross-pollinate ideas and share encouragement, tools, and resources in the future.*)*

2. *The initial congress*

Event planting varies in different cultures. It may be wise to aim at a standard just above what is expected in your culture. Ideally you will have developed a team, including those with administrative gifts, making the task easier.

a.) **Communication**

Those invited will need detailed communication:

- Purpose of the congress and desired outcomes, personal and organizational, to set expectations
- Logistics—arrival and departure times, venue location, and overnight accommodations
- Cost—how and when to pay, and if subsidies are available

---

74 Samples of such booklets are available at http://www.ocresearch.info/?q=resources-accordion-tab and scroll to "Reports." For a helpful overview of what is involved in preparation, see www.gcpn.info/ni/research/Russ-Mitchell-on-Developing-Prophetic-Message.mp4.

- Program schedule. Full details may not be necessary, but many people appreciate them.

    In some cases, sharing "categories" of congress activity—such as worship and prayer, plenary inspiration, regional breakouts, case studies and workshops, and organizational breakouts—may be adequate.

b.) **Program**

From my experience, it would be ideal for some or many of the following to find their way into the final program. These do not represent a template, but are suggestions that could be considered by the program design team.

Plenary: Casting the vision	**Plenary:** Propose a goal (an initial or process goal, or the means of arriving at a goal)	**Plenary:** Worship, commissioning, and communion
Plenary: Laying out the need (research overview of where churches are most needed nationally)	**Breakout—by Denomination, Network Organization:** Review planting growth in the last decade and set goals (numbers and/or planting) processes) for the future	**Breakout—by Denomination, Network Organization:** Develop plans in greater levels of detail, offering them up to the Lord in prayer
Plenary: Prayer and worship	**Workshop:** A variety of practical topics (e.g., planter training, prayer mobilization, movement approach, case studies)	**Workshop:** A range of practical topics (repeat of previous day)
Plenary—Case Study: Demonstrate distinction between planting churches (addition) and establishing movements (ideally, a fourth-generation movement of planting or disciple-making)	**Breakout—Geographic Regions:** Focus on prayer, relationship- building	**Breakout—Geographic Regions:** Explore areas of potential collaboration, set general goals if possible, agree on time(s) to meet again in the region after the congress

Table 2: Program Design Concepts

Each topic above could be developed in detail, although that would run the risk of being overly prescriptive. Alternatively, too little detail could result in confusion over the purpose of a given component. A middle course may be sought, with the following explanatory comments.

c.) **Breakouts**

Breakouts refer to specific groups stepping away from the larger group to work on tasks common to that group, for instance:

By organization: By meeting separately, organizations such as denominations and various networks have the opportunity to review their track record on church planting, including growth rate in the last decade, what they have learned from their experience, setting goals for the future, and planning toward those goals. Denominations typically don't meet with a church-planting focus in a setting broader than the committee officially tasked with institutional growth. Meeting in the context of a national congress brings a broader vision of compassion for the lost and the least-reached, combined with a fresh mix of members passionate for the Great Commission.

There is benefit to scheduling at least two such breakouts. The first will look realistically at the organization's past and current reality, hopefully setting goals to break through to greater heights. The second will pray and plan in greater detail to accomplish all the Lord has placed on their hearts.[75]

If data has not been previously accessible, the first organizational breakout can be supplied with a sheet allowing space for the denomination to fill in previous church-planting efforts and the number of churches by year for the last ten-plus years. In one such setting, a denomination looked back for its last stated church-planting goal and found it in their archives, dated 1936! They responded by setting a fresh goal, supporting it with a $6 million fund, and appointing staff to steward the process toward best possible results. That infrastructure still stands, now nearly twenty years later, continuing to result in regular new church plants.

Many denominations make it a practice to expand the scheduled breakouts to a full day or two after the congress in order to ensure adequate time for this important work.

---

75 A sample of a denominational breakout worksheet can be found in Appendix 7.

By region: It is important for leaders strategizing to reach people with the gospel in the same geographic region to know one another. For this reason, your congress design may bring together leaders from various denominations and networks working in the same state, province, or region in a breakout to share vision, strategy, and passion for the people groups in that region.

It may be wise to gather leaders by region twice during the congress. An initial session may be to make introductions and pray with and for each other. A second session may focus on tools and strategies in which leaders share needs and resources, looking for opportunities for collaboration.

Often these leaders will agree to meet quarterly in their regions to continue the process, deepen relationships, and seek the Lord of the harvest together. I know of relationships formed in this way that have continued fruitfully in mutual encouragement for decades.

There is benefit also for national leaders or members of their team to connect regularly with these regional network leaders. Consider networking the regional leaders in an annual retreat or periodic Zoom meeting to share learnings, increasing collaboration nationally.

By topic of interest: Another fruitful way to help leaders benefit from common interests and growth in effectiveness is to offer workshops, leading to ongoing learning by participants. These conversations can center on disciple-making, developing four-generation movements, church planter training, coaching, Islam, UPGs, secularism, or other relevant worldview challenges in your setting.

This approach is not unlike traditional workshops except that, where possible, those interested in leveraging the impact of the topic increasing effectiveness in a national church-planting process are invited to participate in an ongoing relational working group resourcing its members. Each working group in this way, in turn, serves the wider national church-planting process.

d.) Plenaries

Plenaries have a high but comparatively temporary value in focusing vision and placing encouraging models before participants in a national congress. Although well-known leaders help draw the crowd to the place where ongoing working groups are formed, those groups have a more permanent impact on the effectiveness of collaboration for a national movement.

This is not to say that well-known speakers are not valuable to a national event. They are, and they should be invited. My encouragement, however, is to put comparatively greater effort into building ongoing regional and denominational working groups focused on practical topics and interest areas as the workhorses of the national movement.

A South African leader stated that his most effective experience with a national gathering was an event in which there were only two plenary sessions. Between the opening challenge and closing reporting sessions were five tracks of workshops, of which people could choose three—e.g., youth, unreached people groups, local transformation. Each three-hour workshop, facilitated by a team, was focused on a challenge and what to do about it. Separate gatherings according to state or province provided opportunities for reporting, cooperation, collaboration, and partnership development. Evening sessions were devoted to prayer focusing on needs and regions. The premise of the congress was that big-name speakers don't change people. Adults learn by participating in topics and activities about which they are passionate.

e.) **Goals**

While a national church-planting process cannot make organizations set goals in relation to disciple-making and church-planting energies, it can provide an environment in which organizations are encouraged to do so. This can be done by asking a researcher to calculate the growth or decline rate of each denomination over a short (five-year) and longer (ten-year and twenty-five-year) period. If the information isn't available to a researcher, the denomination can be invited to gather and bring the information to the congress as an aid to discussion and planning within their own circle during "breakout" sessions.

Organizational breakouts can then be devoted to considering their response to their own history and the possibility of shaping a stronger future in disciple-making and church planting focused on least-reached peoples. Some organizations may not be structured to set goals by this means, but perhaps could initiate a goal-setting process to be completed after the congress.

The subject of a corporate national church-planting goal is addressed in chapter 11.

Thinking Forward: Desired Responses and Outcomes

Because a national church-planting process is not an event but an ongoing process, desired outcomes from the initial congress must continue to be pursued, looking ahead to the next annual, biennial, or triennial national gathering. These desired outcomes might be suggested to include, at minimum …

- an experience of personal renewal in the hearts of participants, with freshly enlarged vision and passion for the plight of the lost and least-reached.
- specific goals set in response to this need, by each participant and by each organization. These goals may be end goals or process goals. See the section on the value of different kinds of goals in chapter 11.
- an appreciation of the value of a framework (the image of a trellis or scaffolding may be helpful) or process by which networks and organizations can be supported as they progress toward their respective disciple-making and church-planting goals. For an example of such an organizational process, see appendix 1.
- formation of ongoing shirt-sleeve working groups by focus or by geographic region. Ideally, leadership for subsequent collaboration groups can be identified before or during the congress. If not, a member of the congress organizing team may need to sit in on the first gathering of that regional or interest group to facilitate the choice of a leader by the group.

Value Both Form and Function

Value both minimal but sustained infrastructure and an active environment of encouragement to keep the main thing the main thing in the hearts of leaders to reach the least-reached for whom Christ died.

The balance of basic infrastructure and providing an environment of encouragement can be delicate. It certainly requires regular tending and, from time to time, reevaluation to make sure the balance is right and each component is healthy. Too little infrastructure—and plants in the greenhouse may not climb for lack of support. Too much infrastructure—and the creativity characteristic of a Spirit-led movement may not draw adequately on the God-given imagination of leaders or on the intercession desired by God, demonstrating dependency on the wisdom and power from heaven.

All of us require our vision to be refreshed regularly, perhaps as frequently as every thirty days, due to the pressures and distractions of life that counter our highest aspirations.

Therefore, remember to continually provide a culture of encouragement and to maintain adequate infrastructure within which leaders can share, collaborate, and pray as they press into the harvest.

Next Steps

- What points stood out to you from this chapter?
- What are some practical ways that you can apply or adapt these insights into your context?
- Which of these points do you need to lift to the Lord in prayer?
- What will your next steps be?
- Are there teammates or others you need to talk to about these action steps?

CHAPTER 7

Diverse and Challenging Contexts

"I know how to get along with little, and I also know how to live in prosperity; in any and every circumstance I have learned the secret of being filled and going hungry, both of having abundance and suffering need. I can do all things through Him who strengthens me."

—Paul, Philippians 4:12–13
NASB

YOU MAY HAVE BEEN in a setting where someone was sharing encouraging fruit in God's work in their country. A listener to this good report celebrates the advance of the gospel in that context, and then adds, "But I don't think what you are doing will work here. Our context is different." I can hear echoes of this conversation, having heard versions of it in multiple settings that are still ringing in my ears.

The skeptic, of course, is partly right. At the same time, such persons, recognizing the uniqueness of their setting, are prone to take their conclusion too far. Though their context is without doubt different, it does not follow that an adapted process will not work—albeit by somewhat different means—to engage a broader portion of the body of Christ and increase church planting in their unique context.

Our contexts are different in at least two ways, culturally and politically. Each require sensitivity, wisdom, and perseverance.

Cultural Contexts

Some of us are more aware of our cultural context than others. Some refer to our cultural context as worldview. The differences are slight. Both *culture*, a sociological term, and *worldview*, more of a philosophical term, refer to an environment we don't see when we are in it—like air or water—but which is as foundational in its effect as a rooted tree is to its branches.

The basic idea is that the visible part of a tree, like culture that is noticed and enjoyed, is rooted in a worldview consisting of invisible beliefs and attitudes, like a tree's root system that gives the tree life but is unnoticed.

What does this have to do with leading a national church-planting process? Quite a bit, I would assert. But while this book can't address questions of cultural differences comprehensively, let me suggest a couple of broad examples to encourage you not to set aside a national church-planting process in your context, but to seek ways to adapt it to your culture.

One of the broadest vantage points that helps us see differences between cultures more clearly are the ways people respond to sin—namely, fear, shame, and guilt.[76] While the distinction was developed to assist disciples in more personalized approaches to evangelism, it also has significant impact on how we approach recruitment, leadership, and group decision-making—all significant aspects of national church-planting processes.

For instance, strong leadership in power-fear cultures is often accepted as a matter of course. In guilt-innocence cultures, however, leaders need to be viewed as innocent of major wrongdoing before their leadership will be accepted. In honor-shame cultures, a national process leader needs to be viewed as honorable, a trait more important than whether the strategy he or she espouses is compelling.

In each cultural type, a national process of mobilizing the church for disciple-making and planting is needed, and in each cultural setting the mobilization process requires effective leadership. However, national leadership will require different styles in each cultural type. Most importantly, forming a national team, bringing more leaders on board, and helping church and mission groups come to make strategic decisions are all possible with leaders who respect and value the cultural uniqueness of their country. There is no need to say "Our country is

---

76 Eugene Nida, *Customs and Cultures: Anthropology for Christian Missions* (Pasadena, CA: William Carey Library Publishers, 1975), 150. This concept has been popularized in Jayson Georges, *The 3D Gospel: Ministry in Guilt, Shame, and Fear Cultures* (Timē Press, 2017).

different" or "It won't work here." Rather, energy can be fruitfully expended by asking "What adaptations of tactic or leadership style is wisest in my setting?"

Other approaches help us understand how cultural differences may affect leadership approaches to national mobilization. Let me suggest just two briefly:

KnowledgeWorkx seeks to bring intercultural intelligence to the business community with application also to the mission community. Perhaps you will recognize the power of cultural differences like the following, and where your national culture tends to be on the continuum:

Growth—Do you focus on investment in material growth, or personal growth?

Relationship—Does everything have an effect on your reputation, or are your relationships and reputational risks/rewards compartmentalized?

Outlook—Do you focus on lessons from the past, or potential for the future?

Destiny—Is it in your hands, or are you carried along by external forces?

Context—How broad is the spectrum of acceptable behavior in your culture?

Connecting—The degree to which information is freely shared.

Expression—How open with your emotions are you? What are the "display rules" in your culture?

Decision-Making—Do you build trust through procedures and rules, or by getting to know people and relationships?

Planning—People-focused or time-focused?

Communication—Direct or indirect?

Accountability—How do you view your contribution and belonging to a group?

Status—Is it achieved, or ascribed?[77]

Less widely known may be the insights exposed in the work of Geert Hofstede, whose team has explored seven cultural dimensions and mapped predominant tendencies by country:

1. Individualism vs. collectivism
2. Power Distance
3. Masculinity
4. Femininity
5. Uncertainty avoidance
6. Long-term orientation
7. Indulgence restraint.[78]

Even if you know your culture well, valuable reflection—including self-understanding—will come with an overview of these insights to comparative cultures, particularly in a world of ever-increasing mobility.

---

77 "12 Dimensions of Culture," KnowledgeWorkx website, August 30, 2012, https://knowledgeworkx.com/articles/12-dimensions-of-culture.

78 https://geerthofstede.com/culture-geert-hofstede-gert-jan-hofstede/6d-model-of-national-culture/.

Religious Contexts

Closely related to cultural contexts are religious contexts, since religion is often the primary shaper of a culture's worldview. This is true also of supposedly nonreligious settings, like secularism, both in its milder and more stringent forms of socialism and Marxism. The secular view that there-is-no-god-but-man and—most particularly—the state, at root seek to answer fundamental questions of the nature and purpose of reality. Yet every religious system is in need of Jesus Christ, who, by God's grace, has come to be the divine sacrifice to end all human sacrifices, bringing eternal freedom from the requirements of every religious system. The incarnate Lord Jesus Christ is not only greater than the Sabbath, greater than the temple, greater than Solomon and Jonah (Matt 12:6, 41–42), but greater than all—Lord and Healer, Friend and Savior of all.

What about other contexts—religious, political, or cultural? Is your more difficult environment to be set aside? Or isn't the question, rather, "What adjustments might need to be made?"

Let's look at some challenging settings. Principles discussed here in a specific religious context may be transferable, at least in part, to a political setting; and those in a specific political setting may be applicable to a difficult religious context also.

Communist and Post-Communist Contexts

Communism produces one of the most difficult settings in which to stimulate a national church-planting process, in part, of course, because governments oppose such efforts directly. In addition, the collective mentality works against initiative and vision outside of the party's wishes. In my observation, the corrosive effect on creativity, initiative, and trust remains in the culture even after the political mechanism has officially been set aside, perhaps in proportion to the number of years citizens had been trained to be compliant under the watchful eye of the party.

In one such nation, for example, when freedom emerged for denominations to resume organizational life, those denominations shared the expense of a common administrative building (good news). The building design, however, had separate external entrances to each denomination without a common meeting room (bad news). Outsiders might not be aware that the design simply and perhaps naturally reflected government planned apartment buildings designed to keep occupants from meeting without awareness of the party. Cultural imprints are difficult to see from within and therefore to escape.

Adjustments to national mobilization processes in such contexts, therefore, may involve aspects such as those that follow.

Initiative for a national process may have to wait for newer emerging leaders who, in a culture which hammers down nailheads sticking up even a little, were so forged for comparatively fewer years than their elders.

Unfortunately, because working together for the common good, a stated value of Communist ideology, had not been seen in reality in the culture, it has not been transferred to the church. Another major barrier of Communist ideology is that it produces low trust through a system of informants. While generalizations may be difficult, it may be said that national church-planting processes in Communist or post-Communist nations may best be initiated in quieter disciple-making movements in multiple quieter streams.

Specifically, a leader developing a national mobilization vision can seek out proponents of disciple-making and church planting in each stream (organization, network, and denomination), build relationship, and mentor that person as appropriate to find ways to elevate the priority and practice of disciple-making in that denomination or school.

At the same time, the leader can begin to connect proponents of disciple-making movements and church planting in various networks and, over time, gather an informal relational community of these leaders to share experiences and encourage each other in their respective journeys.[79] To this can be added, in some settings, the contributions of expatriate workers serving in the nation who have earned the trust that enables them to add perspectives and learnings from the body of Christ in mission from outside the nation.

It may take still longer before trust develops to the point where research can be gathered or a broader gathering of leaders can be convened to affirm a shared kingdom task.

The more familiar modus operandi under Communism may make it more prudent to bring together smaller gatherings without fanfare in various regions of the country for some years before considering any comparatively public mobilization of the whole church to disciple the whole nation, as encouraged by shared participation in a national church-planting process.

Because a national process is indeed a process, it will take time, often more time than we would prefer. However, patience in multiple small initiatives with a wide range of organizations and networks, prayer, and faithful tilling will bring fruit.

In highly resistive contexts, further adaptation may be necessary. Even so, initial quiet steps can be taken and opportunities recognized, as God gives grace.

---

79 The story of underground networks of Christian communication, education, strategy, and prayer developed in Poland is wonderfully told in George Weigel, *The Final Revolution* (Oxford Press, 1992).

Islam and Other Non-Christian Majority Contexts

Many countries in the 10-40 Window, and some outside of it, are governed by ideologies that do not distinguish between the state and the religion it sponsors. In these high-control environments, the risk of persecution is well known to followers of Christ. However, a national process may add less to that risk than may be assumed, since caution is already deeply engrained into the practices of believers. If a national process is carefully pursued, it may contribute to a greater harvest than expected.

For the same reason, in religious totalitarian contexts—as under Communism—small, quiet, informal meetings of believers are always necessary. Likewise, trust issues between leaders are generally the norm, requiring patient one-to-one relational approaches. But progress can be made over time.

A national process can be envisioned even by very small groups of leaders. And before it is known how many networks are in the country, initial prayer and discussion can take place during a walk in a park, a drive in a car, or a visit to a nearby tourist destination. Leaders of additional networks can be added as trust issues are resolved. A national team, even though not representing a majority of believers in the nation, can begin adjusting the strategy of a national process to its unique context.

In such contexts, research between leaders of various networks of believers is difficult, for the same reasons that trust is difficult. However, as the number of network leaders grow in trust, knowledge can be pooled. In some settings, research has been gathered by these quiet means, and this light has brought encouragement when more disciple-making communities than expected were discovered. Research, even though partial, can be suggestive of where believers may be few or none. Network leaders can explore ways of focusing small initial efforts in those towns or villages.

Training and gatherings for the encouragement of disciple-makers can be organized in private settings or in extreme cases outside the country. For security reasons, private settings may seek the involvement of a small sector of leadership in the nation, each in a separate private meeting, rather than attempting to bring multiple streams together in the same time and place. In other high-persecution settings it may be wiser to aim for small gatherings in five or ten different locations. Either way, one encouraging effect is to let all streams know that other parts of the body of Christ are present and active in efforts to reach the least-reached. Elijah needed this encouragement (1 Kgs 19:18), as do discouraged, isolated workers in high-risk settings today.

In one Middle Eastern country, multiple networks that are not obviously connected find quiet ways to pray together and initiate small informal Christian communities. Low-paid foreign workers play key roles from within wealthy homes where they are employed. Nationals and foreign workers encourage one another with stories of hope that increase kingdom vision.

Sacrifice, of course, remains a central interest to observant Muslims, with the annual celebration of Eid al-Adha—the remembrance of Abraham's willingness to make the ultimate sacrifice of his son. An effective method of sharing the gospel with Muslims focuses on the "first and last sacrifice story." You may wish to familiarize yourself with this training method, termed "Any 3."[80]

While generalizations cannot be made, in some countries a limited number of public Christian institutions are tolerated by the government. In such cases these permitted buildings host worship and meeting space for multiple denominations and can serve regional endeavors of national initiatives.

Underground house church networks, disciple-making movements (DMMs), and other expressions of church-planting movements (CPMs) can grow independently of the few tolerated Christian institutions. In most nations, underground DMMs and CPMs are most fruitful and public Christian institutions choose to remain unaware. Research has suggested other best practices in such contexts.[81]

A mobilizer in an Islamic country that tolerates a limited number of public Christian institutions summaries his view of practical ecclesiology with images of the elephant, rabbit, and lizard. Elephant churches are the model flowing out of the Constantinian era and may be deeply rooted in Islamic settings.[82] Having long paid the price of faithfulness, these churches reproduce slowly and are hard to miss, but with the right leadership they are able to encourage rabbit and lizard churches. Rabbit churches are smaller, reproduce more rapidly, and are commonly seen as house churches. Lizard churches take their name from Proverbs 30:28. Such churches meet in unexpected places, such as prisons, moving vehicles, nurseries of domestic workers, public cafes, and construction worksites. Like rabbits, they may be short-lived, but they can transform the lives of family groupings for the kingdom, reproducing more easily to the fourth spiritual generation. In some circumstances, small churches will grow to become larger, but often at the cost of future reproduction.

In the end, knowledge of progress needs to be shared by only a few. A small national research team can share macro updates with a small number of representatives of those denominations and networks that are most vigorous and strategic in their disciple-making and church-planting efforts.

---

80 Mike Shipman, *Any-3: Anyone, Anywhere, Anytime—Lead Muslims To Christ Now!* (Monument, CO: WIGTake Resources, 2013). For a summary, see https://www.missionfrontiers.org/issue/article/any-3.

81 See "Fruitful Practices: A Descriptive List," www.GCPN.info\resources\Fruitful-Practices-Descriptive-List.pdf.

82 See "Constantinian" in the glossary.

Post-Christian Contexts

Countries losing sight of the hope of the gospel present a different kind of challenge. Post-Christian countries are largely postmodern: distrustful of organizations and institutions in general and truth-claims of most kinds in particular—specifically the uniqueness of the sacrifice of Christ opening the door that no one else can open, eternally to the Father (John 14:6).

These cultural environments are not only in the West but to a lesser degree also among younger people in some Asian nations that are influenced by similar trends and values disseminated via social media and the Internet. In fact, post-Christian losses to the Christian faith are interestingly mirrored in Muslim, Hindu, and other religious-majority settings also. Young people—perhaps in part due to similar Internet influences or rejection of religious violence—turn away from the faith of their parents. Some wanderers turn to atheism while remaining culturally connected to their roots. Some also turn to Christ. Where these movements within several world religions are heading is not yet broadly apparent.

The greatest danger of post-Christian rhetoric is loss of hope in the church, leading to passive siloing. In my experience, the claim that A or B doesn't work anymore is made by those who have long since stopped employing A or B and haven't yet experimented with Y or Z.

The fact is, a non-Christian generation is emerging in post-Christian contexts that cannot be assumed to be opposed to the gospel, but often is a clean slate that knows nothing of Christ or the cross and is not biased against him or his people, but simply has no personal relationship with a vital Christian community.

In addition, so-called post-Christian contexts are not devoid of multiplying churches. Nor are they without a harvest-ripe segment eager for hope after deconstructionism.

In such contexts church leaders can be gathered, research collected, positive case studies shared, and best practices employed. National and regional gatherings can be convened more easily than in restricted political environments, and both public and private training venues are possible.

Europe's National Church Planting Process community (www.nc2p.org) is evidence of the possibility of vigorous advance in this context. Church Planting Canada (www.churchplantingcanada.ca) continues a fruitful national process also, now in its twenty-fourth year.

Less-structured approaches preferred by many postmoderns can also contribute toward SCP/national goals. Wolfgang Simson applies the images of the starfish and the spider to decentralized disciple-making networks.[83]

---

83 Wolfgang Simson, *The Starfish Manifesto* (Starfish Resources, 2009). The abbreviated "Starfish Vision" is available at www.cmaresources.org/files/The_Starfish_Vision.pdf.

While viewed by some as radical, it may carry valid challenges to institutional weaknesses. It may also provide fruitful alternatives in disciple-making and church planting. But the model also contributes to national goals and processes. In fact, Simson sees his model of kingdom communities as a realistic approach to gospel saturation without the infrastructure of the organized church.[84]

To incorporate church and kingdom movements, along with disciple-making communities, in the national picture, research must find ways to track decentralized movements. This is a challenging task. The goal of research in this context cannot be comprehensive results as much as a prophetic pointer in the direction of the least-reached. The church must always heed this pointer as a pointer to God's heart.

We must remember also that in the West millennials will age, and subsequent generations will offer their own strengths and weaknesses. God is not stymied by trends and fads. Already, it appears, the so-called Generation Z, born after 2002, will be significantly different than their parents, including the tendency to embrace more traditional family values.

Nominal Christian Contexts

Fortunately, many nominal Christian contexts, such as Latin America and some sub-Saharan countries, have few formal barriers to saturation movements. In fact, most nominal contexts will readily affirm the whole-church whole-nation principle. In addition, there is no persecution or need to proceed under the radar of government authorities. This is the good news.

At the same time, nominalism can work against us. In some countries, Christian leaders don't see the need for saturation, since Christians can already find churches. Jesus' point that he came not for the found but for the lost (Luke 15) can be missed. Disciple-making movements and church planting are not for Christians but for non-Christians. In nominal settings, as in others, some Christian leaders become competitive or insecure, which in turn works against collaboration. Further, some leaders are committed exclusively to the expression of church with which they are most familiar. Protecting one's paycheck may even be a factor. But all of this can be overcome.

Prayer summits may be a good place to begin. Prayer summits can begin small. Initial research can be shared and prayer invited for the least-reached. I recall a prayer summit in which little agenda beyond prayer, worship, fellowship, and unity led within a few hours to a leader in one denomination confessing wrong attitudes he had been taught and carried from childhood toward another

---

84 See Simson, "Church of the Future," www.murraymoerman.com\NCPP\downloads\ ChurchoftheFuture.pdf.

denomination. He confessed the attitude as sin and asked forgiveness of a leader in that denomination. This stimulated similar confessions of leaders in other traditions. Soon relationships were such that working together for the sake of the gospel in that nation was utterly natural.

In the bureaucratic ways that can develop in nominally Christian nations, those in higher positions are often, rather than being involved themselves, willing to bless the participation of district superintendents or others in the structure. Most important in such cases is ensuring that lower-level leaders have passionate hearts for the kingdom far beyond their organizational role. When such persons are found and willing to ask a blessing of their organizational head for participation in a national process developing movements among the least-reached, the way forward almost feels downhill.

Remember also that every nominally Christian nation has pockets of migrants, underclass, up-and-outers, adherents of other religions, secularists, and unchurched believers in need of discipleship. Every nominally Christian nation has need of a national process with focus on passionate prayer and multiplicative movements among the lost. *Difficult* does not mean *impossible*. Development of local solutions requires creativity and experimentation.

Large, Complex Countries, Large Populations

Countries with a large population, land mass, or both present special challenges. For example, Russia crosses eleven time zones and Indonesia is composed of 922 populated islands. China and India have massive populations exceeding one billion souls. India has the additional challenge of hosting the largest number of distinct people groups of any nation on the globe. Other countries with large populations, though unique in their own contexts, include the United States, Brazil, Pakistan, Nigeria, and Bangladesh.

Few leaders view themselves as having the capacity for such complexities. Better therefore, perhaps, is to collaborate with other leaders who are passionate about smaller administrative units. For example, Russia may be seen as five distinct regions—the Moscow-centered western region, the Islamic Caucasus region, the animistic northern Siberian region, the Buddhist-influenced southern Siberian region, and the far eastern region. Whether this is the most useful way to view the nation and divide responsibility is, of course, the decision of Russian leaders. More or different subdivisions may be needed in order to be practical and, in the end, comprehensive. Key, though, is that division leaders, however many they may be, connect regularly for prayer, encouragement, and sharing of best practices toward movements in their part of the nation.

Indonesia, China, and the US, for vastly different reasons, may best be viewed in divisions, each facilitated by six or more men and women sharing the heart typified by John Knox for their region, in which they pursue the unity of the body and its mobilization for the lost and for Christ's glory.[85]

Similar principles of division can be applied, and in some cases *are* being applied, in other large, complex nations. It is vital that this be done, especially since the twenty most populous nations of the globe are home to 70 percent of the world's population—in descending order of population: China, India, United States, Indonesia, Pakistan, Brazil, Nigeria, Bangladesh, Russia, Japan, Mexico, Philippines, Ethiopia, Egypt, Vietnam, Congo-DRC, Turkey, Iran, Germany, and Thailand.[86] And it is possible. A national process can start in one region, state, or province, then in another, and another. What will be needed at some point is a person who can envision encouraging and supporting each regional John Knoxer in the nation in the context of a unified team.

Next Steps

- Reflect on a key point that stood out to you in this chapter.
- What are some practical ways you can apply or adapt these insights into your context?
- Which of these points do you need to lift up to the Lord in prayer?
- What will be your next steps?
- Are there teammates or others you need to talk to about these action steps?

---

85 See "John Knoxer" in the glossary.

86 For the sixty most populous nations, see "Top 60 nations in descending population size in 2020 AD" at this footnote number in Appendix 7.

CHAPTER 8

Models on Other Continents

"May ... your ways may be known on earth, your salvation among all nations. May the peoples praise you, God; may all the peoples praise you."
— Psalm 67:1–3 NIV

APPROACHES to multination coordination will vary in complexity and by cultural context. To Eastern friends, I ask: Please consider aspects of Western models. To Western friends, I ask: Please consider aspects of Eastern models. God is building a kingdom culture. Here follows a small sample of models and experiences.

Europe: Health Indicators and Missional Components

Despite an inspiring array of magnificent historic church buildings, Christendom in Europe has declined to levels bringing about deep concern in many hearts, often including desperate prayer and fasting. The unexpected, and in some places nearly uncontrolled, migration of refugees from war and poverty has left parts of Europe reeling.

In this challenging context, God has gathered a warm band of friends nurturing national church-planting processes, NC2P,[87] with great potential for fruitfulness outside of Europe also. Øivind Augland of Norway has provided long-term continuity as the team facilitator.

During frequent conversations over several years, the NC2P leaders have summarized observations of the national church-planting process in their respective countries for simplicity of understanding and evaluation.

Think of the dashboard of your car in which you may see green, amber, or red lights. In Table 3, shades of grey (in lieu of colors) provide an overview of developing health and progress:[88]

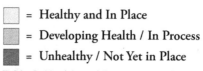

☐ = Healthy and In Place

☐ = Developing Health / In Process

■ = Unhealthy / Not Yet in Place

Table 3: Health and Progress Dashboard

This overview of SCP health and development has two parts—health indicators and missional components. The first of these, health indicators, are viewed as indicators that the second element, missional components, are bearing fruit. Let me share their model in some detail.

The desired health indicators anticipated are monitored with a simple value of red, amber, or green (depicted as shades of grey). It is hoped red (dark gray) will yield to amber (medium gray) and, over time, to green (light gray). If the following example were to represent a snapshot of the health of your nation, province, or city you might be faced with a picture like this:

Health Indicators toward Tipping Point

Net Increase in Total Evangelical Congregations	Increased Evangelical Attendance	Majority Cooperation/ Critical Mass

Table 4: Health Indicators toward Tipping Point

Strengths and weaknesses are summarized in a glance. In the above instance:
1. the number of evangelical congregations are static,
2. evangelicals are growing as a percentage of total population
3. there is some cooperation between denominations but the number of denominations cooperating remains under 50 percent.

It is not assumed the three health indicators will improve in any particular order, but only that the three are related and will affect one another. Experience suggests health is not necessarily a linear process. There are multiple components. Cooperation between a majority of church organizations may precede or follow a net increase in evangelical congregations but all are expected. The key desire in monitoring these health indicators is that a tipping point will be reached. At that point it is hoped that momentum toward making disciples and planting communities will continue and even increase.

---

88 The evaluative colors associated with the "Health Indicators" above and "Missional Components" below do not represent a specific nation, rather show how three universally recognized colors (depicted above as shades of grey) might help show comparative strengths in your national, state or city process.

One health indicator is a net growth in congregations. Careful research is normally required to determine if more churches are being planted than are being closed.[89] The total number of congregations in the nation reaches a tipping point of net growth only when church planting exceeds church mergers and closures.

Another health indicator is increased evangelical attendance. As churches are planted for the purpose of engaging people with the risen Christ, national participation in worship and personal ministry will normally increase. However, church plants start small and growth takes some time. Unfortunately, not all church plants send out spouts to develop into other new churches. And many existing churches add but do not multiply, and some decline. For these reasons, increased evangelical attendance may lag behind net growth in congregations for a season and become healthy at a later time.

Majority cooperation refers to a simple 51 percent-plus (though ideally 70 percent-plus) of evangelical organizations in the country being involved in the process in some way. This involvement could be represented by leaders participating in national conferences organized to encourage church planting, or by the organization giving church planting priority in a new way by setting a church-planting goal, initiating church-planting training, or participating in support networks developed in the nation.

The second element of SCP health and development can be termed missional components. These are expected to contribute to conditions improving health indicators outlined above and can be developed by a national leadership team.

Each missional component can again be assigned a red (dark gray), amber (medium gray), or green (light gray) to indicate current status and progress, as in the sample below. Your own nation, province or city will show different strengths and weaknesses. Over time, it is expected, each will improve. Though experience suggests not always in the linear fashion we may expect. Ultimately, of course, our work and prayer seek to see all components green (light gray) and at the tipping point. Let's take a closer look at the development of each component.

Missional Components

National Leadership Team	Strategic Information	Gatherings/ Learning Communities	Systems/Tools and Training

Table 5: Missional Components

---

89 Christian communities close for a variety of reasons, but most often due to an aging congregation that has lost the ability to engage its community with the gospel or to meaningfully engage the next generation of the members' own children. One of the most effective ways to address this danger is to give a majority voice in the congregation's formal leadership team to disciples in their thirties and to disciples representing the ethnicities in the surrounding community. Such transitions to new leadership are often difficult for current leaders but bring joy far greater than the alternative of fatal aging.

Long-serving national team facilitators increase the likelihood of success. Aim to serve for ten years.

National Leadership Team

The need is great, but don't be intimidated, for the Lord himself enables you. A committed leadership team facilitator is one for whom the initiative and his or her team is a top priority. The leader is a person who has high integrity, who has a kingdom vision above brands and egos, who loves and relates to the whole church, and who has a heart broader than any single organization or model of disciple-making or church planting. Ideally this person is able to keep peace with gatekeepers and continue to move forward with younger leaders who help bridge the generational gap.

It is important also that this leadership role is one with sustained continuity, in contrast with annually rotating leadership.

The leader builds community with a team that, like the leader, values relationship, trusts in the unique gifts and strengths of each member, and enjoys both their work and deep friendships shared in the team. In my experience this team ideally shares a forty-eight-hour retreat at least annually, during which there is time for relaxed meals, an evening out, refreshment, prayer, planning and sharing life, standing together in the challenges, and a deep sense of the Lord's presence and direction.

This kind of community doesn't develop in a fortnight, but is productive and stands the test of time.

The national leadership team is best drawn from representation of a few of the larger organizations in the nation. Larger organizations have greater resources, while often leaders of smaller organizations can find more time to build specific needed supporting components of the national strategy. There are, of course, many exceptions and no set patterns.

Sometimes there is value to both a smaller operational team that meets four to ten times a year and a larger guardian-of-the-vision team that may meet only once or twice a year to hear updates, pray, and help with problem-solving. This team serves also as a sort of fishing pool from which new operational team members may emerge.

The leadership team focuses significantly on the following components, though in no necessary order and not necessarily personally. Sub-teams will often take on specific tasks or larger projects. In my experience effective teams think in terms of serving for a decade or longer. Shifting the momentum of the church in a nation requires long-term engagement.

Gathering places and learning communities

Picture a forum or city square where leaders gather to develop relationships, talk, and hammer out solutions to recognized problems. Those familiar with Spanish culture will appreciate the value and relational bustle of *la plaza*. Other cultures might relate to the concept of a council of elders or a congress where problems are debated, solutions are found, and decisions are made.

> Ensure church and mission leaders have regular opportunities to gather on the national level and, where possible, the provincial level.

It is with such images in mind that national church-planting process teams provide gathering places for organizations and networks, and pastors and planters come to learn, be encouraged, make plans, and develop strategies to make disciples, plant churches, and develop movements.

At the continental level, the NC2P servant-leadership currently brings together national team leaders biannually in learning communities to pray, evaluate progress, plan next steps, and build community. In alternate years, a group consisting of one member of each national team comes together for a shorter period to pray, share, and focus on specific issues.

At the national level, gathering places develop in different ways. In some countries, the conversation may take place for two days every other year. Other countries choose different rhythms, particularly in balancing national gatherings and, where possible, smaller gatherings at the provincial level to involve more local leaders.

National gatherings help build broad recognition that more churches are needed to accomplish the task of making disciples in every geographic, ethnic, and cultural component. This recognition helps networks and organizations refocus on Christ's calling and the means of obeying. Goals are set, plans are made, and passion is rekindled.

Although national gatherings can be organized in different ways, they need ample white space to give time for interaction in a variety of forums for planters, organization leaders, and frontline disciple-makers to meet according to geographic breakouts and huddle with those who share organizational or network affiliations to make plans, reshape organizational culture, and discuss plenary presentations. A range of workshops can provide case studies, resources, or discussion settings to find best practices in difficult contexts. It is vital also to provide time for intercession and to enable fresh connections between new and existing prayer networks seeking powerful spiritual breakthroughs in the nation.

Some countries supplement face-to-face events with periodic days of prayer and fasting. In other countries, NC2P teams offer practical discussions of agreed-upon topics in central locations or via the Internet. Each gathering brings

> Accurate information and an effective communication process are equally important in changing behavior.

encouragement and fresh ideas, resulting in new friendships and partnerships, motivation, and prayer empowerment. As the movement grows, gatherings can also focus on a specific region or city.[90]

A personal practice I have found of enduring value involves these steps:

1) to think long-term, including to

2) ask the Lord at the beginning of each year what he wants me to seek his help to try to accomplish in the year ahead. I then

3) aim for ninety-day objectives, well worth

4) fifteen-minute review at the beginning of each week.

What is best in your country? Ask yourself, "What are the natural segments in my country to which we need to go to complete our work?"

Strategic information

Because the gospel normally spreads along human relational lines, typically some segments of a city or nation are privileged with greater opportunity to know Christ personally. Tragically, other segments remain comparatively barren. It is vital, therefore, that the church knows who has been neglected—and where—and then acts strategically on this critical information.

Every country therefore needs a national research process that identifies and effectually communicates priority locations and people groups for disciple-making and church planting. This information can be shared in booklet form through bulletin inserts emailed to denominational heads for distribution to local churches. Ideally, these inserts provide prayer needs for national days of prayer and fasting, and a form of mapping that gives a picture of the nation to the church that stirs recognition of the need for church planting. Some countries are able to post this information on the Internet, demonstrating the unity of the body of Christ, priority needs for planting, and progress made together.[91]

This research process also normally measures net growth in churches and total attendance. Research can, in addition, identify case studies to stimulate the imagination, encourage the heart, and provide effective models and stories showing the human dimension of hope and lives changed for eternity.

---

90 Out of the NC2P network grew a partnership with Exponential. When COVID-19 required re-thinking the centralized gathering, smaller decentralized roundtables were organized in 100 cities. See https://exponential.eu/.

91 See www.1pour10000.fr/la-carte and http://estar.ws.

Clear and winsome communication is a vital part of the process. While the means of sharing strategic and motivating information within a national church-planting process will vary, it is important to note that aiming at high quality increments of information delivered with reasonable consistency is vital. Remember, communications do not need to be lengthy to be memorable. Accurate information and an effective communication process are equally important in changing behavior.

> Not all support structures are of equal value. Take time to prioritize those which are likely to bring greater fruit for the kingdom.

Systems' support for church multiplication: tools and training

John Caplin, a church-planting leader in Canada, once remarked, "Mission without systems is temporary." While I initially resisted and later puzzled over his view, I now believe it to be true. Passion for mission often gets us, to borrow an image, to the launching pad and through ignition. Later in the process, however, leadership may change or difficulties may emerge, and our dream to move from planting to movements may lose inertia. Mission requires, in addition to passion, support for implementation. What, then, do we mean by support systems?

In many ways, systems are simply a response to needs which emerge as a national movement develops. Problems will arise, and creative and passionate people will pray and look for ways to solve them. These ways could be called systems in that repetition may be involved. The concepts of empowerment, tools, training, and support may be more helpful concepts as you wrestle with the needs in your context.

It can be argued that several basics are foundational, and in fact beneficial in every context. These are, at minimum, prayer mobilization, 4G disciple-making training and coaching, church planter training and support,[92] and communication structures of some kind (ranging from quiet conversations in secure locations to public websites).

Such system basics—despite the image the term may engender—are, it should be pointed out, not impersonal. In fact, support systems consist of warm-hearted persons and of the equipping, support, and encouragement they bring to keep the front lines supplied and expanding in the advance of Christ's purposes.

Disciple makers, church planters, and those empowering peer-learning groups are real people who need to be recruited, prayed over, assessed, trained and coached to be multiplied into the harvest field. Providing for those basic needs can move beyond responding to problems of which we become aware to proactive training and development of teams to serve those who need tools and encouragement. For this reason, this category will always be flexible.[93]

---

92 In Europe this process is frequently supported by https://m4europe.com.

93 Adaptations are emerging—e.g., www.nc2p.ch in Switzerland and https://nc2p.de/ in Germany.

As you advance, remember to keep these means of support, encouragement, and training as economical as possible for sustainability. They must be principle-driven to outlast strong personalities and, as far as possible, accessible to all who can benefit from them to serve with yet greater passion and skill.

A word of encouragement

Yes, this overview is challenging, but don't be overwhelmed! The Lord is great and deeply desires to help you find a way. Our best first response is simply to bend our knees and our heart. The Lord always speaks to a heart listening for his still small voice (1 Kgs 19:11–13), and he will give you courage and show you where to start.

An early goal is for your national facilitation team to make it their concern to find champions who form teams passionate for God's kingdom in these various support roles. In Europe, a helpful graphic has been developed to stay focused and clear.

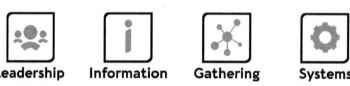

Leadership   Information   Gathering   Systems

Figure 9: Four Components of a National Church-Planting Process

It won't come all at once. The components may not develop in any particular order. There will be fits and starts and returns to the starting gate. But these teams will come as you pray for them, keep them on your hearts and meeting agendas, and invite emerging leaders to serve in these roles for God's glory and the common good.[94]

Kevin Mannoia has also given good thought, refined through experience, to "systems thinking" to accelerate church planting within denominations.[95]

Africa: Growth in Every Region

Africa's contribution is more diverse in approach but no less purposeful. Frequently one nation has sparked church planting initiatives in surrounding nations.

In West and Central Africa, saturation evangelism initiatives in the 1960s (e.g., New Life for All) ignited church multiplication across the DRC, Nigeria, and Ghana. The process was refined in the 1970s into a national saturation church planting strategy by the Ghana Evangelism Commission under the guidance of Ross Campbell. The GEC became an early prototype of an African National Initiative and inspired church multiplication vision across its borders.

---

94 A manual and team worksheets can be found at this footnote number in Appendix 7.

95 Kevin W. Mannoia, *Church Planting: The Next Generation: Introducing the Century 21 Church Planting System* (Indianapolis: Light & Life Communications, 1994).

In Southern Africa during the latter 1980s, the Zimbabwe National Evangelism Task (ZimNET) launched the Target 2000 national church planting process in Zimbabwe involving sixty denominations working together to plant 10,000 churches within a decade. In 1992, a delegation from Eswatini attended the Target 2000 Congress returning to form the Swaziland Evangelism Task, a national research and church planting process involving the three major church associations. Zimbabwe also served to catalyze the formation of The Church Planting Alliance of South Africa in conjunction with The Evangelical Alliance of South Africa.

During the 1990s, the African expression of the AD2000 & Beyond Movement built upon these advances to spread pioneer and saturation church planting initiatives across the continent. Strategic collaboration was fueled by the participation of 1200 African leaders from forty-six nations in the Global Consultation on World Evangelization (GCOWE 97) in South Africa. This convergent moment gave rise to national initiatives such as the FinTask Movement in Nigeria and Finish the Task in Kenya which in turn stimulated national initiatives across East and West Africa.

Building on this momentum, the Movement for African National Initiatives (MANI) was launched in 2001 at the African Millennial Consultation as a grassroots movement, a network of networks, focused on catalyzing African National Initiatives and mobilizing the resources of the Body of Christ in Africa for the fulfillment of the Great Commission.[96] Every five years a MANI continental consultation is held (Kenya 2006, Nigeria 2011, Addis 2016) to encourage collaboration in reaching least-reached peoples and places in Africa and the wider world. Regional gatherings—such as CRAF and MANI Southern Africa 08—served to increase engagement at grassroots levels.

In recent years, disciple-making movements continue to multiply across cultural and national boundaries through a spectrum of organizations and networks. Significant advances are noted in regions such as the Horn, West Africa, and the Islands. Further, African church planting initiatives are flowing outward as African disciple-makers move northward into Muslim-majority nations and as African-initiated churches reproduce throughout the global diaspora.

Southeast Asia: "Gather to Inspire and Go to Serve"

The eleven nations of SE Asia have drawn inspiration, as might be expected, from the national DAWN process, since it has been long and fruitful and is still underway in the Philippines.

---

96 For an overview of MANI principles see this footnote in Appendix 7.

A regional coordinating team, drawn from several nations, continues to gather national church-planting process leaders into a learning community in the region every few years. The gatherings build on established relationships and focus on progress achieved, challenges experienced, and empowering prayer toward a shared saturation goal for the region.

The Torch, depicted on the table in advance of commissioning prayer during a regional gathering, represents the light of the gospel for each nation. The "Torch Challenge" is a doubling of existing churches to 320,000 churches in SE Asia. Judah Cantoria is the current leader of the Global Church Planting Network (GCPN) SE Asia regional team.

Figure 10: The Torch Challenge (used with permission)

A monthly prayer focus undergirding this regional goal for gospel saturation supports the process. The call reverberates: "Set your calendar to pray every eleventh day of the month at 11 a.m. for one of the eleven Southeast Asia nations for eleven minutes!"

The regional gatherings are at a central location, sometimes held in conjunction with larger conferences or sister networks.

At the same time, and on occasion in place of a regional learning community event, regional servant-leaders travel to various nations to serve in more personalized ways. By this means they help strengthen national church-planting processes throughout, and sometimes outside of, SE Asia. These relational visits include informal coaching, prayer support, and assistance in frontline planter training.

One example of this service between nations in this region is Thailand. Several SE Asia nations have been assisting Thailand in their goal of improving the effectiveness of their church-planting training. In this process, Thailand has also become a model of incorporating "whole nation" strategy, DMM tactics, and real-time mapping in an ideal combination. Thailand's mapping tool is now in use and is an example for several surrounding nations.[97] There has also been an exchange with Pacific Rim nations, initially inviting a small number of NE Asia leaders to experience the SE Asia learning community and later visiting NE Asia as it began to gather leaders in that region toward the goal of a national church-planting process in each nation.

There is much reason to be heartened as one observes relationships and encouragement between regional leaders in and between continents. The Lord is marvelously at work to fulfill his word through the prophet Habakkuk: "For the earth will be filled with the knowledge of the glory of the LORD as the waters cover the sea" (Hab 2:14 NIV).

South Asia: Yes, Even the Most Complex Nation on Earth

Made up of vast numbers of people groups, languages, and cultures, India is widely acknowledged as the most complex geopolitical nation on the planet. Some parts of the country suffer from persecution, other parts from a spiritual malaise. It is necessary, therefore, that many organizations and networks labor both together and separately toward gospel saturation and transformation. In the complexity of India, multiple processes are underway, along with several efforts to link them. At significant cost and sacrifice, these initiatives have made great progress advancing the gospel. Yet massive needs for vision, training and coordination, and collaboration remain.

Can a single national process be engaged? The answer is remarkably encouraging. Here is some recent background.

In the first decade of the new millennium, national leaders, standing on the shoulders of earlier pioneers and intercessors, formed the "Compete the Task India Network"—with a "PLUG" goal of saturation, aiming to reach every People group, Language, Urban center, and Geographic (rural) area. The goal was pursued with a "PREM" strategy in four parts: Prayer mobilization, Research to reveal gaps, Equip workers through specific training, and Mobilize workers into those gaps.

After several years of progress, evaluation revealed the network had engaged evangelical, charismatic, and Pentecostal denominations, but not mainline or Catholic workers. To broaden the movement, separate conferences were held, beginning in 2013, for each of these traditions. The vision of reaching the nation in this generation was shared with bishops of each tradition. After the separate conferences for each tradition, the question was asked, "Can we have a combined gathering of leaders of all five streams of the church?" The answer was, "Yes!" As I learned this, the Holy Spirit seemed to say to me, "Let your heart ring with joy!"

---

97 A popularized version of part of this story is available at www.christianitytoday.com/ct/2019/april/missions-data-thai-church-fjcca-reach-village.html.

Love and invite
the whole body of
Christ!

The first combined meeting, held in 2015, was composed of five hundred leaders, including one hundred Catholic bishops. What a milestone in the history of India! Updated research data was shared, along with the vision of reaching India together for Christ in our lifetime. Subsequent gatherings grew in size and unity. These were followed by twenty regional gatherings throughout the nation. In each case the focus was prayer for India and seeking the means to reach the nation in our generation.

The strategy is wonderfully simple, doable, and reproducible in other countries, provinces, or cities. Specifically,

- every church is asked to share one scriptural expression of the Great Commission each Sunday.[98]
- every church is asked each Sunday to pray for five minutes for the Great Commission to be accomplished in the nation.[99]
- every church is asked to adopt three or more villages currently without a church.
- every diocese or district is asked to adopt ten villages currently without a church.

Adoption involves prayer, then prayer-walking, then service and evangelism in that village, followed by formation of Christ-groups. In India, some languages still require Bible translation. Happily, wonderful strides have been made in translation technology. You may be interested in www.adoptaverse.com and https://eten.org. Every Tribe Every Nation works toward the goal that by 2033 95 percent of the people in the world should have a full Bible, 99.9 percent should have the New Testament, and 100 percent should have at least twenty-five chapters of the Bible. This should be viewed in the context of a large majority of the languages that still do not have a *full* Bible in their heart language.[100]

In the vast diversity and need of India, many sacrificial leaders contribute to the effort to train and mobilize for Christward movements. In these efforts both new means of disciple-making and conventional church planting continue and accelerate. One such effort has involved appointing a leader in each of seven zones in the nation, each composed of several states. Each state in turn is served by a coordinator ensuring that all parts of the state have access to a master trainer in the

---

98 Scripture records many such expressions from the lips of Jesus, to his disciples together (Matt 28:18–20; Mark 16:14–18; Luke 24:44–49, Acts 1:4–8; John 20:19–21) and to individuals such as Paul (Acts 26:18). However, many other passages, both in the Old Testament (e.g., Gen 12:1–3) and New Testament (e.g., 2 Pet 3:9), can be gathered by recording during your daily Bible reading the variety of Scriptures, making this portion of worship a rich feast reflecting the Father's heart of love for the *ethne*.

99 A helpful aid to prayer for the region is available at http://pray4ev.org/. Other nations could build a similar prayer guide.

100 See www.wycliffe.net/resources/scripture-access-statistics to track progress.

principles of disciple-making and church planting. Trainers in turn seek to track fruit and report progress.

Make requests of the church very specific and doable.

A respected Indian leader supports national church-planting process leaders in surrounding countries of the subcontinent also. Camaraderie and shared learning among national process leaders in these South Asia countries continues to grow, nurtured by a range of practical aid and personal encouragement.

Perhaps of greatest encouragement is the reality that a national process is both possible and working in what is widely recognized as the largest and most complex nation on the planet. And if in India, then we have reason for courage to say, "Yes, by God's grace, in my nation also!"

Next Steps

- Reflect on a key point that stood out to you.
- What are some practical ways that you can apply or adapt these insights into your context?
- Which of these points do you need to lift up to the Lord in prayer?
- What will your next steps be?
- Are there teammates or others you need to talk to about these action steps?

PART 3

Components of a National Vision

"You can't go back and make a new start, but you can start right now and make a brand new ending." –James R. Sherman

Launching a rocket is one thing. Keeping it in orbit is another. You can probably relate to this metaphor if you are facilitating a national church-planting mobilization process, assisting a team, or applying principles of disciple-making movements in other ways.

In either case, the journey stretches ahead. We proceed with the long view in our hearts.

A young Presbyterian seminarian visited the church he would pastor. An elder showed him the sanctuary and the small room which would be his study. After touring the building, the young pastor was taken around back to the parish cemetery. He was shown the tombstones of previous pastors dating back to the founding of the church. The elder turned to the seminarian: "I expect you'll be wanting to buy a plot, will you?"

You may be feeling what the young man did at the unexpected question. Few serve a church as pastor for a full career. But the great pastors of history and the church of the last century have almost invariably been long-term pastors. You may not lead the national mobilization process through the years. Yet there is something to learn from the attitude that anticipates a long obedience.[101]

A long obedience involves ongoing learning. In my view, learning takes place not only when we reflect on what we think we know, such as spiritual formation and the resulting attitudes, skills, and behaviors we hope for. Learning has not fully taken place in the way Jesus intends until we are acting on what we have learned. This is the nature of personal discipleship and the nature of leadership in organizations and networks. Here too, it is less costly to read books than to follow Christ in ongoing servant-leadership.

---

101 Many will recognize that this phrase is drawn from Eugene H. Peterson, *A Long Obedience in the Same Direction: Discipleship in an Instant Society* (Downers Grove, IL: InterVarsity, 2000).

Deep learning
requires both
humility and courage.

So our focus remains practical, and often personal. I mentioned earlier the view that deep, lifelong learning requires both humility and courage.

Humility is not operating in my life when I am certain, in the wrong kind of way. For example, if I'm having a conversation with my wife and I am certain that I am right and intend not to move, then I cannot learn. This can also be true in mission leadership. To be clear, I'm not speaking of the certainty illustrated in biblical principles or an effective mission tactic, but the *kind* of certainty which can come, unseen only by us, to be attached to ego, producing pride. Such pride is not only sin, but the enemy of deep-level learning.[102]

Wise leaders can hold to a long-term strategic goal—for example, mobilizing for disciple-making movements within national church-planting processes—but continue to learn and adjust tactics.[103] Recognizing when to adjust or change tactics will require humility. Persevering toward the strategic goal in a long obedience in the same direction requires courage. Part 3 deals with two kinds of challenges that require both personal spiritual growth in humility, courage and perseverance: and practical wisdom learning strategies and adjusting tactics.

Wise leadership distinguishes between challenges to resolve and polarities to manage.

---

102 Most of us can bring to mind a conversation with someone set against Christ. The set of our eyes, the mirror of our soul, give away more then we may intend. It is for this reason, no doubt, that Jesus urged his disciples in Matthew 10 and Luke 10 to seek out persons of peace.

103 Because of our calling by the risen Christ to disciple all the *ethne*, our ultimate *goal* remains firm. The "whole nation," "whole church" *strategy* is the framework on which we are focused and within which that goal is pursued. Much of this book, then, is about practical *tactics* within that strategy.

CHAPTER 9

Leadership

"A leader is a dealer in hope."
—Napoleon Bonaparte

EVERYTHING RISES AND FALLS with leadership. Or better, for our discussion, everything rises or falls with the passion, servant heart, and longevity of leadership. Let's develop this reality in some detail, both in terms of character and practice.

The leader of a movement at the intersection of the whole nation and the whole church has often been termed a "John Knoxer."[104] Should that be true in the future? Some have wondered if a better image could be found. After all, many people no longer know Knox's story. Yet the John Knoxer image remains powerful in changing times.

John Knox was a man of prayer with a burning passion for the realities of eternity—for the sake of the lost, for the sake of the redeemed, and for the sake of God's glory. He was a man with a large vision, including encompassing the reform of his nation. Due entirely to his calling, Knox dedicated his life to leaving no stone unturned and doing the needful, despite challenge and opposition, to accomplish the fullness of God's purpose in his hour.

This is the kind of calling and heart I pray for every leader of a national church-planting process. It is the heart of David for his people, as spoken of by Paul at the synagogue in Pisidian Antioch when he summarized David's heart and life with the epitaph: "When David had served God's purpose in his own generation, he fell asleep" Acts 13:36 (NIV).

John Knox was a Scottish clergyman and leader who brought reformation to the church in Scotland. Imprisoned during the late 1540s for supporting the Protestant Reformation, Knox prayed daily, "Lord, give me Scotland, or I die."

Characteristics of a John Knoxer

Are you, or another leader you know, being shaped to be a John Knoxer? How is a John Knoxer called and equipped for endurance and ultimate success in God's eyes? Look in the following directions.

Prayer life

Leadership endurance begins in prayer. "Lord, give me Scotland, or I die." For this Knox is well known, as may be seen in the response at the time of Mary, Queen of Scots: "I fear the prayers of John Knox more than all the armies of Europe."

Passion

In recent conversation, Warren Lawrence, my friend and colleague, commented: "I've been with John Knoxers in Southeast Asia since the 1990s. Some are extroverts, some introverted. Some are high energy A-types, some quieter. Some are strong in administration, some not. But one characteristic has been common to them all: a deep-seated, burning passion for the nation and the lost in it."

Calling

My conviction and experience are that people ultimately become John Knoxers for the same reason they are church planters: because God in Christ has called them. It is God's call that carries us through the dark days, the fiery darts, the misunderstandings and even misrepresentations of our motives, the inner questions, and the lack of support. Apostolic leaders are not volunteers; in fact, they are often reluctant leaders. Paul fell to the ground as a light from heaven flashed around him; other disciples were called while fishing, tax collecting, or even resting under a tree. The work and passion that is enduring through the challenges of a lifetime require this kind of clear call of God. Chronologically, God seems to call John Knoxers before they are recognized by the wider body.

Wartime mentality

Although John Knoxers have frequently been shaped by difficulties, they have learned to stay the course. I recognize that younger leaders often prefer inspiring images for leadership to those of war. It's true that leaders need to inspire those they serve and call to the Great Cause. Yet at least internally, many seasoned leaders come to identify with Paul's image of fighting the good fight (2 Tim 4:7) with the world, the flesh, and the devil (1 John 2:16).[105]

---

105 The contemporary reemergence of the war image applied to mission largely finds its roots in the thought of Ralph D. Winter. See https://joshuaproject.net/assets/media/articles/a-wartime-lifestyle.pdf.

Heart-skills

Skills are usually thought of as practical—and practical skills are needed. Most practical skills, however, can be learned or delegated to a team member. Heart-skills are easier to understand than to learn. However, heart-skills are rooted in love and in passion for God's redemptive purposes over the long term.

> A wartime mentality helps leaders develop mental toughness, keep focused, and stay the course.

- A national SCP process leader appreciates and values the whole body of Christ, not neglecting Pentecostals or non-Pentecostals, Catholics, Orthodox, women, or those with various doctrinal distinctives. The concept is not difficult, the practice more so.
- The leader is able to work with a wide range of leaders, whether or not these leaders are ideal for their role in the denominations they represent. A national SCP process leader recognizes organizational leaders are chosen for a variety of reasons and leadership skills unrelated to church planting. He or she is able to work within this range, seeking to change hearts or seek the blessing of the top leader for a younger leader more committed to church planting.
- The leader takes the long view and is not turned aside by bumps on the road. God's purpose remains compelling through the years—even decades or a lifetime—because of the high calling of him who came to sacrifice and serve (Mark 10:45).
- These, and other heart-skills, particularly for inevitable times of storm or times in the desert, are fashioned and deepened in spiritual formation. This begins, as Benedict was fond of pointing out, with a posture of listening.[106] The spiritual life must be deep and disciplined. This involves being rooted and abiding in Christ, drinking deeply of the Word, surrendering and being repeatedly filled with the Holy Spirit. Spiritual formation inevitably involves our prayer life, vital to the leader's longevity, joy, endurance, and love. No Christian leader can rise above his or her depth of spiritual walk and process of ongoing formation of the image of Christ within.

Primary Leadership: Is This a Part-Time Job?

If leadership isn't the key component of an effective national church-planting process, it comes very close. Nearly everything human rises or falls with leadership.

Some have wondered if the leadership of a national church-planting process can be effective while holding another position. Possibly, but not easily.

My personal view has been that maximizing a national church-planting process in most countries warrants full-time leadership. Leaders with the John

---

106 Listen is the first word and constant theme of Benedict's Rule. Esther de Waal, *A Life-Giving Way: A Commentary on the Rule of St. Benedict* (Collegeville, MN: Liturgical Press, 1995), 46.

The moment of highest vulnerability for a national process is leadership transition.

Knox fire burning in their innermost being of "Give me Scotland, or I die" will find ways to give as much time as possible to this burning priority.

Of course, it's not just one leader who gets it all done. Carol and I were impacted with this truth as we celebrated a recent wedding anniversary. We agreed during an evening out to identify a highlight of each year of our marriage. As we did so, we were amazed at God's goodness and at how often a highlight was related to the gift of friends—people who believed in us and the teams of which we've been a part. This is true of any role in which we may be inclined to take ourselves too seriously: pastor, teacher, movement facilitator. The gift of success in leadership is always about good people in teams, each contributing in their area of strength (Eph 4:11–12).

Finances may make it difficult to devote a majority of our time initially. The practical reality, especially in developing nations, is that many national leaders are also teaching in a seminary, pastoring a church, or holding other responsibilities related both to ministry and making a living for their family. The yearning for full-time or even majority-time engagement in a national process may seem unrealistic, and indeed may be so in the near term. Yet God provides for that to which he calls us. Prayer and patience remain central.

You may sense why a part-time role for such a challenging strategy can push the goal far down the time line. True, circumstances may require part-time engagement for some. If this is the case for you, do all you can to be sure you are supported by a strong, committed team. Your top priority, when limited by time, can wisely focus on developing and encouraging your core team—through which, by the grace of God, both time and needful leadership is multiplied.

Vitally important also is longevity. If this national leadership role is your calling, work at a pace and with a team you enjoy in such a way that you could do so for a decade at minimum, and ideally for most of a lifetime.

Leadership Transition: A Critical Juncture

Whenever it comes, leadership transition is a critical juncture. Steve Spaulding, an early Dawn Ministries regional leader, commented, "I saw cases where DAWN, in the end, didn't 'take off.' It was primarily because of ownership and leadership… When leadership shifts, the national effort can die quickly if the strategy is not really owned in the same way by succeeding leadership."

This is true of the founding leaders of most organizations and movements. The most fruitful engagement of founding leaders is to stay long, build well, and transition carefully to someone you are confident shares your vision and passion.

The moment of highest vulnerability for a national process is leadership transition. When a national leader steps away, don't make an alternate appointment lightly. Pray! Don't leave this critical role unoccupied or left to a committee. Momentum easily fades, and with it morale, or even the entire initiative. My personal view, with which I recognize some will take issue, is that a John Knoxer cannot really be "appointed" by a committee. Rather, we should pray much, asking God to surface the next facilitator. It may be that the person God chooses will "volunteer," testifying to their inner sense of call, or for persons sensing God's direction to speak out their discernment regarding who is to lead in the next season, and for the group to concur with unanimity.

The National Church-Planting Coordinating Team of a John Knoxer

Much has been written about the importance and functioning of healthy and effective teams, most of it highly applicable to ministry settings and reasonably accessible to most readers. I will mention therefore only practical matters directly related to national SCP processes.

Envision your national coordinating team

In some cases, a national team will be formed from volunteers. In other cases, you will have the opportunity to recruit your own team. In either case, because everything rises and falls on leadership, you will want to envision the kind of team you would like to shape or recruit to mobilize the body of Christ in your nation.

One way of doing so is to prayerfully ask, notepad or iPad in hand, "What would the ideal national coordinating team be willing and able to contribute to stimulate the national process?" You will discern your own answers. Let me share, however, some responses made by a group of leaders reflecting on this question. They suggested the team would ideally

1. engender trust and hope, fellowship and authentic friendship, prayer and mutual support among national leaders. Many are quite isolated, even from their own dreams.
2. cast vision winsomely. This would include public speaking and private conversations raising faith for a national disciple-making and church-planting vision and process goals to that end.
3. keep in view the big picture with an almost dogged focus, keeping the main thing the main thing.
4. prioritize appropriate tasks, in light of the big picture, in the coordinating team and outside of it.
5. recruit leaders to strategic roles.
6. organize gatherings at a national, regional, or city level to help mobilize the body of Christ to its highest calling.

7. understand the needs of organizations and help find or develop tools and training to meet those needs.
8. ensure that key processes toward a national movement continue and are improved.
9. serve in reconciliation, if conflict resolution is needed in some section of the body of Christ for it to work together.

Perfect teams don't exist, of course, and challenges will develop. Yet don't be afraid to envision the kind of people you seek, both at the beginning and from time to time as the team is renewed and enlarged. You will be able to pray with greater focus and come closer to finding the people the Lord has for you.

Recruiting your team

Are you looking primarily for gifts, skills, passion, or representation of sectors of the body of Christ? The answer is yes, but among imperfect people.

There is often wisdom in beginning small and using the vision and network connections of your embryonic teams to enlarge your team.

So, in the first handful of friends and teammates, try to set the DNA—willingness, availability, capacity, influence, kingdom diplomacy (people who love the whole church), and servant hearts for the sake of the kingdom. Look for those who value and trust of all parts of the body of Christ. Ask the Lord to lead you to those who believe there is ultimately one church and one mission to which we've been called in Christ.

It will be important that those you invite will be willing to devote time, often weekly but certainly monthly, to relationships and projects to advance the national church-planting process. Knowing the time people are available will help to set to wise objectives in each person's role.

In shaping DNA as you build your team, ensure your friends understand they are being invited not to participate in an event but to preparation for a long-term (five-plus years) process.

You may want to find at least one representative from each major denomination and a trusted pro-church mission agency. The best representative of an organization may not be the top leader, but a person second or third down the organizational ladder who enjoys the blessing of the top leader and access to the resources of that organization.

Some members of the team will have the capacity to lead a small specialty team of their own. Others may be able to take a personal role without leading a secondary team. I'll offer more about secondary teams below.

Core team

The national SCP process teams tend to be small, with many more people involved in sub-teams. Small core teams of six to eight people enable unified decision-making and oversight of the sub-teams. Sub-team leaders can join the core team for a larger gathering two to four times a year, while the core team meets once or twice in a smaller setting between each larger gathering of sub-team leaders.

Sub-teams

The popular business book by Michael Gerber, *The E-Myth*, suggests that entrepreneurial gifts alone are not adequate to sustain a growth in business. This is true also of gospel movements, and even full-blown revival. Inspiration is not enough. Supportive infrastructure must be added. like stakes support a young tree in the wind. Let's call these supports to the national process "sub-teams." Here are some examples:

1.) **Research**

A mission-critical sub-team ensures that motivating strategic information and case studies flow into the larger body of Christ, encouraging them in their mission of disciple-making and church planting. Research is that vital strategic information that provides feedback on progress and needs, assisting in decision-making and keeping the body of Christ focused on the remaining task.

2.) **Prayer mobilization**

Another sub-team is led by a passionate prayer mobilizer to ensure that encouragement in regard to prayer and awareness of spiritual warfare are brought with regularity to the body of Christ. Some intercessors also have the administrative ability to form prayer groups or connect with existing groups, while others will need to add people with administrative gifts to their team.

The team should ensure that specific needs that may be highlighted by the research team or by interaction with denominations and frontline church planters are shared widely among the body of Christ, which is called to multiply disciple-making communities in the nation among[107] those without Christ. Prayer strategies and manuals are numerous. Key to all of this is a national team member to hold up and mobilize prayer in every sector of the body of Christ for Christ's great and final calling.

3.) **Tools and training**

Another vital sub-team takes primary responsibility to ensure seminars and training events take place in all major population centers, bringing together pastors and planters with denominational and mission leaders.

---

107 An excellent example is Brian Mills, *DAWN Europa Prayer Manual*, 1994, available at www.gcpn. info/prayer/DAWN_Europe_Prayer_Manual_Brian_Mills.pdf.

These seminars cast vision, using research to explain the need to multiply disciples and disciple-making communities among the least-reached of every class and kind and location in the nation. In addition, the seminars point to tools and training opportunities, current and future, as well as to ongoing regional collaboration and interest groups that may be planned.

This task, of course, is too large for a single team. The coordinating team therefore needs to visit the major cities as it can and works to form smaller teams to visit smaller centers. It's important to gather contact information of participants in each location in order to build on interest and involvement for the future.

Other roles and sub-teams will also be needed. The following are examples, though you may deem various other tactical roles to be more important.

4.) **Communication**

Communication is the lifeblood of relationships, movements, and national networks. The communication team leader, who obviously has a heart to stimulate communication, will be aware that vision needs to be recast regularly. This means newsletters, email, WhatsApp, Facebook, or other culturally vital connection points need to be identified, used, and expanded. The person who is responsible to keep this important process on the national church-planting mobilization agenda may need to develop one or more sub-groups to focus on areas like the following:

a.) Website

In open countries, a website can assist in many ways. In closed countries, similar information must be handled more creatively and carefully. Depending on security considerations, the following could be considered:

- Priority needs for church planting, mapped graphically
- Encouraging case studies
- Progress reports from denominations and individual planters
- Upcoming church planter training seminars and materials
- Ways to connect to regional and special interest focus groups—prayer groups, church planter peer-support groups, coaches, and fourth-generation movement trainers
- Downloadable books, videos, and links to other sites

b.) Newsletters

In addition to resources that leaders can access on their own initiative, it's important to bring similar material to them. After all, even leaders highly committed to God's kingdom are not always thinking about multiplying disciple-making communities, important as this may be. For this reason, newsletters remain important. As you and your team interact with planters and leaders, you will receive news from planters and organizations, case studies, resources for leaders, training courses, peer support groups, updates from researchers, and more. All can be distributed digitally or on paper.

Printing can be expensive, and likely more so, postage. Therefore, you may also want to consider smaller versions of encouragement and motivation in the form of bulletin inserts that can be distributed through organizational leaders to local churches or downloaded from a website, reinforcing to lay leaders the vision of disciple-making and church planting. Likewise, copy-ready material will almost always be welcomed by editors of organizational magazines, with thanks to them for bearing the expense to advance the cause of your country's national church-planting process.

Communicating with leaders generally involves some form of a contact list or database. Most readers will have casually collected the contact information of friends and Christian leaders for years in more than one way: a stack of business cards, an Excel spreadsheet, MailChimp, or another database. But new questions are arising. Ironically data restriction (in the name of privacy protection), in societies increasingly oriented toward broad surveillance, is becoming more common.

However you view this trend, data-protection laws are growing complex and challenging. In some countries you will be required to have on file a signed form indicating that you have permission to communicate with a person before you can legally do so. In other nations you can hold the contact information of those who are part of an organization or society. A minority of nations have only limited restrictions. Be sure to check the current law in your country.[108]

5.) **Regional focus groups**

Another valuable role for which you may seek a team member is to form a sub-team to encourage regional collaboration groups across the country. In the largest population centers of each state or province, this valuable team seeks to convene leaders from all denominations and organizations who want to become more effective in multiplying disciple-making communities of all kinds and sizes to reach the least-reached.

In each state, province, or region, there are likely people with special interests related to disciple-making and multiplying disciple-making communities who, if gathered, would encourage each other to greater heights. Some of these interest areas may focus on local unreached or least-

---

108 Should restrictive trends develop, it may be necessary to make leadership networks smaller in geographic coverage or ask the Lord for greater means of creativity: see this footnote in Appendix 7.

reached people groups, peer-support groups for church planters, connecting points for coaches and those who would benefit from being coached, and perhaps most importantly from a strategic perspective, practitioners aiming to make disciples and/or plant churches to the fourth spiritual generation, the point at which the potential of a movement a reached.

Depending on culture, size of your nation, and other factors, these focus groups could also have national expressions. In at least one instance, for example, educators eager to contribute to the discipling of their nation by shaping leaders equipped for the task formed a national organization in which to share ideas and resources to make their schools more effective to that end. Another national-level focus group could connect practitioners training others in disciple-making models that aim for multiple generations of disciples.

6.) **A personal touch with organizations**

We want to engage all denominations, networks, and pro-church organizations, encouraging their most strategic contribution toward the task. There is no substitute for personal relationships with leaders of these organizations. It will take a team to connect personally, since each of us is limited regarding the number of personal relationships we can meaningfully maintain. For this reason, one member of the core team may be asked to initiate and deepen relationships with organizational leaders, recognizing that he or she will need to form a carefully chosen sub-team to do it well.

In many countries, denominations, mission agencies, and other organizations have convened "family gatherings," conventions, or other kinds of prayer or training events. While paused or re-structured during COVID-19, these can be opportunities for a more personal connection. Hopefully a member of your coordination team will be invited to be a plenary speaker, provide a display table, or be allowed to bring greetings or brief announcements or updates on behalf of the national church-planting process.

There are many other possibilities. The national coordinating team seeks and adds members as its ministry grows. Figure 11 is simply illustrative as you develop your own sub-teams. Four generation movements, you may remember from chapter 4, are disciple-making and church-planting movements which aim, from the beginning, at a fourth spiritual generation of Christ-followers. When this goal is envisioned from the beginning a spiritual DNA has been inculcated empowering the movement to ongoing multiplication.

Some sub-teams may in time become a national network, adding members across the country who are willing, for example, to call on five or ten key leaders twice a year to listen, encourage, and if possible, help those leaders take further steps in mobilizing their organization for disciple-making and church planting.

Every coordinating team will need to pick from among the opportunities before it or work to create opportunities. A sub-team may host retreats or seminars where

Figure 11: Generating Sub-teams

organizational leaders share how they are leading their organization to give priority to church planting, pray for one another, and share ideas, learnings, and resources.

No one can do it all, and of course not every opportunity is of equal value. This is but one of the reasons we must seek the Lord of the harvest with love and diligence. He will lead and guide into the greater harvest, for this is his heart and the reason for his sacrifice.

Life of the national team

The team convening the first national congress often begins relatively small and focused largely on preparations for the initial gathering. Then joyfully and rather suddenly, vision is extended more widely throughout the body of Christ. An outcome of this is that a larger team is soon needed to build on, maintain, and help grow momentum toward a wider national process. We want the "Amen" of the benediction closing the gathering to be the beginning, not the end! Additional infrastructure will be needed. While this is scalable and can start small, it must not be neglected, and can begin almost immediately.

Vital balance

There are, as on all teams, two vital components, with each giving value to the other. The team must enjoy authentic relationships, rooted in communion with the Trinity and with each other. This is nurtured and manifested in friendship, prayer, eating and laughing together, and reflection on the call to the kingdom. In addition, the team must respond to the call. In the case of a national church-planting process coordination team, this involves committing to outcomes and sharing progress in the journey.

Relational retreats

In larger countries, the team may cover much distance and have difficulty meeting in person with regularity. Therefore, the work and relational life of the team may be lived in the context of less frequent retreat-like settings and more frequent Internet meetings. Generally, teams need to meet at least once a year in a multiday retreat setting to deepen personal relationships, and then six to eight times in addition by Zoom to track progress on mission-critical tasks and directions.

These retreats, in my experience, are most fruitful when about one-third of the time is unstructured for prayer, conversation, rest, and comradery. The other two-thirds of the time can be structured around review and planning.

Zoom meetings also need a balance of renewing relationships and digging deeper into the practical details involved in stewarding a movement.

Purposeful meetings

Even in a Zoom meeting, the balance between spontaneity and "ticking the boxes" can be maintained. The following process might be helpful:

Connecting relationally and spiritually (approximately one-third of time available): Welcome, Scripture, and Prayer

I like to ask, because the Internet allows us to see a person's face but not his or her heart, "What is happening in your life that we can't see, but that may be affecting you—positively or negatively—as we meet?" or, "What personal or ministry high or low have you experienced since we last met?"

You can invite each person to pray for one other person, or the group as a whole to pray for personal concerns as well as the task ahead, deepening bonds and dependence on the power of the Holy Spirit.

Advancing the national process (approximately two-thirds of time available): Task Updates

Each person present shares progress in his or her area of responsibility, followed by time-bound plans for next steps. For example, leaders may be developing sub-teams in such areas as:

- National congress event planning (may be reconstituted every two–three years)
- Regional seminars, consultations, and collaboration groups that aim for geographic breadth.
- Prayer mobilization
- Research of the harvest field and harvest force.
- Relational engagement of organizations and networks—i.e., "drinking tea" with network and denominational leaders to discover needs, encourage engagement, and find key leaders within organizations with a passion to serve.
- Communications and publications—print and Internet
- Tools and training—e.g., developing fourth-generation movements, pre-launch boot camps/incubators for planters, training coaches, peer-support groups for planters that stimulate Bible school and seminaries to assist in training, etc.

This systematic overview may involve about half of the meeting. If the task update rotation cannot be completed, relax—and pick it up next time. Don't neglect to do so.

- *Scrum:* There is always a need for spontaneous input. New ideas emerge. The Holy Spirit speaks. Some liken this part of the meeting to a rugby scrum. It's a quick meeting focusing on solving a problem or floating a new strategy or direction. Sometimes a decision can be made quickly—but if not, return to it at the next meeting.
- *Team development:* The teams mentioned above may need to be enlarged or members may need to be replaced. Each team should have a second, or apprentice, leader, in case the facilitator is unable to continue. It is wise to review team strength and the possible need of forming additional teams on a regular basis.
- *Guests:* It is also wise to invite guests to retreats and Internet-based update meetings, both to broaden the movement and to build potential future leadership.
- *Next meeting:* Setting the time and date of the next meeting is vital and best done while the group can consult their calendar. Leaving this vital step until later is costly.

Relationship comes first. Yet relationship is built on shared purpose. Like the first disciples, some of your team will lean toward the relational. That gift and calling is important. Some will lean toward the vision and task. These gifts and callings are vital also. The wise team leader will sense when the vital balance is healthy and when, even within a single relational retreat or purposeful meeting, the balance is best nudged the other direction.

The Backbone Organization

In support of the coordinating team and its leader, an effective national church-planting process will normally, over time, require the services of an organization in which to nest functions like financial administration. This and other support are provided by what is often termed a "backbone organization."

While this support is vital for a movement to have effective longevity, it is important that the support organization does not view itself as owning the national process in a controlling way. It is involved only to serve the movement selflessly. This support organization must also be perceived by leaders across the country as being neutral in not advancing its own name or reputation. The heart of Jesus celebrated in Philippians 2 is the portrait which often comes to mind and heart.

> The national process is best "nested" within a broadly trusted supportive or "backbone" organization.

Let's address this needed balance of service and selflessness both positively and negatively.

Positively, as implied, it is critical that a trusted hosting or nesting organization serve the day-to-day operational functions of a partnership of this national scope. Unfortunately, a national team without a backing organization frequently does not actually have the capacity to accomplish its vision. We seek not overworked servants, but a servant organization to maximize effectiveness.

A national Evangelical Alliance (EA) or Lausanne Committee is generally supportive in principle, but in daily reality often has a wide range of interests and priorities. Its best role may be to host or convene an initial gathering launching a national process, giving its moral support without attempting to give practical attention to all the details of a national church-planting strategy. The EA, however, should be asked for its blessing, and the hosting organization should be a part of the EA or other national association of Christian churches.

Let's touch on some functions of a trusted host or backbone organization. Financial administration is often related to national gatherings. Registrations need to be collected, bills paid, and bookkeeping managed. The coordination of research and its effective dissemination to church-planting leaders is often managed from a hosting organization, as is the gathering of progress reports from denominations and networks and case studies of effective models. While some of these activities can be delegated to volunteers, evidence suggests not all can, particularly in the long term.

For this reason, the support organization needs not only to serve in a Barnabas fashion but also be selective in the way it does so, not doing for denominations and mission agencies what they can do themselves, but where necessary freeing them from administration to focus on their central task of planting and multiplication.

Fundraising for the national movement—in support of research, for instance— if the coordination team deems it necessary, should be led by a member of the national coordination team, in my view, rather than directly by the backbone organization. The backbone organization is wise not to (overly) monetize the national process lest its motivation be misconstrued or an unsustainable dependency be developed. The backbone organization's financial role is best limited to administration of initiatives taken by the national coordinating team. While this distinction may seem hairsplitting, the way finances are initiated and organized can send unintentional messages, so financial issues are worth thinking through and reviewing from time to time.

Some may wonder how the backbone or nesting organization comes into its support role of a national initiative. Often it simply sees the need and begins to serve. Sometimes its people make themselves available as volunteers. The support organization should not simply assume this role, however. In my experience, it is wise to offer to serve and to be welcomed into the role by the coordinating team—the group of national leaders who give the team its initial mandate—or even by the larger body during a national gathering.

While it may not always be necessary, my practice has been to give the national SCP movement's leadership opportunity to reaffirm the backbone organization's service role every two years. This way it retains a volunteer service role, without control. Generally, as the relationship deepens, the agreement loses its need for renewal.

In a small number of settings, the SCP movement, in lieu of a volunteer backbone organization, opens a new organization with its own board to serve the movement. This may also become the best way forward in your setting for some political reason. This course, however, is more work than inviting a willing backbone organization to serve.

In either case, one of the support functions of the backbone organization is to provide, if possible, personnel to support the SCP task on a volunteer basis. These personnel may include expat workers who raise personal support in order to serve. Loaning personnel to a larger kingdom cause may not make business sense, but it makes excellent kingdom sense.

In country after country, I find expat workers serving in vital roles—not always leading formally, but often in a leading support role. Why? Often because pastors and denominational leaders (in many countries these are dual roles) don't have the energy to add another role, even though the role is valuable to the growth of the kingdom. Local leaders are wise to view expats as valued partners. Expats are wise to serve humbly and well.

In most cases I've observed missionaries to have demonstrated that they are nonthreatening to national leaders (i.e., "They really are here to help and not try to control us") and have demonstrated they can be trusted with important tasks ("They have paid their dues").

It is interesting to note that a secular sociological study has also recognized the role of the hosting organization for community service, summarizing the importance of this role in these terms:

> Backbone organizations essentially pursue six common activities to support and facilitate collective impact which distinguish this work from other types of collaborative efforts. Over the lifecycle of an initiative, they:

1. Guide vision and strategy
2. Support aligned activities
3. Establish shared measurement practices
4. Build public will
5. Advance policy
6. Mobilize funding[109]

Denominations, Organizations, and Networks

A final key leadership role is played by the church itself. Church leaders serve in denominations, mission agencies, networks of various kinds, and, of course, local churches.

A primary calling of the national coordination team is to stimulate, motivate, and support the vision of these church leaders. The task may seem challenging—and it is—but it's easier if you see them in two primary categories.

Jim Montgomery's "13 Steps to a Successful Growth Program"[110] sought to address leaders of denominations, organizations, and networks capable of planting churches. While the full text is available in appendix 2, given its importance, let's summarize the steps:

1. Dream great dreams; see large visions.
2. Develop, maintain, and use a solid base of data on the church-planting ministry—past and current—of your organization.
3. Set challenging, realistic, and measurable goals in your organization.
4. Achieve goal ownership by coming to your goal in a careful process.
5. Give a name to your initiative and the goal representing it.
6. Develop functional infrastructure to support your organizational initiative.
7. Depend on prayer and the power of the Spirit.
8. Keep members informed and motivated through quality and regular communication.
9. Train your members for their task and calling.
10. Create sound financial policy.
11. Send out workers, planters, and missionaries.
12. Regularly evaluate progress.
13. Update and make new plans.

---

109 "Understanding the Value of Backbone Organizations in Collective Impact: Part 2," *Stanford Social Innovation Review*, https://ssir.org/articles/entry/understanding_the_value_of_ backbone_organizations_in_collective_impact_2.

110 www.gcpn.info/resources/13_steps_to_SCP.pdf.

The process will seem challenging to those not called to organizational leadership. But those called to such leadership often have access to forming teams and gathering resources to undertake this process of multiplying transformational disciple-making communities. The process itself, outlined and adaptable, gives organizational focus to kingdom growth among the least and the lost, the highest priority for existing as a denomination.

Local pastors, arguably the primary leadership category in the national church, can be engaged in heart and spirit both by leaders of their denomination and by direct communication from the national coordination team, highlighting the unfinished task and inviting them to national and regional gatherings for prayer and training.

Local pastors must be convinced of three practical realities:

- The local church is the frontline of kingdom growth.
- No local church, no matter how vital it is currently, will exist forever.
- Therefore, every local church must plant at least two daughter churches— one to replace itself in advance of the day when it may cease, and the other to extend the kingdom in a community or among a people group where the church does not currently hold out the light of Christ.

Local pastors are key to mobilizing the church to her calling to be the gospel incarnate in every location, cultural space, and high-rise apartment complex. How will this come about? Pastors hear, on behalf of your community, the call of Jesus to the sheep and goats in Matthew 25. Ensure that your people hear it; and move your people out to form new disciple-making communities to bring the lost to Christ and Christ to the lost.

Next Steps

- What are practical ways you can apply or adapt these insights into your context?
- Which of these points do you need to lift to the Lord in prayer?
- What will your next steps be?
- Are there teammates or others you need to talk to about these action steps?

CHAPTER 10

Harvest Field, Harvest Force, Harvest Fruit

"The goal of research is to turn data into information, information into insight, and insight into action."
—Russ Mitchell

THE PURPOSE of national research is to change behavior. The changed behavior is to plant churches by those who have not planted churches before. In addition, we want to plant churches that make new disciples and plant new disciple-making churches, ideally to the fourth spiritual generation. Further, we desire those planted churches to be healthy and to have transformational impact at minimum locally and ideally regionally. That's a tall order!

But there is more. We do research not simply to plant churches where we find it easiest to plant churches, but to plant churches where they are most needed to give everyone equal opportunity to be engaged by the gospel, which brings Christ's grace, radical renewal, and eternal life to the lost.

Initial Research: How Much Information Is Enough?

When we speak of national research in the context of a church-planting movement, a question often asked is, "How much research is needed for a national process, and how accurate must it be to move forward?"

The answer varies by stage. To begin a national process, research can be cursory. It should be accurate as far as it goes, but it doesn't need to be comprehensive. A preliminary survey can be drawn in some countries from government census data, and in other countries from a sampling of denominational data. It could be as brief as five to ten pages, but it must draw applications that motivate discussion and action. Presenting accurate, though initially limited, information in a way that engages hearts as well as minds has been termed the prophetic message flowing from the research.[111] The motivational message, based on accurate information—as modeled by Nehemiah in his call to rebuild Jerusalem's wall after the exile—is an attempt to hear and communicate the Lord's heart, who wept over Jerusalem (Luke 19:41), as Christ looks over the reality of your nation.

Preliminary research should be offered in humility, readily acknowledging it is incomplete, but maintaining, however, that it suggests valid initial directions to disciple the nation. As much as giving information, preliminary research also should call for unity, for obedience to the Great Commission, for courage, for working together as "hands and feet" of one body (1 Cor 12), and for discipling the nation.

As unity and commitment to next steps are evidenced, a second stage with more detailed research will be needed.

Establishing a National Research Team

To track progress toward the goal of placing an outreaching, disciple-making community within reach of every one thousand persons, and to direct wise and practical decision-making to that end, is a considerable task. But it is worth it! For both reasons, every country should consider establishing what Bob Waymire, founder of Global Mapping International, termed a "permanent national research function team."[112]

The role of this team is to find ways of addressing the research needs of the national process in which helpful comparisons can be drawn over time to see progress and specifics of the task that remains. In addition, this team aims to present its findings and case studies of successful models of multiplication in a form to motivate godly hearts to strategic action.

Technical details of the work of this team are beyond the scope of this book. Excellent work has been published to assist your national research team and to provide practical tools for its work. Please consult the reading list at the end of this book in the section "Strategic Information."

---

111 Jim Montgomery devoted an entire chapter to the power of a wise and motivational prophetic message in *DAWN 2000*.

112 Bob Waymire, *National Research Mobilization Handbook* (Etna, CA: Light International, 1994). See this footnote number in Appendix 7 for a downloadable scan of the *National Research Mobilization Handbook* manual.

Effects of Culture and Human Nature on Recognition of the Need for Research

It should be acknowledged that establishing a research team to serve this mobilization function may come more easily to some cultures than others.

In many countries, an individual with a passion for the task can simply begin to work, recruit a team, and share results with leaders at a later point, with reasonable expectation that findings will be received respectfully and taken seriously. These cultures are characterized by low power-distance assumptions.[113] In higher power-distance cultures, researchers are more likely to need someone at the top to request, commission, or mandate the needed research.

Regardless of where your country falls in this continuum, it is helpful to communicate with leaders, either to let them know of your heart and intentions, or to ask permission, or both.

Then there is the element of simple human pride. In one nation, research was commissioned and completed to a high standard. However, an advance copy came into the hands of leaders who found the results did not reflect favorably on their organization. Sadly, pride found ways to boycott release of the study. Church planting in this country continues with energy, but planters are like pilots flying blind, planting where they think churches are most needed, but uncertain—doing their best without the proper intel of strategic information.

Three Vital Sectors of the Harvest

To produce an accurate picture, strategic information involves linking what predecessors have called the harvest field and the harvest force. These terms are drawn from images used by our Savior in passages like this in John 4:

> "My food," said Jesus, "is to do the will of him who sent me and to finish his work. Don't you have a saying, 'It's still four months until harvest'? I tell you, open your eyes and look at the fields! They are ripe for harvest. Even now the one who reaps draws a wage and harvests a crop for eternal life, so that the sower and the reaper may be glad together. (John 4:34–36 NIV)

In this harvest image, the harvest field is readily seen as those waiting to be invited to know Christ and the harvest force as laborers in the fields of the world.[114] Following this image, the harvest field then comprises all the *ethne* in Jesus' heart in this passage in John 4, as well as Matthew 28 and other passages. In addition to Jesus' words in the Gospels, other New Testament writers often use the agricultural images of harvest fields, the work force, and the fruit of the harvest.

---

113 A map comparing countries relative to "power-distance" can be found at https://geerthofstede.com/culture-geert-hofstede-gert-jan-hofstede/6d-model-of-national-culture/.

114 Raised in a family with a farming background, I've appreciated the video "The Harvest," available at this footnote number in Appendix 7.

Harvest force

The harvest force is about the workers. Who is available? Where is the church active in the harvest? Where isn't it engaging the harvest yet?

There are several specific aspects to harvest-force research, each equally important.

First, researchers focus on finding all vital denominations, mission organizations, educational organizations, networks, and other groups in the nation committed to the gospel and to reaching the lost. In some countries, directories of Christian organizations are readily available and only need to be updated. In other nations, such directories (digital or print) may have never existed, and your work will represent a breakthrough.[115] In some countries, organizations are relatively public and open; in others countries, they are purposefully quiet.

After ten years of tracking the directories of such organizations, my experience reveals that new organizations continue to surface, at least in part because new networks and organizations continue to be born. For this reason, the discovery task, including the development of relationships with leaders of new organizations, is never final.

The second aspect in relation to research is the discovery of active congregations themselves. This is not about helping Christians find a church. In most cases, Christians can find a church with little help when they move into a new community. Nor is it about whether there is a church building within physical reach of non-Christians looking for a church. This is so because those who are still in the harvest field are generally not looking for a church building, and therefore do not see it.

If not to help non-Christians find disciple-making communities, why does the research team look for and map active congregations?

The purpose is to see where there are enough existing churches with capacity to reach the lost adjacent to them within their people group, and where the church does not yet have adequate capacity to reach the number of lost near them. To do this effectively, researchers need to identify local churches ministering in

---

115 In some nations a list of Christian organizations and their leaders exists only in the minds of a few strategic leaders. The reason for this may be a lack of trust or even pride. Workers may conclude collaboration based on shared knowledge is impossible for security reasons. In severe cases this may be the case for a season. In moderate cases, collaboration will be slower, partial, and require careful trust-building. Even so, I am convinced that God wishes to gather leaders who choose to know each other and to learn to trust each other as much as possible for the sake of the kingdom. We can pray and be patient, losing sight neither of the goal nor of the reason for our desire for collaboration for the sake of those yet "strangers to the covenants of promise, having no hope and without God in the world" (Eph 2:12). In God's timing, collaboration can be pursued fruitfully, even if initially in smaller installments until wider opportunities open, as at least a partial example to others toward an answer to the Lord's prayer in John 17 for unified mission among his disciples.

categories like those uncovered in national harvest-field research (e.g., language group, ethnicity, people group). The importance of these parallel categories will become more apparent in the section on mapping the harvest field.

In addition, it is valuable to discover which denominations and mission agencies are growing most healthily, where, and if possible, why. Organizational growth is generally measured in average annual growth rate (AAGR). Most organizations will be interested in their growth: whether it is increasing or slowing, why, and what this may mean.

Organizations with healthy growth rates can be studied further to see which methods of training, leadership development, disciple-making, and church planting seem to be effective in their context.

It is true that not all denominations and mission agencies want to learn from their peers, or even about themselves. Yet taking the time to learn about the harvest force in your nation is valuable for those most eager to engage with the harvest and therefore generally most eager to learn from their peers who are demonstrating sustained growth. Sometimes one district of a denomination will begin to apply learnings from another denomination, followed later by other districts.

Harvest field

Harvest-field research seeks to make clear who remains without an active gospel witness, and in which districts they live. There are initial general ways and more specific practical ways of bringing this needed clarity to intercessors, nearby churches, and church planters.

Initial harvest-field research can be aided by government census results in those countries where such information is made public. Many governments gather census information regarding the language spoken at home, ethnicity, religion, and other factors that help church planters better understand those whom they are seeking to engage in conversation to know Christ. In open countries, maps are often available, sometimes for a fee, from which such key factors of identity can be gathered.

Where census data is not available, other efforts to draw pictures of people in each locale must be made. Sometimes the sociology department of a local university can help. On occasion, undergraduate or graduate students can be recruited to assist in part of the task for a paper or project. If a Christian college or Bible school is nearby, this assistance may be more easily acquired. At the local level, the chamber of commerce, the planning department at city hall, the library, or the office of a marketing firm may also provide insights.

Then comes the exciting step of preparing pictures of existing churches as part of the harvest force in their context of the harvest field.

Mapping the harvest field

Most people understand information visually better than conceptually. Lists and numbers become more meaningful when converted to maps and charts. The next step is to bring together—in the way most helpful to decision-makers in your nation— information about where least-reached people groups, languages, ethnicities, and other cultural subsets live in relation to local churches. This shows where the church is not yet present, and where disciples most need to plant churches. This important visualization can be prepared in steps from views of the whole nation to details within a city.

> Most people understand information visually better than conceptually.

Static mapping

Static maps, showing the ratio between the population and the number of churches currently providing a gospel witness to that population, can be prepared to provide a snapshot of a nation, province, city, language group, or people group. These ratios, in turn, show the comparative need of prioritizing prayer, disciple-making, and church planting in this region or among this people group.

Here are just two visual examples.[116] First, from Romania, where a national overview brings comparative church-planting needs into stark relief in a largely monoethnic context.[117]

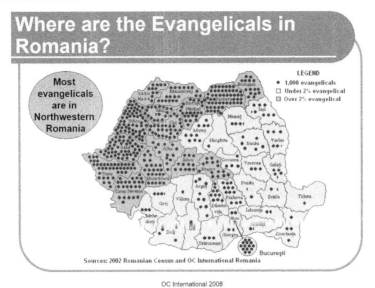

OC International 2008

Figure 12: Where Are the Evangelicals in Romania? (used with permission)

---

116 Links to additional examples can be found at this footnote in Appendix 7.

117 The full research presentation by Russ Mitchell is available from www.gcpn.info/ni/Romania_ CP_needs_research_2008_in_English.pps.

A second example shows the comparative need for church-planting among counties in Taiwan.[118]

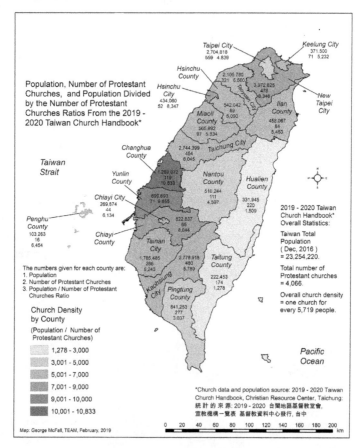

Figure 13: Taiwan Comparative Needs for Church Planting by County (used by permission)

The goal of effective mapping is the most helpful level of detail for decision making. Too much detail can be overwhelming; too little detail can aid only minimally. Other map possibilities will occur to you.[119] Don't miss high-density housing crying out for microchurch-planting or "invisible" groups like the deaf![120]

If you have the capacity, static maps can be prepared in a customized way as new questions and needs arise. Depending on your security context, you may want to post them behind an online password. Bear in mind, however, that while

---

118 Map by George McFall from www.tmf.org.tw/all-taiwan-maps.html (accessed Nov 1, 2020).

119 In an earlier stage of Canadian SCP ministry, I gathered harvest field, harvest force, mapping, and other PPTs for presentation. See Appendix 7 for the links.

120 There are seventy million deaf people worldwide, the largest UPG in the world—hidden "in plain sight." See https://doorinternational.org/.

the technology is available and many maps are possible, not all are necessary or equally useful. Therefore, your research team may wish to engage small focus groups to discern which maps are of highest value and usefulness in your setting.

Interactive mapping

Interactive mapping organizes the proportion of active churches in a given harvest field into real-time depictions of church-planting needs and priorities. These can be posted on the Web when security allows, so that the entire church can see its responsibility. Good examples have been provided by leaders serving national church-planting processes in France and Thailand.[121]

The examples are interactive, showing more detail as you zoom in, and in real time so that multiple organizations can provide updates simultaneously, producing a map that is likely to be more accurate at any given time. This approach lessens the data entry required of the research team and increases the engagement and involvement of each denomination.[122] In addition, the responsibility for accuracy lies with each contributing organization.

Naturally, there are advantages to both static and interactive maps. The best solution is to provide church planters with the use of both kinds.

An essential advantage of static maps is that it is easier to depict a wider range of harvest field realities. Almost any condition tracked in a national census can be isolated and highlighted. Such maps can be labor-intensive to produce and can become outdated, but they also can often be updated online for the widest benefit to church planters.

Interactive maps depict population-to-church ratio, usually by shading, to show priority needs for church planting, which is vital to drawing attention to high-need locales. To my knowledge, however, interactive maps currently don't yet show UPGs, ethnicity, language, or other primary cultural groupings important to providing more nuanced understanding of those people groups who most need new churches planted to reach them. In years ahead, we may expect to see technology develop to include selectable layers to better understand ethnicity, language, and other social realities—in addition to overall population-to-ratio interactive maps.

Security issues in some countries will continue to restrict public access to interactive maps via the Internet. Technology will likely allow for thumb drives for computers or the use of microSD cards in smart phones as an alternative, but in some cases static maps will remain best. Software has also been developed to track multigenerational

---

121 France: www.1pour10000.fr/la-carte; Thailand: https://estar.ws. Some countries will have those with the expertise to produce their own mapping software, using tools like QGIS or Philcarto, which don't post online but work on Mac and PC, or industry leader ArcGIS.

122 Reality is such that a member of the research team will still need to check periodically with denominational representatives to ensure that data is current.

disciple-making movements.[123] The means of tracking disciples who make disciples can be simpler, but face the same security concerns in some contexts. You are in the best position to evaluate changing security realities in your own setting.

I know a country where a single static map is stored on a thumb drive and viewed privately by trusted leaders. Another country posts information on the Internet. I've watched church planters place Xs on a rough, hand-drawn map to show new disciple-making communities and resulting churches. Some use smart phones and GPS coordinates. Technology varies, and sophistication itself is not the issue. Rather, the point is that the church, large or miniscule, free or persecuted, knows its harvest field and calling, and with much prayer and passionate hearts, obeys with great love for the lost and a desire for God to be glorified.

A caveat

Because interactive maps, as valuable as they are, give the impression of sophistication, they may be accorded such authority that can reduce motivation to do needed local research. For this reason, you may wish to offer comments and suggestions such as the following to strengthen the effect of your interactive map.

- Post with your map a brief guide with practical suggestions for church planters as they engage their neighborhood at ground level in shoe-leather research by prayer-walking, exploring cultural spaces, and engaging people in conversation street by street.

- Post a disclaimer explaining that the map presents only a partial picture, since some churches may cease ministry but appear on the map for months before removal. In addition, new churches may not appear immediately.

- If necessary in your context, you might explain that interactive maps show only a ratio, rather than depicting church street addresses. The population-to-church ratio for each municipality (census tract or other governmental administrative unit) keeps church locations private, while yet making clear priority population centers for new disciple-making and church-planting needs.

While providing disciple-makers and potential mother churches strategic information about where the lost have least opportunity to encounter Christ, it is also important to reflect on decision-making we still want to facilitate by our presentation of data. We want the data we share to stimulate planters to think further for themselves, do additional research, and come to their own conclusions regarding the best strategy as they engage the harvest.

---

123 At the time of writing, helpful tools include GenMapper and iShare. Technology develops quickly. For updates please see this footnote number in Appendix 7.

For example, a church-planting mobilizer knew that data pointed to high-density housing near a shopping mall as a primary need area. Yet he knew this information alone wasn't enough to engage the heart. He then gave those working with him a clipboard, a neighborhood to research, and five questions with which to engage residents:[124]

1. Are you actively involved in a local church? (If the answer is yes, thank them for their time and move on.)

2. Why do you think most people in your neighborhood are not involved in a church community? (Note negative stereotypes that might exist but do not need to be countered now, since your heart is being opened to hear the cry of the community.)

3. What significant needs are you aware of in the community? (Programs may be able to be developed to meet these needs. It is premature, however, to make promises.)

4. If circumstances were to change in your life in such a way that you were open to involvement in a Christian community, what would that church need to be like for you to consider it? (Listen for positive images which may be legitimately reinforced in your church plant.)

5. What advice would you give to leaders developing a new church in your community? (Listen with humility.)

Though this process is not particularly comfortable, it is very valuable. It gives church planters a feel for the community's greatest needs. The style of new churches planted are impacted by responses reflecting local perceptions of the Christian church. For example, the theme "Come as you are" was initiated in one church plant out of the inaccurate impression that nice clothes are needed to visit a church. The decision not to pass an offering plate but to make an offering box available on the wall grew in response to the common perception that the church is primarily after people's money. Your experiences, growing out of your willingness to become uncomfortable as you listen, will help shape your approach as you make disciples and begin churches and movements in your context.

These specific questions may be applicable only in comparatively open cultures where the gospel has a measure of acceptance. I share them as an example of how street-level research moves us from abstract assumptions regarding the location and culture to which strategic information leads to a deeper engagement of the heart. Less-open cultures may require other means, such as reaching out in coffee shops or community groups (sport, arts, debate) or visiting schools, hospitals, or refugee camps. The point is to connect with a community to which research points, and then to explore and engage that community with both your mind and your heart.

---

124 Adapted from one of Rick Warren's first seminars, which I attended some years ago.

Multicultural churches

What about multicultural churches, or what some call intercultural churches? Can multicultural churches fill the gap in a way that sets aside the need to focus on cultural distinctions and preferences and unique people groups? Why not just plan multicultural churches until all have been reached?

Christians are rightly passionate about an end to racism. In the gospel lies a vision of one people, equally loved by God, redeemed by Christ, brothers and sisters who are made one family in the cross (Gal 3:28). In addition, the realization of history in the immediate presence of the Lord is one in which every tribe, tongue, people, and nation are gathered in worship to express the beauty and justice of God's kingdom (Rev 5:9–10). Why, then, plant churches for different cultural and ethnic groups on earth?

The answer, which I recognize will not satisfy everyone, is largely practical. The day revealed in the Revelation of Jesus Christ and communicated to John the Apostle will come. Of this we have no doubt, and we eagerly yearn for the day of completion when every knee will bow and every tongue will confess that Jesus Christ is Lord (Phil 2:9–11). We also recognize and celebrate every multicultural church that testifies to the power of the gospel in the face of sinful racism, demonstrating now that which is to fully come. We also recognize and celebrate that some members of some ethnic groups are already drawn to multicultural churches that demonstrate the coming of the future.

The reality remains, however, that some for whom Christ died, especially seekers, are not drawn to such churches. Many people prefer their own *ethne*, are not inclined to let their children marry outside their *ethne*, and don't really understand or trust people, including Christians, who come from other cultures. For this reason, our preferences notwithstanding, distinct efforts to reach each culture, language, and ethnicity must continue to be made.

That is not to say that multicultural churches shouldn't also be planted within reach of many *ethne*. We should do so. We should also compare the effectiveness of multicultural churches versus predominately homogeneous churches to reach each *ethne* in the community. Sometime the younger generation is more responsive to the discipling efforts of a multicultural church, and we rejoice as they come to Christ! Yet as long as sociological realities remain barriers to turning to Christ for members of any group, we are being compassionate to plant churches within their culture to reach them.[125]

---

125 Donald McGavran, in *Understanding Church Growth* (Grand Rapids: Eerdmans, 1970), articulated the power of what he called the "homogenous group principle" in the human community. C. Peter Wagner, in *Our Kind of People* (John Knox Press, 1979), developed the concept further. Some have taken issue with this assertion, arguing that the new humanity in Christ must be multiethnic. While this is ultimately and gloriously true, it remains a sociological fact that many

Harvest fruit

Researchers can also serve the body of Christ by discovering what is working best to bring the harvest to Christ, and hopefully why. It is this part of the research task that Jim Haney, Director of Global Research for the Southern Baptist International Mission Board and author of *Fruit to Harvest* (missionbooks.org), calls a focus on harvest fruit. This entails measuring the effectiveness of planting efforts and discovering the most fruitful tools and methods being utilized to multiply new disciples and disciple-making communities.

> Street-level research moves us from abstract assumptions ... to a deeper engagement of the heart.

This is not to focus only on groups and locations which are most responsive—that is, on low-hanging fruit. Indeed, emphasis on fruit can lead us in that direction. The Lord of the harvest, however, loves both responsive and resistant populations. The purpose of harvest-fruit research, therefore, is not to find responsive populations. Rather, it is to find those means which are most fruitful in responsive populations and those means which are most fruitful in resistant populations. Every population requires our best for the sake of the cross.

This is done in two sequential processes. Initially, researchers seek to learn which denominations, networks, or organizations are generally planting most effectively, particularly in the longer term. This part of the study involves learning the number of congregations in the denomination at the end of each year, or if annual statistics are unavailable, then every five or ten years. From there, calculation is possible for growth rates of various denominations or movements.[126]

At this point, we can group denominations and networks into small, medium, and large, and identify the three denominations or networks multiplying disciple-making communities most effectively in each size grouping. Smaller denominations and networks generally plant most effectively, but there are lessons to be learned from larger denominations and networks that continue to plant effectively also.

An important question, then, becomes something like "Why are these nine denominations and networks planting effectively? What is it about their prayer life, shared vision, leadership, planting models, training, or other factors that enable them to extend the good news of the gospel more widely than most?"

---

people prefer their own "kind" of people. This preference may indeed be rooted in insecurity, distrust, racism, classism, or other attitudes rooted in the fall. Yet we do not require people to come out of their own people group and join another before they can be saved (Acts 15). Fuller recognition of the new humanity in Christ often comes later. In the meantime, new believers, rooted in their historic people group, are far more effective in reaching others for Christ within their people group than if they depart from it.

126 Bob Waymire and C. Peter Wagner, *The Church Growth Survey Handbook* (Colorado Springs: OC International, 2006). This and related helpful tools can be found at www.ocresearch.info.

Share with the
wider church
what you learn
from leaders of
organizations
that are planting
effectively—in
responsive as
well as resistant
populations.

Such questions provide fruitful opportunity for case studies to uncover best practices in responsive and resistant peoples. These case studies can be shared in seminars and training events, equipping others to similar effectiveness.

It is vitally important to call the church to those difficult settings where it will likely take longer to establish disciple-making movements. Jesus ministered to both Jews and Gentles. The apostles and missionaries through the ages have done the same.

In our generation, funders of frontline church planting have come to value efficiency. In their desire to see fruit, funding has become time-limited. This forces church planters to choose more-receptive people groups over less-receptive people groups. While efficient, this approach leaves peoples who are more difficult to reach without workers. The funding approach for disciple-makers among more-receptive and less-receptive people groups may therefore require reconsideration.

Case studies

Case studies are like guiding people to a good fishing lake—but more. Sometimes a fishing lake has many fishers at work, but some doubt that there are fish in the lake or if the fish are biting. Perhaps you've been in that situation. What happens when someone begins catching fish?

Theoretically, two vital questions are answered: Yes, there are fish in the lake. And yes, the fish are biting. Practically, those who haven't caught any fish come to those who are bringing in the catch with questions like "What are you doing that I'm not doing?" and "Why is your method working so well?"

Good case studies have this effect. While fishing isn't equally effective everywhere and with all methods, case studies can help bring focus, or at least raise worthwhile questions.

Case studies are useful to highlight many possibilities—planting a church, an old mother church planting a church, a young mother church planting a church, one mother church planting multiple churches, one mother church and each of her daughter churches planting multiple generations of churches. Studies of denominations and networks which have seen high percentages of congregations planting are highly instructive.

What is a good case study? Preparing a helpful case study, in my opinion, involves a presentation that devotes one-third of its time to the good outcome which has taken place and a third of its time to sharing the transferable principles which the researcher believes underlie those happy outcomes. A final third, if the presentation is to a group, should allow participants—individually or in small groups—to discuss and plan how to apply those principles in other contexts. If the presentation is published, the writer, following his or her understanding of the transferrable principles, should offer a series of questions or a worksheet in

> Good case studies help stimulate greater effectiveness of the whole church.

which readers can apply their learning in practical ways to their own context. Case studies, in the context of disciple-making movements in national church-planting processes, are never of mere academic interest only, but rather for the purpose of making the ministry of a reflective practitioner more effective.

Studies that clarify the difference between rapid addition and multiplication are important.[127] Case studies of church-planting movements, disciple-making movements, lay-led movements, T4T, or other specific tools and methods leading to multiplicative processes are likewise vitally important.

Tell the stories. Share important details. This is not about honoring personalities, but about sharing principles and how the Lord of the harvest is at work for his glory. Let no one say that the fish aren't biting!

Research challenges due to changing forms of church

The church, and the way the church makes disciples, is changing. Yes, change has been a constant of history, and *how* the church is changing in this critical area also affects the research task. Much of this change in how the church makes disciples appears to be rooted, at least loosely, in the Reformation and its implications. I see not one, but three "reformations" initiated, at least embryonically, by Martin Luther, who believed public debate brings change.[128]

The first reformation was essentially doctrinal, leading to needed theological change. The second reformation took longer to develop, but resulted—as William Carey reflected further on the practical implications of *Sola Scriptura* (by Scripture alone), *Solus Christus* (through Christ alone), *Sola Fide* (by faith alone), *Sola Gratia* (by grace alone), and *Soli Deo Gloria* (glory to God alone)—in a global missions movement, of which this book is a part.

But a third reformation is also still underway, though unintended by Luther, who wished not to start a parallel church but only to reform the existing church. This change is a reformation of ecclesiology that began with the formation of

---

127 Neil Cole, *Church 3.0*, chap. 4.

128 There is reasonable evidence to suggest Martin Luther's "95 Theses" were initially simply offered to debate, in the academic setting of the day—vigorously and without fear of offending Johann Tetzel—the principles underlying the practice of selling indulgences.

> Changes in the form of church require changes in the way we measure progress.

denominations and continues with significant changes in the structure of local churches—ranging from megachurches to house churches and to many Christians for whom their only church is their prayer group, Bible study, or disciple-making group.

Our purpose is not to evaluate these changes, but to reflect on how they affect our research task.

Steve Spaulding, previously of Dawn Ministries and author of *Obedient Nations: What's So Great about the Great Commission,*[129] observed in a recent survey of whole-nation strategists,

> We are almost in a post-denominational era. In the past, the primary measuring tool tended to be *denominational* growth; these are less and less primary movers in nations worldwide. Increasingly *independent* or nondenominational groups or networks of *simpler structures* like house-churches are surfacing. Adding to this complexity, I see *insider* movements as a great advent, but they will also make it harder to measure who is "in Islam" for instance, and who is not, given many are now converting to Christ but not institutional Christianity. [italics in original]

Spaulding points to ways that change in the church is making the research task difficult. At the same time, he also points to reasons why research is more important. New tools and approaches will need to be developed.

A fresh and more accurate approach to the question of saturation church planting, for instance, is one which better recognizes the tremendous range in size of disciple-making groups today. I'm aware of thousands of Christ-groups in one country, often consisting of just five believers in size. The same country, however, has also seen the rise of megachurches. It may be wise to develop a range of weightings related to average group size. For instance, conventional churches may best be given a weighting of 1, house churches or DMM groups a weighting of .1 or .2, and megachurches a weighting of 5 or more.

---

129 Steve Spaulding, *Obedient Nations: What's So Great about the Great Commission* (Sisters, OR: Deep River Books, 2020). In regard to the increase in independent and nondenominational groups, Patrick Johnstone estimates the growth of independent/post-denominational churches at 15 percent of global Christianity in 2000, having grown from 1 percent in 1900, and on track to reach 25 percent in 2050; *The Future of the Global Church: History, Trends and Possibilities* (Downers Grove, IL: InterVarsity, 2011), 113.

Surveys of Muslims, Hindus, and other religious groups may also be useful to evaluate the percentage in that group who trust in Christ alone, in grace alone, and in faith alone for salvation, to use theological reformation principles. Such believers may not yet be gathering into disciple-making communities, but such research could point to where such communities should be formed.[130]

This is new ground for the church, but we cannot avoid the joyful reality that the leaven of the gospel is spreading among adherents of other faiths, as global mobility, the influence of the Internet, and personal witness grows. Some of this kind of research will be seen as less precise than measuring conventional churches. This may be so, but it does not diminish the need. Research will always need to adjust as it aims the church toward the greatest needs in the harvest field.

Strategic information continues to be vitally important to point both churches and church planters to those places in the harvest field where the Lord of the harvest has yet "many people in this city" (Acts 18:9–11 NASB) and to show where we can give thanks and celebrate progress. It is to the joy of gospel advance that we now turn.

Next Steps

- Reflect on a key point that stood out to you in this chapter.
- What are some practical ways you can apply or adapt these insights into your context?
- Which of these points do you need to lift up to the Lord in prayer?
- What will your next steps be?
- Are there teammates or others you need to talk to about these action steps?

---

130 Compared to earlier periods of history, Muslims and Hindus are increasingly trusting Christ without leaving the religious culture of their birth. This brings both danger and opportunity. The obvious danger is the risk of syncretism. The opportunity is the penetration of the gospel of Christ into other faith groups. A survey of those faith groups in your country could help determine to what degree that penetration has taken place and to what degree syncretism may be occurring.

CHAPTER 11

Purposeful Planning: To What End?

"Begin with the end in mind."
—Stephen Covey

AT A FUNDAMENTAL LEVEL, goals seem essential to life. As individuals, we need to know what we aim to do with the day when we wake up. Corporately, we need to articulate the purpose of our organization and the vision we exist to pursue. The need for meaning is so deep that psychologists tell us purpose and vision are required for mental health. Those who have studied victims of unjust imprisonment tell us that purpose and even the smallest goals help maintain sanity. God has made us with purpose and given us high callings.

Two of these callings are the Great Commandment and the Great Commission, the latter being Jesus' final post-resurrection expression of divine love for our lost world. As such, discipling the *ethne* in the nations where we live is not a goal we've chosen or set. The calling is Christ's, and it is not given to an individual, but it is incumbent on us, his followers, corporately.[131]

Our response to such a calling, therefore, cannot remain in the realm of vagaries. For instance, many churches speak of their mission in general terms, such as "the glory of God," "knowing Christ and making him known," or even "making disciples." Each statement is true and compelling, but

---

131 All the verbs in Matthew 28:18–20 and other expressions of the Great Commission (Luke 24:45–49; John 20:21–23; Acts 1:8) are plural.

they face great restriction of actualized potential if clear and sustainable pathways aren't articulated, scheduled, and regularly evaluated.

A national vision of discipled urban and rural areas, universities and high-rise apartments, business leaders and immigrants, likewise must be followed up with plans to draw nearer, in practical terms, to that goal which compels our hearts to obedience.

Such a call to obedience takes us into the realm of planning our work and working our plan. A large goal is broken up into smaller goals, or action steps, taking us in the right direction.

The idea is simple—which makes the following story surprising. A consultant was promised a given sum to solve an organizational problem. Upon analysis, the consultant challenged a certain leader to make only one change in daily practice—to begin each day by writing the three most important things to be done on a three-by-five-inch index card and doing them before pursuing other tasks. The result was so fruitful that the agreed fee was willingly paid.

At the micro level of our personal missional calling, the story would be trivial if many leaders didn't in fact live by drifting or running from one pressure point to the next, seemingly unclear on how to make real progress on their central goal. I have too frequently been taken back by the discovery of respected leaders who don't keep a calendar of their commitments.

Likewise, at the macro national level, clarity about how we will expend limited energies on our primary calling—organizationally and practically—is a vital stewardship in the brevity of life. Not everyone is equally gifted in breaking down steps toward their vision into bite-sized pieces, goals, and action steps. So, invite the help of a teammate if this isn't your forte. Use your teammates' gifts—be they coach or trainer or in a group process—appreciatively and regularly with some of the resources on goals and planning readily available as aids to developing your own skills.

While there is a plethora of excellent material available on the distinctions between *vision, mission, purpose, goals, objectives,* etc., you will find that the terms are not necessarily used consistently. For this reason, it may be wise to choose the terms you prefer to use, and to use them consistently in tracking your progress in obedience to your calling.[132]

What, then, is the role of the Holy Spirit? Some leaders argue that they wish to seek and obey the guidance of the Holy Spirit only, making goals and planning unnecessary. Indeed, listening to the Holy Spirit is mission-critical. I am confident the Holy Spirit seeks to lead us in full obedience to the Lord of the harvest. In this process, each directive given by God's Holy Spirit, as experienced by Paul,

---

132 Further reflections: www.murraymoerman.com/home/the_value_of_time.asp.

Use goals and planning as a mental discipline to sharpen daily focus.

for example, in turning to Macedonia (Acts 16:6–10), sets before the listening disciple a new goal in obedience. While the change of plans in Acts 16 was very specific, Paul's earlier mandates (Acts 13:2–3; 26:15–18) were more general. A study of Paul's developing strategy on his three church-planting missionary journeys shows unfailing focus on the goal and several adjustments in tactics as he learned, guided by the Lord of the harvest.

Paul's missionary career speaks also to those who believe our world is currently changing too fast to make the effort involved in five-year plans worthwhile. Even if this were so, I would argue that mid-range goals and planning remain useful, if only as a mental discipline to sharpen daily focus.

Plans can be reviewed and adjusted. The difference between a slow-moving world and a fast-moving world is that in a slow-moving world we can make long-range and mid-range goals with less need to adjust as we go along. In a fast-moving world, we may need to make more adjustments as we go along, but we still need to stop periodically to look at the big picture and at least tentative long- and mid-range goals. The reality is that both East and West live in the same fast-paced world. However, political systems in China, for example, make five-year plans in the context of much longer-range macro goals.[133] In Western democracies, by contrast, time frames for goals rarely exceed the distance between elections, generally producing only short-term tactics. It seems clear that long-range goals and planning are proving more effective than short-term tactics. Certainly the advance of the kingdom of heaven is of higher value than nationalism.

Having argued for long-term goals and planning, let me offer a word of encouragement. Many of us are inclined to overestimate what can be accomplished in one year and underestimate what can be accomplished in five years.

There are, of course, many excellent goal and planning processes to be commended. My encouragement here is simply to commit to the value, due to our high calling, of a goal-setting process worthy of that calling.

---

133 Further reflections: www.murraymoerman.com/home/the_value_of_time.asp.

The Value of National Goals

The value of working towards national goals and using research to keep us apprised of progress are significant:

> We tend to overestimate what can be accomplished in one year and underestimate what can be accomplished in five years.

- A national goal helps disciple-making ministries of the church keep the main thing the main thing amid the pressures and distractions of life and ministry.
- National goals remind us of our calling and need for obedience to our task, and for reliance on the Lord in difficult circumstances.
- National goals help stimulate prayer, creativity, and new, more fruitful models.
- National goals focus our limited energies and resources in the disciplined long obedience in the same direction involved in discipling the *ethne* of our nation.
- National goals provide "a stake in the ground," enabling us to know if we are progressing.
- National goals, to a degree, may even manifest in a public way the wholeness of the body of Christ as we pray, learn, collaborate, and work together toward the shared goal given to us by our risen and returning Lord to disciple the nations.

At a more personal level, a national goal encourages all churches and organizations to ponder prayerfully and individually the part each might play as part of the body of Christ toward discipling the nation. Each congregation might consider planting a daughter church every five years. Each denomination may aim to increase the rate of church planting in its circle by a certain amount. Each training institution could consider how to adjust its program to better equip planters and pastors of new churches. In each of these areas, a national goal can stimulate the body of Christ to take steps toward healthier teams and organizational health, leadership development, disciple-making processes, and approaches to multigenerational and multisite ministries.

In each area, making progress toward national, organizational, or congregational church-planting goals gives wonderful reason to give thanks and celebrate mileposts along the way. Progress toward each of these goals can be measured. Why measure? Ultimately because we measure what we value.

Yes, goals can be set and used wisely! Let's explore this possibility further.

While there
may be one
primary goal,
there can be many
supportive goals
which contribute
to it.

Kinds of Goals

In this section we focus only on national goals. By national goals we simply mean statements like "Our goal is to provide an outreaching church for every five thousand people in every people group in every census division within twenty years."[134]

Such a goal can be scaled to a provincial or city level. In each instance, discussion with leaders in the region will bring creative and practical alternatives.

The point for now is that when a goal statement is refined into a form grasping the heart and imagination of your country's leadership community, it tends to cascade into organizational and personal goals more easily. These supportive goals tend to bring further benefits, raising the bar of missional focus more widely in the body

While there are many kinds of goals which have value, my suggestion is that the number of goals set be few—perhaps three or four at most to start. Many countries will not set goals in each of the following areas, but these are presented to stimulate prayer and discussion. Most goals are likely to be set around discipling the *ethne* within your country, with fewer goals set around the churches in your country sending workers to help disciple the *ethne* in other countries.

A. *Mission goals inside the country*

There are three kinds of goals to consider in regard to discipling the nation.

1. **Numeric goals**

   Numeric goals can focus on the end goal, interim steps toward the end goal, or activities in the process which lead towards an incremental or end goal. In addition, several qualitative goals are worthy of consideration.

   a. End goals: An end goal focuses directly on the conclusion of the process leading to a discipled nation. This may be expressed numerically in ways like:
      • A church for every one thousand persons in every geographic and cultural space, language, ethnicity, and high-rise apartment building in the nation.

      The purpose of such a goal, of course, is not to have enough churches to accommodate those who are already Christians living in these spaces. There are already, by definition, enough churches for those who are already committed disciples of our Lord Jesus.

---

134 Such a goal requires a good research process to measure progress. I will touch on this below.

Rather, the goal is to have enough biblical, active, healthy churches to actually and effectively reach the lost around them in the near future, to complete the Great Commission, and to bring deeper restorative change to local communities and the broader culture.

Martin Robinson has suggested there are assumptions, perhaps open to question, about the number of churches that need to be planted in order to engage urban, mobile societies fully. I agree. One thousand persons may be too high or too low, and further research would be useful. Anecdotally, I've observed both highly Christianized communities and communities that are close to 100 percent Islamic settle close to the ratio of one church or mosque serving four hundred people.

It is important to note also that such a goal, either higher or lower, is not to be viewed as a universal average for all nations and cities. To avoid this misunderstanding, it's helpful to unpack such a summary goal into its incarnational application to every nation, city, language, race, social segment, cultural space, etc. We cannot be satisfied with the goal being reached in one such social segment while missing the one physically adjacent to it. A well-known example is the wonderful growth of the gospel among the Berbers in Algeria, a movement that has not widely crossed over to its Arab neighbors.

b. Interim goals: Regardless, in many countries the end goal seems too distant to approach directly. For this reason, some choose an interim goal. The evangelical leaders of twelve denominations in France have set the interim goal of planting a church for every ten thousand people in the nation. When the incremental goal is reached, these leaders may adjust the goal to a church for every five thousand people or define the goal in somewhat different terms. The point is that in the course of a national process, it is likely that several goals will be set, passed, celebrated, and refocused further down the horizon of God's purposes.

Russ Mitchell likens this process of moving through several goal stages to shifting a five-speed transmission. It is normally best to start with a low goal (first gear), but not to stay in first gear indefinitely. The time will come to set a higher goal (second gear), and so on.

First-gear goals might include:
- Winning 1 percent of the population through effective evangelism.
- Planting churches in towns and cities having more than five thousand inhabitants without a single evangelical church.
- Planting churches in urban areas so that there would be at least one evangelical church for every twenty thousand inhabitants.

There is wisdom, while keeping "the end in view," in "gearing up" from small to larger goals.

Second-gear goals might include:
- Planting churches in towns and cities having more than two thousand inhabitants without a single evangelical church.
- Planting churches in urban areas so that there would be at least one evangelical church for every fifteen thousand inhabitants.
- Planting churches so that there would be at least one evangelical church for every five thousand people in each county or province of the nation.

I commend to you further details of Russ Mitchell's article and to prayerful reflection on the needs and context of your own nation.[135]

c. Process goals: Another kind of numeric goal can be called process goals, because they are part of the process helping move the nation toward its end or interim goal. Some prefer to call these activity goals. Here are some examples:
- We want to see 50 percent of evangelical congregations plant a daughter church in five years.
- We want to see 50 percent of daughter churches plant a daughter church in five years.
- We want to see 80 percent of denominations set a church-planting goal in two years.
- We want to see 80 percent of training institutions add to their curriculum a church-planter training component in four years.
- We want to see 80 percent of church planters being mentored or coached in a personal or small-group setting.
- We want to see ten (or one hundred!) disciple-making movements grow four spiritual generations deep in five years.
- We want to encourage 50 percent of denominations to offer training in disciple-making movement principles in two years.

Such activities are measurable and contribute toward an interim or end goal.

135 Russ Mitchell, "Setting Contextually Appropriate Goals for Evangelism and Church Planting,"www.gcpn.info/ni/best-practices/Setting%20Contextually%20Appropriate%20 Goals%20for%20Evangelism%20and%20Church%20Planting.pdf.

Qualitative goals: Many important goals cannot be measured. These qualitative goals, however, are also highly important and can be held high up to rally church planters and movement leaders. Even so, many qualitative goals have measurable components that can help encourage us as signposts to celebrate. Let's look at a few.

Process goals contribute to interim or end goals.

Prayer is so vital to God's blessing on the redemptive mission of his people that some movements have aimed to increase the number of hours of prayer focused specifically on the Great Commission in a given country or people group. Because hours can be counted, progress in prayer empowerment can be measured.

Likewise, church health, which is generally viewed as a highly valued qualitative goal, is measurable in large part. While less than peak health is not an adequate reason to postpone disciple-making, church planting or initiating movements, church health in categories such as those suggested by Christian Schwarz (e.g. empowering leadership, holistic small groups, need-oriented evangelism) are important goals for both mother and daughter churches.[136]

The transformational impact of the church in the community is another highly valued and largely qualitative goal. Community impact for good may seem difficult to measure, but we can learn to measure outcomes over time. Even if outcomes are difficult to measure, activities invested (with prayer for positive kingdom outcomes) can be measured, particularly when transformational impact in turn contributes to new disciples and planting more churches.

A young denomination in Russia was founded and has grown entirely through recovered and recovering drug and alcohol abusers. Church planters who themselves are recovered drug or alcohol abusers establish a drug and alcohol support group in a community. They know both the culture and the power of the gospel. As members of the support group come to freedom in Christ, their family and associates are impacted and come with questions. A church community is formed in conjunction with an ongoing drug and alcohol recovery ministry and often forms another ministry in a nearby city, in time planting a daughter church. When I last spoke with leaders of this network, three hundred churches had been planted through transformational impact.

---

136 Christian Schwarz, *Natural Church Development: A Guide to Eight Essential Qualities of Healthy Churches* (Saint Charles, IL: Churchsmart Resources, 1996).

Every church planter is aware of deep needs in his or her community. A visit with local police, social workers, schools, or hospitals can more sharply focus our hearts on God's calling.

In these three kinds of qualitative goals—prayer, church health, and transformational impact—I am being suggestive of only a small sample of possibilities, seeking to show how qualitative goals can be included in a national plan and, if desired, measured at least in part. Measurement itself is not our goal, of course, but serves only but importantly as a pointer to the greater goal of discipling the *ethne* of our nation.

B. *Mission goals outside the country*

In addition to goals toward discipling to Christ the *ethne within* your country, you may consider goals assisting disciple-making efforts in *other* countries.

Evangelical leaders in the Philippines, for example, focused their first twenty-five-year goal entirely on planting fifty thousand churches within the island nation. By the grace of God, they were successful! In 2000, the nation then turned to increasing its internal church-planting goal of sending workers to help make disciples and plant churches in other nations.

Filipinos are well known for their smiles and ability to adapt to other cultures, often as domestics. Sometimes they are treated marginally or abused. A wealthy family in a Muslim-majority nation hired several Filipina as maids and as nannies to help with their unmanageable children. The nannies loved the children, prayed with and for them, and shared Christ. When the parents learned of the gospel in their home, they insisted the Filipinas never again mention Christ. They refused and were fired.

Some months passed before communication was reinitiated by the parents, whose children missed their nannies and who found themselves again unable to manage their children's behavior. The nannies were invited to return. They agreed, on the condition that they would be allowed to pray with the children and read from the Injil. The parents accepted these conditions and invited the Filipinas back, who then continued their ministry to the children.

Evangelical leaders in Romania likewise set national goals to send workers to countries in the 10/40 Window, eventually becoming the first Eastern European country to do so.

Setting goals can be both numeric and strategic, such as: "By the grace of God, we aim to send X missionaries in the next ten years," or "By the grace of God, we aim to plant X churches in X UPGs in the next ten years."

The question of where mission goals outside your country might be best focused is largely beyond the scope of this book. However, you might want to consider comparative national needs, as illustrated by the global map produced by Chris Maynard.

> A national church should hold itself responsible not only for goals inside the country, but also outside.

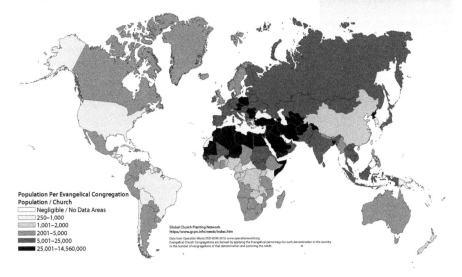

Population Per Evangelical Congregation
Population / Church
Negligible / No Data Areas
250–1,000
1,001–2,000
2001–5,000
5,001–25,000
25,001–14,560,000

Global Church Planting Network
https://www.gcpn.info/needs/index.htm

Data from Operation World DVD-ROM 2010, www.operationworld.org
Evangelical Church Congregations are derived by applying the Evangelical percentage for each denomination in the country to the number of congregations of that denomination and summing the result.

Figure 14: Population per Evangelical Church Comparisons Globally (used with permission)

C. *What about time frames?*

You may have noticed that many of the goal examples included a length of time—for example, two years or ten years. Adding a time frame helps make the goal more specific and useful.

Some leaders prefer not to include time frames in their goals. Though I am personally inclined to include them, I acknowledge potential downsides. One of these is the view that a national SCP process is a time-limited project that is completed when the allotted time expires, regardless of the outcome. That is certainly not the case!

A target date simply suggests the importance of a point for evaluation of progress, a review of the harvest field and harvest force, regrouping, and a refining of the goal for the next season. Sometimes the refinement involves an upshift of gears, to use Russ Mitchell's image, perhaps refocusing the goal on an underserved location, ethnicity, or subculture left behind during previous efforts.

> A target date simply highlights the importance of a point for evaluation of progress.

D. *What if we fail to reach our national goal in the anticipated time?*

Some suggest that setting a national goal is demotivating if the goal is not met. I can recall one situation where this was the case. A challenging national goal, unmet at the end of the decade, gave national leaders pause, questioning what may have gone wrong. That's certainly a fair question—in fact, a necessary question. Learning from disappointment can bring much benefit. Could the goal-setting process have been done differently?[137] Could a leadership transition have had negative impact? Should there have been additional national congresses or regional seminars and consultations? What else could reasonably have been done? Many other questions can and should be asked for full benefit. *The purpose of questions is not to assign blame but to learn and grow.* The only failure in this regard would be the failure to examine the past decade carefully for learnable lessons to honor the King moving forward.

Even aside from lessons gained, the effort was worth it because lost souls came to Christ as the body of Christ demonstrated its unity by praying and working together to plant many new churches. This is to be celebrated without reservation, whether the increase in disciple-making communities introduced some or many to Christ and reached 20 or 60 percent of the nation's challenging goal.

What then is to be our attitude? In the end, we do our best. We seek the Lord. We experiment. We learn. We make advances. There is, then, no such thing as failure. There is, however, a failure to try.

Each nation is certainly different. In another case, an eighteen-year goal period that ended in 2015 fell short and hardly caused a ripple in the national movement, with no discernable loss in either motivation or morale pressing forward. Didn't the leaders care? Some clearly did. While there was no survey of the leadership community in this regard, several factors seemed to be at play. There was definitely joy over several thousand net new churches reaching out in the name of Christ. Leaders also recognized that the cultural environment had become more difficult during the past eighteen years and that new approaches were needed. Encouragement was also drawn from a vastly more unified national leadership community.

---

137 In this case, the goal was carefully and collaboratively set. Intercessors prayed for guidance. Denominational leaders were asked their goals for the decade. The aggregate total of denominational goals was compared with the goal intercessors felt they were hearing from the Lord. The two were the same. Leaders felt this to be confirmation of the goal.

We have a choice about how to respond to unmet goals both in our personal lives and in the national church. Unrealistic time lines and time lines interrupted by unexpected developments, leadership transitions, and the like will require adjustments. Such circumstances are best seen as learning environments, as opportunities to draw wisdom from experience needed in the future.

> We do our best. We seek the Lord. We experiment. We learn. There is, then, no such thing as failure. There is, however, a failure to try.

E. *What, then, is a good goal?*

Let's attempt to summarize in this way: A good goal is *medium to long-term*, particularly in larger nations. It takes time to mobilize the church to a large task. The time range may be ten to twenty-five years. Even so, a good goal is best viewed also as an *interim goal*, understanding it to be the next step in a larger context and longer-term process necessary to disciple the nation to Christ.

A good goal is one with *multiple components*. A primary goal is likely to have a higher public profile and to be the goal toward which the other components contribute—for example, an interim goal of one church available to serve every five thousand persons in the nation. In addition, there will be *process* (or activity) *goals* that are a means toward the interim goal.

A good goal is one that *invites each organization to set its own goal* as a contribution toward the larger national goal involving the whole body of Christ. This is where a range of process or activity goals can make it easier for all parts of the body to see how they can contribute in a practical way.

A good goal is one which has *evaluation and review points on the calendar*. A national congress every two to three years can provide natural review points. The national facilitation team can set calendar points more frequently to evaluate their own progress in encouraging a national SCP process.

A good goal is one which *reflects more than the vision of a single leader or simply the lowest common denominator* of a larger number of persons in the room. This leads us to the question of a goal-setting process.

F. *How to set and ratify good goals*

The process of setting and agreeing to motivating goals is important but can be difficult. Spiritual forces arrayed against the extension of Christ's kingdom oppose concerted prayer and action. In addition, group dynamics can vary considerably. Sometimes one vocal leader in the group proposes inadequate interim goals, and the rest of the group is willing to agree on the lowest common denominator, reflecting the anxieties of that one leader. Spiritual discernment, patience, and skill in the group process is needed.

In the end, a good goal will be *broad* enough to engage the vision of a large portion of the church without being the *lowest common denominator* in the sense that everyone agrees easily because the goal is not challenging.

For this reason I encourage you to pray as you consider application of the principles that follow in your own setting.

As a leader or part of a small group of leaders, you can suggest an interim goal and/or a range of process goals for discussion. Only the very highest and very lowest goals should be set aside.

You can introduce this range of proposed goals to a larger group of leaders. Don't feel pressured to make a decision if the group isn't close to consensus, but encourage prayer for the Lord's guidance. Ultimately your ratification process can parallel that of Acts 15:28: "It seemed good to the Holy Spirit and to us ..."

Encourage a season of reflection and prayer. Some leaders might point with caution to the possibility of national goals being set too hastily or by too few people, or they might view measuring numbers as unspiritual or incomplete if lacking in qualitative counterparts. All such concerns are worthy of discussion. Ask others in the room to respond to questions or concerns with their own views. You need to facilitate the discussion without being drawn into the position of personally debating those with hesitations.

Encourage those who are quiet to speak. Sometimes the Holy Spirit is recognized in the voice of a quiet leader who has been praying.

If needed, allow an unhurried process within a reasonable time frame. In some cases, several weeks or months may be needed. Have patience, even if the process takes a year. If it takes longer than expected to find consensus, don't become preoccupied with the process. Work as if the goal has already been set. There is much training, communication, relationship building, prayer, planning, and other work to do!

Wait in expectation for that moment when the Holy Spirit is recognized by those in the room to confirm the goal of his choosing. This is a time for holy reverence and fresh submission to the Lord and to his gracious, redemptive purposes for your nation. This is a time to celebrate!

Next Steps

- Reflect on a key point that stood out to you in this chapter.
- What are some practical ways you can apply or adapt these insights into your context?
- Which of these points do you need to lift up to the Lord in prayer?
- What will your next steps be?
- Are there teammates or others you need to talk to about these action steps?

CHAPTER 12

Engaging Leaders Across Your Nation

"Alone we can do so little; together we can do so much."
—Helen Keller

LEADERS SERVING in smaller communities might feel somewhat distant in culture, or even disconnected relationally, from leaders in the national or even provincial capital.[138] Happily, some leaders in outlying areas, though not all, will travel to a gathering in the capital city every couple of years.

Some of those leaders who don't travel to meetings will be generally aware of efforts to focus church planting on least-reached locations and people groups, but they will remain in great need of a personal connection if they are to mobilize their local church to plant daughter churches. Even leaders who do attend a key meeting but live more distant from the city where national gatherings take place will need fresh encouragement and relational connection between these centralized events.

It is vital, therefore, to engage pastors and church leaders in each region of the nation emotionally and practically to share the vision of making disciples and planting churches among the least-reached, to offer some level of training, and to model an environment of prayer and collaboration.

---

138 The term *provincial* is used recognizing that other terms are also used—e.g., state, oblast, prefecture, etc. Smaller units like county, township, etc., can likewise contain significant populations. A national church-planting process should consider how best to engage church leaders of every level for the purposes of vision-casting, training, and collaboration.

Russ Mitchel points out that "seminars and consultations" is the second-most significant factor contributing to an effective nationwide disciple-making process. Let's offer several models to consider.

Provincial Visits by a Trained Team

In some nations, a seminar or consultation is offered at a central location in each province. A single team can travel in the course of one or more years, presenting a simple one-day program. Local research can be shared and small groups can convene for discussion and prayer, followed by lunch and a short training program. The event can be hosted by a respected local leader, who ideally will make his or her church available for follow-up gatherings to build on the interest and commitments of participants.

Provinces in some nations are so large or heavily populated that such a local gathering will be more effective if held in two or more cities.

Toward the conclusion of each gathering, committed local leaders can be sought to continue the process. For example, volunteers can be invited to convene church planters in their city every month or two for encouragement, sharing, and prayer. Likewise, a local leader can be sought to convene those who want to learn more about disciple-making.

Ideally, this kind of provincial rotation to mobilize and encourage local pastors and leaders will not be a single cycle. Hopefully the visiting team will return to build further among committed local leaders—sharing testimonies and progress. Even better, of course, is that several teams are trained so that each province or major city can be visited more quickly or more often.

Local Fellowships of Denominational Leaders

Another approach to regional mobilization is to build community among denominational leaders, particularly those with responsibility for church planting. Denominational leaders are typically busy and focused on the needs of their own constituency. But they will build interdenominational community when they come to recognize these relationships will give them ideas, resources, and expertise that will help their own denomination also.

In my experience, this model works best when an opportunity to gather—ideally every thirty to ninety days—is provided in a location involving no more than two hours of travel. The initial purpose is to receive training, input, and encouragement; to share progress and challenges; and to pray together. Over time, deep friendships will form and a local denominational leader will facilitate an agenda formed by the group. Interdenominational perspectives and experiences are mutually enriching and bring fresh opportunities to focus on each denomination's initial purpose for formation.

In one such experience, denominational district superintendents in a province recognized that they would benefit from training they didn't currently have resources to supply. All of them wanted to learn how to better access potential church planters. They recognized that the denomination would benefit from a "boot camp" training experience for church-planting teams. The superintendents also surfaced a need to train more coaches to help church planters be successful. They recognized that they were wrestling with questions and experiencing challenges that other denominations were also facing.

> Provincial groups can most easily be formed in breakouts during a national gathering.

In the course of the conversation, the leader of church-planting efforts for one denomination said, "We're happy to organize training event A to serve us all." Another said, "We'll plan training event B six months later to serve us all." Because of shared vision and mutual trust, in a matter of minutes four important training and support components—an assessment process, a boot camp, a coaches' training event, and a planter peer-learning process—were undertaken to benefit everyone, with less effort than if every organization was required to do all the work themselves. In a contagious display of kingdom priority, the group organized training events that also served denominations not represented in their group. The core group, which was not large—perhaps four to six leaders—continued to meet fruitfully for multiple years, resulting in many healthy new churches.

In other settings, regional gatherings have focused on training pastors to plant daughter churches. Local needs and vision will, of course, determine focus, the frequency of gatherings, and the geographic scope served. In my experience, some regional groupings become strong and effective, some need frequent encouragement, and some don't really gain much traction.

Launching Provincial Groups at the National Gathering

One great way to get regional expressions underway is to schedule program time for regional breakouts at each national congress, where leaders from their respective provinces meet, pray, discuss challenges unique to their region, and make plans to meet periodically and locally when they return home. In my experience, these groupings tend to become most productive and sustainable when refreshed every two years during national gatherings.

Supporting and Building Provincial Leadership Groups

Each of these approaches to engaging and connecting local leaders regionally for the purpose of building relationships and initiating, strengthening, or accelerating disciple-making and church-planting movements can begin the process in that region. Whichever initial approach best fits your context, you or a member of your team will need ongoing relational connection with the leader of the regional group, in my experience, minimally twice a year. This can be done by phone or in person, centering on listening, praying, encouragement, and sharing stories and ideas from other regions that may be of interest and applicable. In some cases, it may make sense to invite these leaders together, in person or by Internet, to share learnings, recast the vison, and pray together by phone or in person—centering on listening, prayer, encouragement, and sharing stories and ideas from other regions that may be of interest and applicable. In some cases, it may make sense to invite these leaders, in person or by Internet, to share learnings, recast the vison, and pray together.

Scanning the provincial horizons for need, opportunity, building, and rebuilding is ongoing, but the benefits are great. The point of this short chapter is not to suggest one best way to serve your regional leaders. Rather, the role of the national facilitator, personally or through part of his or her team, is to surface regional needs and stimulate ways to help regional leaders engage at a practical level, where the harvest is ripe and ongoing frontline encouragement is needed.

Next Steps

- Reflect on a key point that stood out to you in this chapter.
- What are some practical ways you can apply or adapt these insights into your context?
- Which of these points do you need to lift up to the Lord in prayer?
- What will your next steps be?
- Are there teammates or others you need to talk to about these action steps?

MANY LEADERSHIP CHALLENGES require resolution. Other challenges, however, may wisely not be approached as problems to be overcome, tasks to complete, or signposts to be passed. Some involve rather dynamic tensions, best held in balance.[139] Balance is not static. Both polarities have value and require attention in turn. But to give all one's attention to either pole for too long would not produce a balanced national process.

Take, for example, the relationship of water, dikes, and sailboats. Each represents a strength or beauty to affirm, but each also reaches its highest purpose when in right relationship with each of the others. From a leadership perspective, sometimes it's time to refit the sailboat and other times to repair the dike.

Similarly, Jesus used "just in time" learning. He taught his disciples just before he sent them out, but he didn't linger with extended teaching or wait long after they returned to do extended debriefing (Luke 10).

We now address leadership issues where choosing one polarity over the other is less wise than emphasizing each in season, moving between them and seeking to make progress toward both seemingly opposite needs.

---

139 The book to which I am indebted for helping me distinguish between problems to overcome and polarities to manage is Barry Johnson's *Polarity Management: Identifying and Managing Unsolvable Problems* (Amherst, MA: HRD Press, 1992).

CHAPTER 13

Building the Kingdom Locally and Nationally

"There is no limit to the amount of good you can do if you don't care who gets the credit."
—Ronald Reagan

> Each pole has value, but neither should take permanent center stage.

We begin with the tension some Christian leaders feel between the needs and interests of their own organization and the sometimes uncomfortable call to put the resources of their organization at the service of a broad national movement. This tension can exist for a denominational leader, as it can for a pastor who wants the best for his or her local church. Helping organizational leaders work healthily with this tension, though the issue remains unresolved, is a vital skill for you as a facilitator of a national church-planting process to mobilize the body of Christ to disciple the nation.

This polarity exists not only for you as the national facilitator or as a member of the team, but for the leader of every denomination and local church. Let's look at it from the perspective of a pastor considering the cost and potential of planting a daughter church. During my years as a church planter, I was deeply aware of the needs and shortcomings of the congregation I loved. We sometimes referred to the church as a hospital for broken people. It was more than that, but it was certainly a hospital. As such, the church required much prayer, pastoral care, building, and rebuilding. Energy taken from this vital task might well keep the church from maturing to where we could successfully plant a daughter church.

At the same time, I recognized that focusing exclusively on church health could result in a church that would not become a mother church. So we had to initiate a second Sunday worship service, and later a third, before most agreed we were ready to plant. We needed to grow in health. We needed to grow in faith to risk planting when we were not fully "ready." And in the end, we needed to value the kingdom as much or more than our personal preferences.

Denominational leaders reading this book will recognize the same tension. They deeply desire the health of the denomination they serve. At the same time, in all likelihood, they equally desire the growth and enlargement of the denomination, both at home and in world mission. Yet church planting, at home or abroad, requires at least a measure of health.

A congregation or denomination can concentrate on both church health and church planting, but not all leaders feel able to juggle both balls at once. In addition, organizations often need time to consolidate gains after seasons of growth.

Gaining Organizational Support for a National Vision

I have noted that if a church or organization doesn't stay healthy, it will have little to contribute to a national movement. So the pendulum cannot be solely on the side of the national process. Yet if a church or organization is preoccupied with its own health and unwilling to plant costly seeds for the kingdom (John 12:24), it honors not the King who gave his love and life for them.

Even if organizational leaders believe that giving time and energy to a national movement is part of their biblical calling, a friend expressed this common perspective: "Getting national cooperation is challenging. So many (good) projects want everyone's attention."

We are often invited to try a new special sauce to bring spice and success to our work. With all the options, why should we give energy to a national church-planting process?

The answer, in principle, lies in the fact that new disciple-making communities planted among the least-reached are good for the organization(s) planting them, while honoring our shared biblical mandate to disciple the nation in the spirit of unity for which Jesus prayed in John 17.

One leader who understood the benefits of collaboration rightly—both for her organization and for our shared biblical mandate—was Marge Osborne, who led church-planting efforts in her denomination. She challenged other denominations this way: "If we (Nazarenes) go in (to a certain city) and plant ten churches, some will be saved, but the city won't notice. But if ten denominations go in and plant one hundred churches together, the city can't help but be impacted for the kingdom." Then she dropped the gauntlet: "We won't go in without you." That city continues to be one of the most influential for Christ in the nation.

As we lead toward broad collaboration to disciple and plant among the least-reached in the nation, there are several ways in which to affirm support both for healthy organizations (the individual good) and ask for their contributions to national progress (the common good). Let's look at several ways to engage every organization.

Stirring Motivation for National Collaboration

In some denominations and church families, internal concerns have held priority for a long time. Many denominations were born in an environment of passion. When passion wanes and life becomes routine, fresh stirring is needed. A national process of disciple-making and church planting among the least-reached can serve and refresh many denominations with renewed motivation and vision. There are several ways a national process can help.

First, we can call for a shared commitment to Jesus Christ and obedience to his call to engage in his mission to the lost [140] It's not just about me or about the

---

140 The gospel, in fact the entire Bible, is God's "love and rescue mission" to his lost and broken world. Jesus' Great Commission is not limited to its most often quoted expression in Matthew 28:18–20, but repeated in many settings, beginning with Genesis 12:3, Psalm 67, Luke 24:46ff, John 20:21, Acts 1:8, and the specific expression to Paul in Acts 26:15–18, NASB: "I am Jesus whom you are persecuting. But get up and stand on your feet; for this purpose I have appeared to you, to appoint you a minister and a witness not only to the things which you have seen, but also to the things in which I will appear to you; rescuing you from the Jewish people and from the Gentiles, to whom I am sending you, to open their eyes so that they may turn from darkness to light and from the dominion of Satan to God, that they may receive forgiveness of sins and an inheritance among those who have been sanctified by faith in Me."

Prayer summits, retreats, and congresses stir hearts for collaboration.

organization I find myself in or have founded. It's about Christ's calling, purpose, and mission that creates one body in mission. This basic truth is often readily affirmed by churches and denominations who were born out of this commitment, but whose passion has waned. Older denominations and movements can benefit from gratitude for this call reminding them of their roots and reason-for-being.

Second, you too may have seen prayer motivate powerfully when leaders of different organizations or parts of the country come to realize their hearts yearn for the same kingdom reality and are in fact knit together by the Holy Spirit.

On one occasion, leaders serving in one region of the country in separate organizations came to a national congress aiming for saturation church planting. During breakout sessions bringing together leaders working in various geographic areas, these leaders for the first time prayed together for the salvation of their region. After prayer, one said to the others, "It's amazing that we had to come to a conference to do what we hadn't done during twenty years of working independently in another province." The group began to meet regularly in their own province to pray and wrestle with common issues pertaining to church planting and multiplication, with great effect!

Prayer summits have also been powerfully used by God to bring unity of spirit and collaboration of resources in mission. In prayer summits, Christian leaders of various streams and organizations meet simply to pray, without an agenda, for several days. They share their stories, worship the Lord, pray for God's kingdom to come in their churches and organizations, listen to "what the Spirit is saying to the churches" (Rev 3:22 NRSV), and share table fellowship, communion, and often tears. I've seen public repentance of sinful attitudes toward various sectors of the body of Christ, personal and organizational reconciliation, and practical love overcome benign neglect. Even before the subject of church planting is raised, leaders in the body of Christ emerge ready to share in his mission.

In another relational setting that God uses for similar outcomes, leaders from various denominations meet annually for an informal thirty-six-hour or forty-eight-hour retreat. Leaders recognize denominational loyalty is often thin among their members and that they are wrestling with nearly identical in-house issues. During the retreat, the leaders share vulnerably, without the presence of the boards to whom they are accountable. They share family, marriage, and family pressures. Relational and organizational challenges are shared, as well as visions and experiments forward. Deep bonds of prayer and comradery develop and deepen. Barriers to working together are left behind.

Third, regular national gatherings, sometimes called congresses, help leaders grow in motivation and deepen commitment to their common calling to disciple the nation. Research updates, highlighting both progress and the work yet remaining, as well as case studies of planting models that are taking root and multiplying among those who have had the least opportunity to be engaged by winsome followers of Christ, are important to share in these regular national gatherings.

Vision Agreement between Leaders of Diverse Organizations

It's fair to say that it is easier to find agreement on biblical vision—the end goal, than on strategy—how to reach the end goal.

Therefore, vision agreement on a national church-planting process is a good place to begin. Most church and organizational leaders will agree on the vision of planting among the least-reached. When faithfully pursued, this vision will result in churches being more evenly distributed among the people groups and geography of the nation, providing nearly equal opportunity for everyone in the nation to become a mature follower of Christ.

For a national strategy to gain traction and momentum toward this goal, an early step is to cast this vision with pastors and leaders of diverse organizations across the nation. Since there are a variety of ways this can be done, it's probably best to pursue multiple ways rather than depend on one way to reach and convince a majority of national leaders.

In countries without significant security issues, a beginning point might be to prepare a pamphlet to leave with denominational leaders when visiting them or mailed to denominational and organizations more broadly.[141] The pamphlet could outline the basic need; the ethnic, cultural, and geographic spaces where churches are most needed; and why working together is the best way to reach the least-reached.

A more detailed summary of research findings can be powerful follow-up, gaining vision agreement of organizational leaders. A PDF version emailed to leaders brings broad coverage at low cost. The research summary, as well as further details, can be posted to a central website.

Getting an article published annually in national and denominational magazines and ezines that summarizes a corporate vision and draws on research and steps forward can bring broad awareness and progress toward national vision agreement.

In an African nation, the facilitator, who was seeking vision agreement among national leaders, took a very relational approach—applicable in open cultures as well as those with security issues. He tried to schedule a one-on-one meeting

---

141 While communications are now widely digital, I suggest considering a personal visit and printed media where possible until relationship and commitment are in place. This initial personal touch still has most impact in many cultures. Email and websites then follow naturally.

every week with a different influential Christian leader in his nation. During these conversations, he focused on three topics—asking questions like these:

1. "What is God doing in your life, organization, and church?" The facilitator positioned himself as a listener and learner, affirming what he heard.
2. "Can I share the vision God has put in my heart and what I'm doing in response?" The facilitator then shared the core vision of a national church-planting process.
3. "Every day, three thousand of our people are perishing without Christ. What are some ways we can partner together in light of this?" The facilitator then offered to preach or share with the leader's church or organization, hoping to find agreement for a follow-up point of connection.[142]

I shared, in chapter 6, about an initial gathering using discussion of a research piece to bring organizational leaders together to discuss ways forward in light of national needs. Such one-time events can be followed up with a full national congress or with small meetings according to state or province.

There are certainly multiple ways to promote national recognition of a need along with vision of a way forward. It may be that only a few of the steps above will be needed. It may be that persistence and more creativity will be needed.

Remember, initially only a comparatively soft vision agreement is needed for a transformational national church-planting movement to begin. Ideally, most organizational leaders will come on board, at least in principle. More work on how to proceed practically will follow. It is neither wise nor fruitful to expect 100 percent of leaders to agree, or to wait for full agreement before proceeding. Typically, a healthy minority or small majority can be rallied together and much can be achieved. It is important to try to get a few larger, respected organizations included in that loose consensus. Move quickly then to the next steps while continuing to invite leaders who might still have some reservations or just be busy.

Ownership within Organizations

It is possible, of course, for organizational leaders to agree in principle, even in a heartfelt way, on the strategic importance of a transformational national church-planting movement without having gained broad support from their own organizations. Gaining this support may take time.

Bringing gatekeepers, those who hold formal or informal power in their organizations, on board is vital in the process. It is important that they come to bless the organization's full involvement in the national process, even if that particular leader does not participate personally.

---

142 I recognize that this exchange is an example from one culture and that leaders and cultures vary in style and approach. However, I believe this initial conversation is a good model for many cultures.

The goal of ownership of the vision will have taken place when the church or organization has come to believe that it will honor the King and the kingdom and that it will flourish locally if its internal goals are in broad alignment with the calling of a national church-planting process.

> One facilitator met with a different influential Christian leader each week.

To this end, Jim Montgomery offered organizational leaders in the Philippines a process by which their denomination could be motivated and led effectively in a way that—together with other denominations—would powerfully impact the nation for Christ through new disciple-making communities.[143] In other settings, I've seen organizations motivated by a national vision held in common with other denominations and organizations add an entire department to their structure, raise major funds for new church-planting initiatives, and add training courses to their Bible school and seminary curriculum—even adding a core curriculum requirement and the offer of a new major in church planting. Another denomination set for itself public church-planting goals for the first time in nearly a century!

As organizations are stimulated by their own leadership to contribute to a national church-planting process in practical ways, each organization soon discovers in its own way that its contribution to the national movement directly benefits its own organization, network, or movement. It's a principle of the kingdom!

For example, some organizations may view church planting too costly. Yet, as Curtis Sergeant pointed out in an email exchange, the most multiplicative methods in fact cost very little. DMM approaches require no buildings and some CPM approaches likewise require no funds for buildings and little if any for staff. In these models virtually all church-planting activity is done by unpaid volunteers living out their faith in a more intentional manner. The only real sacrifice is that existing structures need to be open-handed about what happens to the people who come to faith through this ever-expanding witness of ordinary believers. There is relatively little sacrifice involved other than changing how disciples are equipped within the existing structures. The existing believers can even remain as part of the existing churches, but simply help catalyze new house churches of which they need not even remain a part after roots take hold.

A significant challenge to ownership of the vision within organizations is that "whole church efforts" can be complicated by nominalism, even a measure of syncretism, in some cases touching the very hierarchy of the church.

---

143 A statement of seminal principles to serve denominational leaders in this effort can be found in Jim Montgomery's "13 Steps to a Successful Growth Program" in appendix 2 and digitally at www.gcpn.info/resources/13_steps_to_SCP.pdf.

Highlight examples
of collaboration
to stimulate more
collaboration
to advance the
kingdom.

Some "legacy" or "traditional" churches, yes even evangelical churches, require full revival! A national disciple-making process with focus on church multiplication helps by touching on Jesus' point in the Parable of the Sower in two ways. First, it challenges leaders and organizations which do not produce "a crop—a hundred, sixty or thirty times what was sown" (Matt 13:18 NIV) to examine their core purpose, perhaps even the soil of their hearts and pray—pray for revival and pray for laborers to be sent out into the harvest (Matt 9:38). Secondly, it challenges organizations overly reliant on clergy to throw open the doors to laity—through invitation, training and empowerment—to join in making the harvest, as it was for Jesus, their primary concern.

Willingness to Work Together

There is a third level of engagement in a national process beyond initial vision agreement. This level of discovery involves working together with and contributing to the success of *other* organizations.

Working together doesn't mean multiple agencies collaborating on planting one church. This may happen occasionally, but Baptists generally still plant Baptist churches, Pentecostals still plant Pentecostal churches, and university disciple-making communities still plant university disciple-making communities.

Ways of working together can take many practical forms. I've seen a large denomination develop a first-rate church-planter training curriculum, debrand it, and give it to all other planting organizations with the freedom to contextualize and rebrand it in ways that would serve them best.

In another setting, several organizations collaborated on a single church-planter assessment center involving a range of interviews and inventories to help all denominations identify the best of their church planter candidates. In an alternative assessment process, several denominations agreed to interview and approve one another's planter candidates. They did so believing that another denomination would be more objective than themselves, since a candidate is often a friend or relative of decision makers in the denomination of which he or she is a part.

Some organizations collaborate in providing for a broad range of training for coaches to serve frontline church planters. In the West, there is increasing recognition of the practical and spiritual value of coaching for church planters. Training, certification, and oversight of coaches have risen to higher levels in recent years. By contrast, the term *coach* is viewed with some caution in the eastern hemisphere. However, the enduring value of "uncles" to mentor and encourage planters is well established. Whether coaches or uncles are found along relational or organizational lines, denominations will benefit from encouraging the use of this key role widely and even training for it collaboratively.

As I mentioned in chapter 12, denominations can also collaboratively provide initial training for church planters in a "boot camp." In this experience, church planters from various denominations who are preparing to engage the harvest spend several days together with a facilitator. During this time, church planters—or better, full teams—share and learn from one other's ministry plans, which ideally include planting a daughter church soon after the mother church is established. The range of approaches to planting and learning from one another enriches all planters and their plans.

In my early planting experience, I invited other church planters within an hour's drive to bring a bag lunch to a ninety-minute gathering. The time was generally divided between planters sharing challenges likely to be faced by others; helpful resources; small group discussion; and prayer in circles of three or four. Over the years, several planters testified that these simple monthly gatherings kept them in the battle through times of spiritual attack and discouragement. Informal, independent, and interdenominational groups can easily be organized in most cities to the ongoing benefit of all and to the growth of the kingdom.

Another area of collaboration where I've seen benefit accruing to a national process is among Bible school and seminary educators. Initiating engagement between providers of formal and nonformal training of movement leaders can be served, in my experience, by an Engel-scale approach to understanding where incremental process may be possible. At the low end of the scale are schools that don't train for mission. Higher are those that offer a single course in church planting. A still higher level is offering a major in church planting. As a school chooses to become more practically engaged in assisting students to become effective church planters, coaches, and trainers, it benefits increasingly from collaborating with other schools in course-development, field assignments, internships, and the like.

The interaction can begin in a small way—such as instructors from two or three schools sharing over lunch—and grow to include more schools until the entire ethos of mission education in a nation has been measurably increased.

A missional conviction is that organizational and kingdom interests, at the deepest level, are ultimately the same. Think of Nehemiah, as he arrived at the holy city of Jerusalem, which had been devastated by the Babylonians nearly a century earlier. Some years earlier, the exiles who had returned had built or rebuilt a house to protect it from the elements. Nehemiah's survey of the city wall showed broken sections, walls, and gates. What to do? Each household focused on the needs of the portion of the wall nearest it. If the wall wasn't repaired to protect Jerusalem from enemy attack, the houses they had built would also not stand. The national interest and the household interests were not at odds, but ultimately the same.

Relating to Unengaged Organizations

A reasonable working goal may be to engage initially a small majority, and later 70 percent or more of denominations, church networks, and educational institutions in the transformational national church-planting process undertaken in your country. Let's consider opportunities to engage several kinds of unengaged organizations.

Parachurch mission agencies [144]

At one level, mission agencies can be quick to engage in a national process. They are often already equipped to offer training, coaching, research, prayer mobilization, and the like to serve those engaged in frontline church planting. At another level, however, mission agencies that draw financial support from the church community are often hesitant to plant churches directly, since they are not denominations. Church planting is often seen as an activity belonging to the church. In some countries, therefore, there is an unspoken agreement that churches and denominations plant daughter churches, while parachurch missions organizations support local churches in the process, without in fact planting churches directly.

Fruitful ways forward can be found. One way to engage the energies of parachurch agencies in direct church planting is to explore models and find areas of agreement in direct conversation. Some years ago, I organized two meetings at opposite ends of a country, to which I invited leaders of larger denominations and prominent mission agencies. First we discussed whether it was good for the kingdom for mission agencies to plant churches directly. Case studies were then shared of mission agencies that were planting churches. Denominational leaders were asked which models they saw as most suitable to healthy relationships with the leadership community of denominations generally.[145]

Here are the models, or examples, that were most strongly affirmed:

Several mission agencies worked in the aboriginal community. The aboriginal community had formed a denomination, which at that point did not have

---

144 Some leaders challenge the "modality" (local congregation) / "sodality" (mission organization) distinction within the body of Christ, first proposed by Ralph Winter in the *Perspectives on the World Christian Movement* course and reader (4th edition, chapter 19). These leaders argue that local congregations are also "on mission," though admittedly often with less focus and intensity than mission organizations. While the line between the two structures can sometimes blur, a reading of history suggests the two forms are likely to stay.

145 The PowerPoint used is available in Appendix 7.

a strong history of church planting. Agreement came easily. When a church plant in the aboriginal community reached an agreed benchmark of maturity, the mission agencies would transfer oversight and support of that aboriginal church to the denomination. There was joy on the part of the aboriginal denomination and among mission agencies empowered to do that which was in their hearts for the kingdom.

> Find ways to encourage parachurch mission agencies to support and plant alongside of local churches.

Another agency worked in the rural north of the country in small blue-collar communities. They reached out to children and planted churches among their parents. When the church grew to a certain size, the members were given the option of relating to the denomination of their choice. No representatives of the mission agency attended the meeting in which the decision was made, but they were available afterwards to assist in the connection with that denomination if needed.

In another model, certain denominations contracted with specific mission agencies to plant churches that would become a part of their denomination or network. Memos of agreement were worked out to ensure clear expectations, boundaries, and exit processes.

Planting within parish structures

There is also much value in seeking to engage denominations organized in the parish model, which, by definition, allows only one congregation in the geographic bounds of the parish. In addition to high-church structures, some large evangelical denominations, which are satisfied with one congregation of their tribe in every town or administrative unit, lack motivation to plant additional churches when they meet their goal.

While the relationship between Catholic and evangelical communities varies significantly by country, I should comment on the challenge of the parish structure. This approach, which places a church in each parish and cannot then plant an additional church in that parish, presents a problem, regardless of which group structures itself this way. Changing parish boundaries is difficult. More fruitful is the practice of planting communities beside existing churches.[146] Within the Catholic tradition, this is being done most broadly through its lay-oriented, non-residential charismatic communities,[147] which are missional and tend to hold many evangelical characteristics.

---

146 National church-planting movement researchers generally do not dispute geographic or ecclesiological nomenclature, viewing the matter an internal denominational matter.

147 Officially termed the Catholic Fraternity of Charismatic Covenant Communities and Fellowships, the communities are affirmed by the Pontifical Council for the Laity to encourage renewal in the Spirit and intensification of apostolic activities for a new evangelization of the world; www.nsc-chariscenter.org/about-us/other-ccr-groups/fraternity.

Respect ecclesiology as you help parish structures find ways to multiply disciple-making communities.

While the definition of "evangelical" is debated in some quarters, the Evangelical Fellowship of Canada has found the four characteristics offered by David Bebbington useful:

The Bible: Devotion to the Bible as God's Word;

The Cross: The centrality of the cross of Christ in teaching and preaching;

Activism: Cooperating in the mission of God through evangelism and charitable works;

Conversion: The conviction that each person must turn from their sin, believe in the saving work of Christ, and commit themselves to a life of discipleship and service.[148]

Regarding the Anglican tradition, one leader observes, "While the Anglican church can be hostile to church planting, it yet has been very welcoming to the opening of 'resource churches' and 'Fresh Expressions' of church because they can see how these fit within their ecclesiological framework."

Large evangelical denominations, without formal policy but in practice not planting in locations where they already have a church, also need to seek ways around their informal tradition. This may be done by seeking to view the harvest field not as geography but as *ethne*. In this way, churches can be planted in each *ethne* within a town or section of a city, multiplying churches among the least-reached.

Separatist organizations

Some denominations are hesitant to engage in a national church-planting process, not because they lack passion for church planting or the harvest, but because of their passion for doctrinal and moral purity. Their passion is not to be derided.

In seeking to engage the largest denomination in a region, I invited its leader to a gathering of other denominational leaders, but he did not attend. Following the meeting, I took a taxi to his office to brief him on the conversation and points of agreement between his peers and invited him to the next quarterly meeting. He didn't attend that meeting, so I again took a taxi to his office for a brief, friendly visit and update of the developing process. This pattern repeated three or four quarters, after which I saw a new look in his eyes. Upon my arrival he smiled and said that he was busy but would send an underling to the next regional meeting—and did so! Over the next several years he attended personally from time to time, but always ensured he was represented. His denomination gave generously of their energy and resources to the common cause of the body of Christ in his region.

---

148 www.evangelicalfellowship.ca/About-us/About-Evangelicals.

Some denominations may not engage in the national process publicly. They may not accept invitations to public meetings, participate in training, or appear to be interested. Why?

Be patient, serve, and keep connecting with separatist organizations.

Sometimes they are unable to reconcile perceived differences in their church or agency agenda with a national strategy. Some may not want to be compared unfavorably with other organizations or networks with more effective church-planting processes or leadership-training programs. Or they may find the challenge to plant first among the least-reached too difficult, choosing instead to work among more responsive populations.

Whatever the case, you will need to decide how to relate to unengaged organizations. True, some may not move. Sadly, over time they are likely to die. Some will move easily with personal care and attention. Others will move with a bit more effort. Don't make assumptions about reasons for disengagement or about God's ability to move them. There are several ways of continuing communication with unengaged organizations. The following steps could be of use:

1. Annual face-to-face visits

Keep making personal contact, ideally over lunch or coffee. The initial visit might consist mostly of you asking questions about the vision and ministry of the leader's organization, an invitation to an event, and prayer for the leader and organization. Hopefully you will eventually be able to speak directly about any perceived polarity between the needs of the organization and engagement with other denominations at a practical level in a national church-planting process. If the leader acknowledges this is a manageable polarity, invite them to engage at the level at which they feel comfortable; then make a return visit the following year to assess progress and to encourage participation in future meetings.

2. Encouragement in their own goals

While some denominations and organizations may be unwilling to share church-planting goals publicly, a first step is to encourage them to set either end goals or process goals and to offer assistance in that process. When a denomination or network has begun the process of setting church-planting goals or encouraging congregations in their circle to set church-planting goals, half the battle is won. Even if the leaders never share those goals with you, church planting has been engaged and people are being invited into the kingdom.

3. Share the benefits of research and other tools and resources

Although the leaders of an unengaged denomination or organization might not contribute the locations of their congregations and thus further the national church-planting process, share freely the results of your research with them.

Doing so will enable these leaders to benefit from seeing where new churches are most needed and to see why the contribution of the locations of their own congregations is necessary for compiling a comprehensive database. Whether or not an unengaged denomination invites sister denominations to training events offered within their own tribe, invite the unengaged denomination to training events for church planters, intercessors, coaches, researchers, or educators offered by other denominations or by the national church-planting facilitators themselves. Share newsletters and invitations to national process leadership gatherings and training events, wherever these may be held.

4. Keep them on your mailing list

Whatever your normal means of distributing invitations, news or announcements, continue reaching out in that way. Some relationships take time. Love is patient. The cause of the kingdom is worth it!

We've covered a lot of ground. The ground can sometimes be difficult to traverse because we're dealing with leaders who are responsible for the good of their own organizations. Often their paycheck depends on it. Sometimes they view this responsibility as contrary to contributing to the efforts of the whole church to disciple the nation. Yet it's not an either/or decision. Every disciple-making process that multiplies disciple-making communities moves the church nearer the goal of its calling.

The process of engaging organizational leaders in a national process is relational—requiring love, patience, and perseverance. Don't give up. Share the relational task with your team, as far as you can, using Jethro's example of delegation (Ex 18). At the same time, recognize the 80/20 principle: engaging 80 percent of national leaders is a magnificent accomplishment, and even 51 percent is a highly significant marker on the journey.

Next Steps

- Reflect on a key point in this chapter that stood out to you.
- What are some practical ways you can apply this chapter's insights into your context?
- Which of these points do you need to lift up to the Lord in prayer?
- What will your next steps be?
- Are there teammates or others you need to talk to about these action steps?

CHAPTER 14

Prayer and Action

A FRIEND WHO LEADS a mission-mobilization movement in my country, Canada, told me the Lord directed her to read the book of Acts as often as she could in the course of a summer. Doing so surfaced an indelible pattern: prayer, boldness followed by the power of God in advancing the gospel, and opposition—leading to more prayer, boldness, and advance—and repeating continuously. My spirit cries out for this pattern in my own life and ministry. It is the root of the proper relationship between prayer and action. The relationship between the two in the work of God both in our nations and in our personal lives is essential.

Historian and preacher J. Edwin Orr made the study of church renewal his primary life's work. He declared that he could find no revival of the church that was not preceded and sustained by "united, concerted prayer."[149]

It has been argued that prayer alone is adequate to disciple a nation. I believe this assertion to be true at its most foundational level. At the same time, when I pray I often feel the Lord urging me to take steps to advance his mission. This urgency is generally specific and personal: "Apologize to Carol for that comment." "See how so-and-so is doing." "Keep that promise you made but has slipped your mind."

"Every Church-Planting Movement (CPM) and Discipleship-Multiplication Movement is also fundamentally a prayer movement."

—Steve Smith

---

149 J. Edwin Orr's brief and widely respected lecture, though dated, is available at www.gcpn.info/video/EdwinOrr-role-of-prayer.mp4.

Don't pray alone. Recruit others to pray for and with you.

I like to divide my prayer time between open-ended listening prayer, items suggested by phrases in the Lord's Prayer,[150] and the use of lists relating to the requests of others, my own requests and goals, and my schedule. As I pray, the Lord often prompts me to take steps related to my prayer requests—reminding me that prayer and mission is a partnership between the Lord of the harvest and me, a laborer in the harvest.

When I pray, I often have pen and paper within reach, jotting down items stirred in my heart that go to the top of my to-do list for the day or are incorporated into my calendar for the next few days.

Prayer Shield

Peter Wagner once said to a class I took at Fuller Seminary, "I don't pray enough. I wish I prayed more. I do, however, have a great prayer life." With this seemingly contradictory statement, he introduced his book *Prayer Shield*.[151] External prayer support, in addition to your personal prayer life, form a prayer shield for the church-planting movement ministry in which you may be on the frontlines. Furthermore, Wagner describes external prayer support in three levels. Let's consider these levels, in inverse order.

The third level of prayer support, which Wagner calls I-3 intercessors, is familiar to most mission leaders. These are the people who receive prayer letters or prayer requests by mail, email, text, or other means. You may have fifty people on your list or five hundred or more. In most cases you don't have such a close personal relationship that you know how many of these people actually pray. Some pray only when they receive your communication, others pray occasionally, and some more frequently. Together their prayers make an eternal difference.

Closer relationally and geographically are those whom Wagner calls I-2 intercessors. This might entail a small group of friends with whom you meet weekly, monthly, or otherwise. Carol and I intuitively recognized our need for such prayer support when pointed to its high value. (While planting we had experienced significant spiritual battle but, surprisingly, hadn't thought of gathering such a group.) Even when traveling or away for an extended period, we continue to meet with these friends via Zoom.

---

150 I've found praying through the Lord's Prayer to be a fruitful process for many years. For each phrase, I add in a Word document several items expressing, in additional personal detail, points relating to that portion of the prayer. The Internet will yield many resources to a search for "Using the Lord's Prayer as a pattern for prayer."

151 C. Peter Wagner. *Prayer Shield: How to Intercede for Pastors, Christian Leaders and Others on the Spiritual Frontlines.* (Glendale, CA: Regal Books, 1992).

This group prays more specifically because of a high trust level whereby we can share needs and challenges that may not be appropriate to make known to I-3 intercessors. This group often asks follow-up questions because they know many details of our ministry. They care deeply for us and for the ministry for which they have prayed—some now for over twenty years!

In addition, some leaders are blessed to have the support of one or two individuals, whom Wagner refers to as I-1 intercessors, who are called to a ministry of intercession. These are spiritually mature believers, sometimes intense in personality and prophetic in spiritual gifting. Because of this closer relationship, it is important that the leader's spouse feels comfortable and connected with a person who serves in this role.

Monica, an I-1 intercessor, approached Carol and me and said, "I was praying for you. I don't even know you exceptionally well, but the Lord told me I was to walk with you, like Aaron with Moses, and pray for you." She would go into solitary prayer retreats on behalf of our ministry, and then often tell us about dreams she had relating to our work, usually in regard to open doors. Although Monica didn't often pray *with* us, she consistently prayed *for* us. It was her calling, for which we were grateful.

Retreat to Advance

Our personal prayer life, regardless of the prayer support of others, remains critical. I have found prayer retreats, both alone and with the national process facilitation team, to be vital.

In a personal prayer retreat, I take just my Bible, a notepad, and a book through which I believe the Lord wants to speak to me. Sometimes I bring food, sometimes I fast. I pray, I worship, I listen, and I rest in the Lord's presence. In each case I leave with a sense of who our Father wants me to be and what he wants me to do personally and in ministry.

When our core facilitation team goes on a retreat, we pray, listen, and make plans to implement what we sense to be the Lord's direction. I recognize that some people are drawn to action and some to intercession, but throughout my ministry I have found a vital and empowering interplay between the two.

Training Others to Pray

Training others to pray for a national process is vital in many ways. Russ Mitchell's study in chapter 5 suggests this is especially true for traction and impact immediately after the first national gathering (congress or la plaza) and at the heart of every further stage. Brian Mills of England whose prayer manual is rich in practical tools and examples is the first person I know to write specifically in prayer support of discipling a whole nation (DAWN).[152]

---

152 Mills, "DAWN–Europa Prayer Manual," August, 1994, www.gcpn.info/prayer/DAWN_ Europe_Prayer_Manual_Brian_Mills.pdf.

Mobilize prayer triplets and prayer-walkers for broader reach.

Mills aimed to mobilize the nation to pray for specific neighbors in prayer triplets, asking three people to gather regularly to pray for three not-yet followers of Christ—for up to two years, before regrouping into new configurations. When one of a triplet's nine people came to Christ, that person would be replaced by another pre-Christian to pray for; and the new believer would be invited to join a triplet to pray for three of his or her pre-Christian family members or friends.

These small groups of intercessors are also prayer-walkers, choosing regular times to walk and pray for blessing and spiritual light for their town or community. In these ways, prayer triplets seek to saturate the nation in prayer for a harvest of disciple-making communities.

In addition, intercessors prepared for spiritual warfare are recruited to pray for specific prayer breakthroughs in a specific city or for the national process as a whole.

24-7 Prayer

Through the leadership of Pete Greig, the 24-7 prayer movement has produced a wonderfully strong and healthy balance of prayer and mission.[153] The concept is simple: invite those in your church, network, or community to sign up individually for an hour of prayer, aiming to pray around the clock in a room set apart for that purpose. The room might focus on prayer for local mission issues on one wall, for national issues on another, and for global issues on a third. Worship music could be playing in the background and prayer maps and other prayer and worship aids could be scattered about. People could be invited to jot down on pieces of paper the sins that they would like to bring before the Lord—and then destroy in a paper shredder, "sin bin" (waste paper basket) or even small burning pit outside.[154]

Managing the details of a 24-7 prayer room might well involve more than many movement leaders can engage personally. For this reason, you might want to ask the person or team mobilizing prayer as part of your mobilization ministry to consider forming a prayer room themselves and then asking the Lord to raise up 24-7 prayer-room leaders across your nation.

Many nations have been influenced by 24-7 prayer and, before it, by the story that birthed it, the Moravian one-hundred-year prayer meeting, in which a band of refugees prayed in one-hour shifts around the clock. In the twentieth century, South Korea was a prayer furnace for advancement of the kingdom at home and for a broad missionary movement abroad. China's prayer movement, despite

---

153 www.24-7prayer.com.

154 See Pete Greig and Dave Roberts, *Red Moon Rising* (Colorado Springs: David C. Cook, 2015).

being difficult to access directly from outside, has become legendary. New efforts, such as the three-thousand-member intercessors' network in South America which is focused on national disciple-making and church-planting movements, are growing.[155] In addition, God has worked in Indonesia to apply the vision of national prayer for the advancement of the gospel in a wellspring of amazing blessing even in a challenging context.

Prayer Towers

Indonesia has become a light of prayer for the lost in its own nation, which is home to more Muslims than any other country, and an inspiration to other nations seeking to grow in corporate prayer. A week-long national prayer conference in May of 2005 mobilized half-a-million Christ followers to unite in fervent prayer for national renewal through church revival and growth, evangelism, marketplace ministry, and uplifting the poor.[156] Other initiatives include national 40 Days of Prayer campaigns and many prayer towers uniting the body of Christ in prayer.

These prayer towers are expressions of the well-known 24-7 prayer movement, but in a powerful, symbolic way they are typically situated in one of the points of highest elevation in the city, including high-rise apartments or even in structures purposely built to serve the city as a meeting place for 24/7 prayer. Each prayer tower is a meeting place for intercessors from congregations throughout the city. Many prayer towers continue in intercession around the clock. The dynamic and effect of dozens of such prayer towers continues to change the spiritual atmosphere opening doors and hearts for the gospel.

One prayer tower has multiple levels, three of which were complete at the time of my visit. On one floor, believers aim for around-the-clock prayer and worship of our Lord and King. Six to ten instrumentalists and singers worship spontaneously as first one, then another, leads out in a song of praise.

Figure 15: City Prayer Tower (used with permission)

---

155 To be connected to this intercessors network, please go to this footnote number in Appendix 7.

156 Such prayer events continue, organized by the World Prayer Assembly in 2012 and 2020. For a recent report see www.christiantoday.com.au/news/worlds-largest-prayer-gathering-concludes-in-indonesia-drawing-over-9000-evangelicals-globally.html.

In the level above it, a similar number of intercessors pray in shifts around the clock for needs in the city, global evangelization and church planting, other restricted-access nations, and breakthroughs in political crises current in the world. A coordinator receives emails and texts from around the city and, in some cases, around the world.

The third level demonstrates the devotion and creativity of this movement. Absolute silence and reverence are practiced in order to listen to the Lord. A model of the ark of the covenant, representing the presence of the Lord in the Holy of Holies, is in the center of the room. Worshipers and intercessors sit around the perimeter of the room in silent prayer and listening to God's Spirit. I've visited this room several times and have never seen it empty or heard an audible word spoken. The presence of the Lord is palatable. Is it any wonder that a disproportionate number of the children of Ishmael who have come to know the Lord Jesus around the world in recent years have come to know him in this prayerful nation?

Prayer towers exist in many nations. Some consist in a modest single room in a highrise apartment tower, another in a spacious meeting room on the top floor of a seniors residence. While seeking a location overlooking the city has symbolic and inspirational value such a location may not be available when you start. The point is not a particular style or location but a gathering point for intercessors from all churches to pray for the city and nation. Can you mobilize a team to establish a prayer tower in your city?

Nurturing the Activist Soul

When submitted to the lordship of Christ, the activist soul is a powerful instrument in the hand of God. I use the term *activist* here not in the common political sense, but in that of a soul passionately gripped by the call of God—like John Knox—who cannot remain passive while his or her nation languishes without Christ. Such a person displays breadth of vision, a prophetic urgency, entrepreneurial initiative, and difficulty in not responding to—and often creating more—opportunity.

Yet the activist soul can, like the brilliant but problematic Wankel rotary engine, rev to impressive levels but at risk to self. I can relate to this from personal experience, having reached burnout speed in 1995. Prior to the need to step away for six months, those close to me had attempted to point out my imbalance. Sadly, I didn't listen adequately to make the needed changes. The Lord used my burnout for good, as he graciously always does, but if I had found the balance in this vital polarity earlier, I could have saved much pain for myself, the church I served, and others dear to me.

Jedd Medefind reflects helpfully on the need for a vibrant inner life to sustain the activist's soul. He warns of the short-lived fruit of remarkable effort rooted in zeal alone. In his *Christianity Today* article, "The Fight for Social Justice Starts Within," Medefind quotes prominent pastor John Ortberg:

> Schedule and protect your times of solitude.

> Increasingly we find Christian people who are involved in ministry ... experiencing stress and burnout and overwhelmed by compassion fatigue. I can be tempted to think I don't really have to pay much attention to my spiritual life, since I'm working for God all the time.[157]

Jesus' mission and passion issued from his eternal position at the right hand of the Father. Yet Christ himself gives us our model of a man who did not succumb to the need to respond to every need, but took time to rest, to grieve, and to hide to be alone with his Father in heaven. If this doesn't come naturally to you, do what activists must do—put it in your schedule and protect your times of solitude in the Word, in prayer, and, if possible, in nature. Not only does our physical health depend on it, as was my experience, but our ministry, our family, and, ultimately, the very contribution to the kingdom that we so deeply desire to make.

The polarity bringing together the strengths of prayer and action is not, it seems, like most other polarities we are considering. On the one hand, prayer almost inevitably motivates changes in the actions of the person or community praying. Activism, on the other hand, does not inevitably lead to deepening prayer, but to challenges and spiritual opposition. Yet I have more often seen idealistic Christian activists press forward in their own strength than I have seen intercessors, not satisfied with quietude, be drawn into activism.

Facilitators of national disciple-making or church-planting processes live in this polarity personally and in community. Sometimes you will urge other leaders and yourself to pray, and sometimes you will remind praying leaders and yourself of what you've asked the Lord to enable you to do—and to do it!

In addition to the Bible, one of the first books I read after committing my life to the lordship of Christ was Dietrich Bonhoeffer's *The Cost of Discipleship*. The burden of this call remains in my heart to this day and may be linked to my propensity to activism (which I like to rationalize, in Christian circles, as obedience). Most deeply, however, Bonhoeffer calls us to balance in this polarity with which many movement leaders struggle: like alternating footsteps—prayer, action, prayer, action, prayer, action—each in the power of the Father, Son, and Holy Spirit.

---

157 Jedd Medefind, "The Fight for Social Justice Starts Within," *Christianity Today*, June 21, 2017, https://www.christianitytoday.com/ct/2017/july-august/fight-for-social-justice-start-within.html.

A wonderful aid to the interactive nature of prayer is suggested by the image of the Trinity as a community of persons, as in Andrei Rublev's fifteenth-century icon.[158] The holy, triune God invites you and me to join with them in conversation—as an undeserved but honored fourth party, so to speak—in which we make petitions, seek wisdom, gain direction, and are empowered to live out God's holy purposes on the earth.

Does your personal "wiring" predispose you to surge ahead as an activist or to devote many hours to passionate prayer? Take a moment to reflect and plan for any needed adjustment. Whether you are inclined to quietude or activism, fill any needed balance out of your passion for the lost and your desire to glorify God!

Next Steps

- Reflect on a key point that stood out to you.
- What are some practical ways you can apply or adapt insights from this chapter into your context?
- How does this challenge and deepen your prayer life?
- What changes will you make beginning this week?
- Are there teammates or others you need to talk to about these action steps?

---

158 See https://en.wikipedia.org/wiki/Trinity_(Andrei_Rublev).

CHAPTER 15

Quality and Quantity

> *"It's the little details that are vital.*
> *Little things make big things happen."*
> —John Wooden

SOME EXPRESS THE CONCERN that a national church-planting process can be too concerned about the quantity of people engaged with the gospel, disciples made, and new churches planted. Furthermore, whether or not the leaders are overly concerned about numbers, they have too little concern about the quality and the health of new disciples and new churches. Is the concern legitimate?

Some people suggest that quality and quantity in church planting are mutually exclusive goals. The assumption is sometimes expressed as "I'm not interested in numbers. I'm committed to quality—to fruit that remains."

To be honest, having tried my hand at church planting, I've wondered how this view has emerged. Certainly, all movement leaders desire not only fruit that remains, but in addition, fruit that multiplies. In twenty years of planting experience, having struggled through seasons of low-quality ministry and rejoiced in times of high-quality ministry, I have found far less correlation between quality and numerical growth than with prayer. The task and challenge of every church planter is to offer and develop maximum quality, since this is necessary to engage, retain, and hopefully grow more mature disciples and start new churches. I've never seen low-quality groups or churches expand and multiply quantitatively!

> Wisdom is the ability to know when to resist either/or thinking and when to hold fast to principle.

Jesus on Numbers

When we look to Jesus in the Gospels, we find the shepherd leaving the ninety-nine to find the one (Luke 15). We find Jesus' expectation of a harvest that yields a hundred, sixty, or thirty times what was sown (Matt 13). Jesus is urgent for more workers who care about the harvest (Luke 10) and urgent that the gospel go to all the *ethne*, so that God's kingdom may be established (Matt 24:14).

Does Jesus not care, then, about the quality of discipleship? If anything, Jesus' uncompromising call to a high bar of discipleship leaves us trembling (e.g., *Matt 5–7; 16:24–27; 25*), acknowledging our sin, and seeking greater grace. There is no reduction of the high expectation of "quality" allegiance to him for the sake of reaching all the *ethne*.

Either/or Thinking

An older friend was reflecting on the American church-growth movement of the 1980s. Some have viewed the movement as willing to sacrifice growth in quality for growth in quantity. He wistfully said, "I will not reopen the debate but only point to it as one of many sad examples of the human personality using either/or thinking to reject an important contribution which could be retained and benefited from by both/and polarity management."

An astute observation it is. To those drawn to either/or thinking, whether by personality or by the identity politics of our world, we might urge abandonment of inductive reasoning as a tool for confirming broad conclusions. The inductive process reasons from a specific example to argue for a general principle. For example, one could find a poor-quality, mass-produced shoe, and reason from it that mass production produces poor-quality shoes.

It is certainly true that mass production of cars, houses, or widgets— coupled with quick production deadlines—can pressure those responsible to skip important steps in planning, design, testing, and assembly. Poor quality can result, and memorable examples can be found.

It must also be acknowledged, however, that mass-production car makers also frequently produce high-quality cars. The point is that mass production can produce high-quality or low-quality shoes or cars. The use of inductive reasoning is not the best way to determine the quality of cars or shoes. Most consumers will suggest a better way to determine if their shoe or car is of high quality.

Likewise, the quality and quantity of national church-planting processes, disciple-making movements, or other ways of training or supporting emerging disciples and leaders is not best determined by inductive logic. Quantity vs. quality is not an either/or question. More effective ways to evaluate the quality of movements can be found. Let's abandon either/or thinking!

Growing in Quality

Ultimately, quality is that which most closely reflects the beauty, righteousness, and holiness of God's kingdom. No leader, church, disciple, or movement reflects this quality fully. For this reason, we remain passionate for a greater measure of God's reflected glory. This passion is the fire in our bellies issuing forth in prayer for greater grace, internal discipline, and discerning spiritual warfare.

Quality grows in communion with the Father.[159] Quality grows when we visit high-quality churches with a heart to learn and take time to interact with leadership. Church planters are wise to discuss with their leadership team permission to be absent for this purpose an agreed amount of time—e.g., monthly or one Sunday every other month. The quality of the church plant is likely to reflect more fully God's purpose that we thrive.

Helpful input also comes from guests, particularly a guest you invite to visit unobtrusively, with the purpose of providing afterwards an informal SWOT list (Strengths, Weaknesses, Opportunities, and Threats) based on their observation and experience. Such input from the loving but objective vantage point of an outsider is invaluable, since those who visit and do not return generally do not provide the benefit of their observations and impressions. This list can become your prayer list and then agenda items for your leadership team as it seeks to move the church to be a more faithful reflection of God's heart. Examination of the barrel staves of a healthy church suggested by Christian Schwarz remains fruitful for growth in quality and quantity.[160]

One of the best ways to ensure quality and depth of discipleship, like the approach modeled by Jesus, is to start small, go deep, and train for multiplication.[161] I am personally convinced this model of Jesus, deliberately returned to by CPM, DMM, and T4T applications, shows higher quality disciple-making than most traditional Constantinian models. At the same time, such disciple-making processes also show more people being reached.

With those who remain unconvinced, I share this antidote. Westerners questioning whether so many disciples made by these means could in fact be of high quality understood a study in an Asian country. Followers of Christ into many spiritual generations were asked their understanding of Christ, the cross, the Bible,

---

159 www.murraymoerman.com/2mission/renewing/renewing_missional_communities.asp.

160 www.ncd-international.org/public/natural_church_development.html.

161 This principle is very helpfully applied by Curtis Sergeant, *The Only One: Living Fully In, By, And For God* (Littleton, CO: William Carey Publishing, 2019).

Quality of impact can be measured if we are clear what we are looking for.

church and morality. Disciples from many spiritual generations from the movement's fountainhead were solidly biblically orthodox. In fact, the same questions were then asked of members of a Western megachurch. Sadly, the results were not as encouraging.

Externally, we must ask also. "What is the transformational impact of the churches we plant to bring support and healing to our communities?" A national church-planting process cannot, of course, control transformational impact. But we can certainly encourage purposeful effort by several means.

One way is to highlight in conferences and publications those church plants that make community impact a high priority. Another way is to provide a transformational impact measurement tool at national gatherings of denominational and mission agency leaders. These are being improved, and an Internet search may help you identify a tool to help your church understand the needs in your community and identify steps to be taken.

Having said this, I confess that I have mixed feelings about many measurement tools for community impact (certainly not about the need for community engagement and impact, nor about our calling to bring the light of Christ to bear on these needs). My experience is that inventories offered by prophets and strategists tend to hold the bar so high that a sense of inadequacy ensues. We may be inadequate, but God is wholly adequate to work through his people, weak though we may be.

For this reason, my encouragement is to begin with a simple measurement tool, make some progress, and then apply a slightly more challenging measurement tool. Begin with questions like these:

1. A survey of our community brings to light these three needs that we can meet with practical expressions of the love of Christ:

   a.

   b.

   c.

2. The ways we will know if we are making a positive impact in one year are these (one measurement for each need):

   a.

   b.

   c.

For the average church, very little more will be needed the first year. Remember, most people overestimate what they can do in one year and underestimate what God can do in five years. The place to start is the willingness to start, and to evaluate the community impact of that which has been initiated.

One church plant serves the poor well with a "free store" and with childcare to provide safe space for children of working parents. Another is located near a school in a community with high suicide rates. Gratefully, the school welcomes a simple program of church engagement with students who are needing and willing to talk about the pressures and concerns in their lives.

All biblically healthy churches are missional, embracing loving community engagement, whether or not they identify with the rediscovery of "the missional church" in the West.[162]

Shortly after one of our sons was married, he and his new bride traveled to serve with a small church in Lebanon, helping to meet needs in a refugee camp of 1,200 families. As he told of their experience, he said, "I fully expected to be moved by the plight of the refugees, just across the border of war-torn Syria. And certainly I was moved. But I was equally or even more deeply moved where I hadn't expected: with the daily love and sacrifice of that small church, engaged far beyond their means, under great pressure, day-in and day-out, in the massive needs of the camp—physical, emotional, and relational. Such love, such sacrifice!"

Quality of care. Quantity of care. How can we speak of polarities to manage when human need is so deep? It seems foolish to speak of choosing between planting a few high-quality churches or many low-quality churches—if that were possible—when the harvest remains so vast and the human cry for the kingdom of God, recognized as such or simply experienced as a wordless and aching emptiness, remains so great.

Yes, there are times to press for quality. Yes, there are times to press for reaching more of the *ethne*. There are times to pray with tears and groans beyond words (Rom 8), because there remains such a great and painful need for more and better disciples.

Pray and work for more disciples. Pray and work for more multiplicative movements. Work and pray for greater maturity and quality leadership. Don't remain locked in one direction.

Regardless of the needs in your community, there will be encouraging advances and periodic setbacks. How do we engage the ebb and flow of local ministry and, in all likelihood, that of the national mobilization process being stewarded by your national coordination team?

---

162 The jury may still be out on the Western "emergent" church movement, which seeks to engage postmodernity while broadly accepting the premises of postmodernity—so far, at best, with mixed results.

Next Steps

- Reflect on a key point that stood out to you in this chapter.
- What are some practical ways you can apply or adapt other insights into your context?
- Which of these points do you need to lift up to the Lord in prayer?
- What will your next steps be?
- Are there teammates or others you need to talk to about these action steps?

IN PART 3 we've been unpacking aspects of leadership relating to perseverance in pressing through to a high calling in a long obedience in the same direction. We are mentally and spiritually committed to a marathon rather than a sprint. Not everyone who has begun with us will finish with us. Leading a transformational national saturation church-planting movement is as challenging as we expected, but the Lord is with us as we introduce thousands and even millions to him whom to know is eternal life.

Starting Well

The national process may begin with comparative ease. Not all eight cylinders (see appendix 1) need to be firing at the start, but just enough to begin moving. This book has touched on several approaches to begin simply.

We considered the fruitful model developed in Europe that focuses on four missional components, which can be reviewed at www.nc2p.org.

CHAPTER 16

Consolidate and (Re)Build

"The elevator to success is not running; you must climb the stairs."
—Unknown

Leadership   **Information**   **Gathering**   **Systems**

Figure 9: Four Components of a National Church-Planting Process

The NC2P four-step process helps SCP startups understand a simplified "What shall we focus on first?" question, which is vital to engaging a broad transformational national-saturation church-planting movement.

Outcomes of Russ Mitchell's research, shared in chapter 5, revealed that four of the eight cylinders often provide mission-critical strength to get underway:

- National leadership team that is focused, capable, and committed.
- Seminars and consultation, surfaced by research. Local leaders are engaged and pointed toward further training and other resources.
- The support of a capable, committed backbone organization to assist in areas such as research, communications, and financial administration (see chapter 9).
- Diversified action plans developed by denominations and mission agencies throughout the body of Christ. These action plans are along the lines of the example in appendix 2.[163]

As the initial foundations are established and national growth toward a church-planting movement begins in multiple denominations and agencies at nearly the same time, there is often a bit of euphoria, as when a rainbow or sunrise gilds the sky. No one expects it to last forever, but it's a joy to celebrate. This often lasts through two or three national gatherings, assuming congresses, la plazas, or gatherings by other names continue—ideally every couple of years.

Slippage

In the Philippines the DAWN movement grew in momentum for a decade or more, then plateaued as many churches switched priority from church planting to church building and health for a season. This change was surfaced by research and faced squarely. The national movement then regrouped and pressed on to meet its AD2000 goals. Following this there was again a plateau until new goals were set and fresh wind filled their sails.

---

163 Russ Mitchell also provides a helpful summary of four initial phases of developing a national process in his paper "DAWN 2.0," prepared for international SCP leaders gathering for the www.nc2p.org learning community held in Berlin in February of 2018. Available at www.murraymoerman.com/mm/downloads/DAWN2.0-RussMitchell.pdf.

Other countries have reported slippage following a change of leadership. The highest risk-moment to a movement is during and immediately following leadership transition. Sometimes leadership transition is a result of burnout, health issues, or spiritual problems. Whatever the eventual cause, it must be recognized that no one leader will stay through the entire process, because the national process needed may well be longer than a single leadership career. Some serve with distinction for a season, others for nearly a lifetime; but the day inevitably comes when a founding leader or team leader steps down and needs to be replaced.

Similar to the case following the founding of a church by a successful church planter who stays to pastor the church for multiple years, founding leader's syndrome often sets in. Founding leaders frequently serve with uncommon passion and urgency and are so admired that their successor has a difficult time measuring up. Measuring up, of course, is not actually the correct goal. Leaders are differently gifted, but those they lead don't always understand this and expect of the successor the same skills, gifts, and even personality of his or her predecessor. This all-too-human trait makes the national process vulnerable to a few bumps before enjoying smoother skies.

A national process can be compared to rock-climbing. We gain some elevation, but can slip back or need to move laterally to find another way to advance. Organizations also exhibit a normal, healthy pattern involving growth, consolidation, problem-solving, leadership development, and building again to make further advances.

Renewal as a Normal Part of Life

Of course, everything needs renewal. Our bodies need eight hours of sleep; our spirits need refreshment in the Lord when wandering or depleted; our homes need upgrades if they are to provide comfort and protection as long as they have the potential to do so; and our organizations, networks, and movements need renewal. This is not a reason for discouragement.

We've all heard people say, "It didn't work the way we expected," and this representation is doubtlessly truthful. The question, however, is not "Is everything still working as expected?" but "What adjustments need to be made to build or restore the organization or movement to maximum potential?" The need to rephrase the question and engage the inevitably needed tactical changes with courage and perseverance, without losing the core, will be faced by every leader.

Periods of consolidation can last for two to three years without undue worry. Continue to pray, encourage, and cheer national leaders of every kind in their effort, creativity, and diligence. But during a season of consolidation keep a close eye on the colors in the health indicators evaluation form (see appendix 4) and continue to focus on low areas. Doing so on an annual basis will help smooth out the inevitable bumps or turbulence involved in the ebb and flow of a decentralized national movement of many streams.

Paul's missionary journeys were largely composed of consolidation of gains and rebuilding where the ebb and flow of spiritual warfare required focused attention. Much of the Pauline correspondence can be seen in this light.

There will certainly be attrition in one or more of your teams—national coordination, research, seminars and consultations, or elsewhere. It is unwise to expect that all who start with us will finish with us. Restoring team strength or health following the departure of team members will be critical in any national process. This is not merely a challenge, but an opportunity to trust and train younger leaders for wider fruitfulness.

Further, some denominations or agencies who start well may suffer internal difficulties, leadership transition, or spiritual attack. Persecution may erupt or Satan may attack the unity of the body. Renewed prayer focus and energy may become a visceral need. This is not the time to quit, but to recognize the turbulence of real-world ebb and flow, retreat to pray, and recalibrate—but then to be strong, bear down, and press for victory.

Many have observed that national movements launched with joy in the context of one or more strong national congresses later find the frequency of national and provincial events waning, for a variety of reasons. This again may not be damaging for a short season of rest, evaluation, and creative planning. However, the time will come to refresh and rebuild the process with younger leaders and fresh vision.

Time to Experiment

In the process of growth, consolidation, and (re)building you have time to experiment. This is a gift. Consider the first round of national gatherings, for example, as an experiment. You evaluate and next time aim for small improvements. This applies to other components of your work. There is nothing that cannot be improved.

In this undulating process you need not aim at perfection or be discouraged if you don't reach it. In the first round, aim to do well, certainly; but give yourself room and time to learn. Rest, pray, follow up with and regather leaders to encourage them further in their journey deeper into the harvest field, building on what you have learned together in the previous round. In the second round, aim higher, yes; but progress is sufficient, and take another step as you are able.

This is the gift of a long obedience in the same direction. You have time to experiment, consolidate learning, and relax in the process. This is a blessing of taking the long view.

Readiness to Engage Additional Components

I began this chapter by encouraging satisfaction in building on several strong pillars. Many gains can be achieved by doing so. Nevertheless, more gains can be achieved by implementing additional components, as outlined in appendix 1.

> Even the disappointments of ebb and flow give opportunity to add a component, rest, and consolidate.

Perhaps your national process hasn't clearly identified least-reach people or locations, or hasn't set a clearly measurable goal to enable the church to evaluate progress in love and obedience to the Master's call to disciple the *ethne*. A national goal helps everyone stay focused. Without goals, subsequent congresses can devolve into good church-planting conferences. National congresses include the "good conference" component, of course, but national congresses can and must be more: the ardent pursuit of the least-reached and last-reached placed in sharp prayer focus by research, directing the priorities and stewarding the resources of the church on mission.

Your country may have reached one or more of its end or process goals. It's time to call the church to look at fresh goals further down the road or even outside the country.

It may be that you began with a national congress or la plaza gathering and hosted a second event three to five years later. To maintain what was started and to keep the vision alive and growing, more frequent national congresses or la plaza gatherings will engage incoming pastors and leaders.

Or perhaps a few decentralized regional seminars and consultations have had good success engaging lower-range leaders, but many regions of the country haven't yet been visited; or there has been good coverage, but a second round would now be fruitful.

If one or more of these components were added, a season of consolidation will likely follow in the natural growth process of ebb and flow.

When you return following a season of rest, the time may be right to deepen and broaden personal relationships by recruiting a larger team with capacity to engage denominational, mission agency, and apostolic leaders on a semiannual basis. Everyone needs encouragement! Listening hearts learn new ways to serve and new ways to pray.

It may be time to add an emphasis on transformation. Initially, this would mean local-community transformation. Later, ways can be found to form teams to engage local government, business, social workers, education leaders, etc. Chapter 21 may be helpful.

Have movement thinking and practice been owned by most of the church? If not, four-generation movement training and coaching circles could be added.

Has prayer become national and passionate? What could be done to add a powerful component releasing power from heaven? Neighborhood lighthouses as introduced in chapter 3? Prayer towers?

The time may now be right to encourage churches and organizations to set goals. Some critics will likely suggest that the encouragement of goals implies that it's all about activities or numbers, rather than about people. This is not true, because we all measure what we value in life, and what we value organizationally is people coming to Christ. We then measure and count people and the communities that nurture them, or the activities that lead to reaching them, just as Jesus counts his sheep to know who may be missing or found. Don't hesitate to lead simply because some may not join in the journey.

What else does the Spirit quicken to your heart and mind that could add a more comprehensive harvest process; the acceleration of that process; higher-quality disciples, leaders, and disciple- making communities; or greater transformational impact on culture, its components, and the institutions of society?

Unreached People Groups and Unengaged People Groups

Mission leaders rightly point to the need to adopt and engage every unreached people group. This is important both for larger and smaller population people groups. Strategically, larger population groups are sought first to be engaged with the grace of the gospel; then, as committed sponsors can be found, smaller population groups are targeted. Every UPG must be engaged, with multiple indigenous movements discipling the people group to its fringes. The long-anticipated goal is within reach, and the day is coming near when the last unreached people group has been engaged. When you read this, it may be that the coming of that day has fully come and is being celebrated!

At the same time, two things need to be remembered and to remain a matter of passionate prayer.

The first is that when a people group is engaged, it is not fully reached. The urgency of the need is not removed when the work begins. Figure 16 depicts the disciple-making and church-planting process taking place simultaneously within several people groups.

Every **people group**
requires a **church-planting movement** (inner circle)
to disciple it to its **fringes** (outer circle).

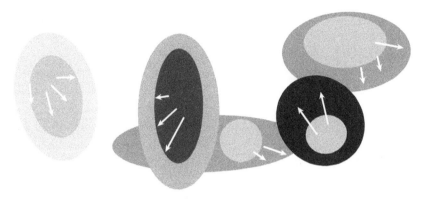

Figure 16: Every "People Group" Requires a "Church-Planting Movement"
to Disciple It to Its "Fringes"

Each of the larger ovals represents a people group. People groups frequently overlap geographically, as in this diagram. The inner circle represents the discipled portion of that people group, and the arrows represent efforts to enlarge that portion. Those primarily responsible for discipling the people group to its fringes are the believers who are indigenous to the group. If 10 percent of the people group has been discipled, rather than sending missionaries to that group, they should be deployed to people groups who are unengaged, or engaged to a far less degree—e.g., under 2 percent. Research is needed to make wise, practical decisions. In many cases, such research has already been done and only needs to be sought out or updated.

The second thing to remember and commit to prayer is that even after the last unreached people group has been engaged, vast numbers of lost souls remain—much larger numbers, in fact, in terms of the unreached—among people and language groups already engaged, including some engaged centuries ago. For example, the largest language groups on the Eurasian continent are Chinese, Hindi, Bengali, Russian, and Japanese. All are engaged (i.e., the disciple-making process has been started long ago) but in majority not yet reached (i.e., vast numbers are not yet disciples). In addition, there are many who speak Spanish (460 million), Arabic (315 million), French (280 million), and Portuguese (234 million), to say nothing of English speakers, who know the church but not him whom to know is eternal life (John 17:3).[164]

---

164 www.babbel.com/en/magazine/the-10-most-spoken-languages-in-the-world.

The reason we pause to reflect on larger and long-engaged people groups is that *every* lost soul is infinitely precious to the Savior and Shepherd who leaves the ninety-nine for the one.

So here is the polarity to be managed. It is always right to seek out and engage unreached people groups, and it is always right to disciple engaged people groups to their fringes. But which is more important—to engage a small-population unengaged people group or to disciple a large-population people group that is already engaged but still massively unreached? The answer is yes! There is a time to do both, and often at the same time. The enemy would insist that we choose one, leaving the other to languish. But the kingdom is always both/and—unengaged and engaged in an appropriate balance of focus and energy and prayer.

Some will argue that we should evaluate groupings of undiscipled peoples, somewhat like a triage situation. Yes, but instead of leaving some without needed disciple-making movements, let's call out more laborers into that field of the harvest. A majority of new deployments should go to those who have not yet had opportunity. More about strategic deployment in chapter 18.

A Celtic Rhythm

I am concluding this chapter on the ebb-and-flow, advance-and-evaluate nature of the national-discipling process by recounting the wonderful pattern of life developed in an early season of Irish mission history.

Celtic Christians of the first millennium developed a healthy pattern of life and mission, including three elements repeated in an ongoing way because each was important.

Preparation—This included prayer, the reading of Scripture, and worship and communion with Christ, whom they loved and represented in a dangerous world. This season often included fasting and preparation for spiritual warfare. The Morning Prayer of St. Patrick is one of the enduring gifts of this element to the global church.[165]

Mission—This involved hazardous travel, praying for the sick, establishing monasteries, and proclaiming the good news of Jesus to those had their own gods and often strenuously resisted God's grace. There were frequent dangers and hardships. These times required all the courage, strength, and faith that could be renewed within during the season of preparation.

Heaven—Upon returning from a mission, there would be feasting, celebration, rest, expressions of joy, and replenishment. Celtic believers called this phase *heaven* because they viewed such activities as foretastes of heaven. This element was unhurried and deeply enjoyed before returning to the next season of preparation and the steps of obedience, struggle, and joy that followed.

---

165 www.murraymoerman.com/3downloads/prayers/prayer_of_saint_patrick.asp.

Next Steps

- Reflect on a key point that stood out to you in this chapter.
- What are some practical ways that you can apply or adapt these insights in your context?
- Which of these points do you need to lift up to the Lord in prayer?
- What will your next steps be?
- Are there teammates or others you need to talk to about these action steps?

PART 4

Where to ... Globally?

The question may sound audacious. How can we know how to best move toward a national process of disciple-making and church planting in every country on earth? How can we say with confidence what we will do in this season of the shaking of the earth (Heb 12:26–29)? Certainly "the heart of man plans his way, but the LORD establishes his steps" (Prov 16:9 ESV).

Nevertheless, we must not overstate our weakness. We serve a great God. We remain confident of eternal, unshakable realities. God is establishing his kingdom. It is his unswerving purpose to bless all the *ethne* of the earth (Gen 12:1–3). The *missio Dei* preceded God's revelation of it to Abram. God's redemptive purpose in Jesus Christ remains sure. God's Word does not return without accomplishing its steadfast purpose (Isa 55:11). The gospel will continue to go out in power and humility as God's offer of grace, healing, and forgiveness to all *ethne*. And Christ will come again to establish his glorious kingdom (Matt 24:14)!

For these reasons we can ask these global questions and have confidence that God will answer them. In addition, God is likely to use us in those answers for national processes everywhere, and to do so in surprising ways as we step forward in obedience.

SERVING AS A LEADER in mobilizing a national church-planting process can be lonely. I've been there! Challenges can be many, and those we feel truly understand us are often few. Yet, for the sake of sustained movements, longevity is vital and encouragement is its lifeblood.

How can movement leaders be encouraged, retain perspective on the task, continue to be learners, and benefit from interaction with other national process leaders? There is no more important component in your national mobilization process than leadership.

Let me share some possibilities and propose others. While we recognize that some models may come to be dated from the perspective of readers in future years, we may be confident that God will raise up other leadership-support possibilities, because his desire to mobilize his church to reach the least-reached and to disciple the nations will not change. It is the heart of the *missio Dei*.

If one of the following opportunities for support and learning doesn't currently exist in your region, consider if the Lord of the harvest might be calling you to bring it about for your own benefit and for the encouragement of your peers.

Let's start with the simplest.

CHAPTER 17

You Are Not Alone

"Moses' arms soon became so tired he could no longer hold them up. So Aaron and Hur found a stone for him to sit on. Then they stood on each side of Moses, holding up his hands. So his hands held steady until sunset."
—Exodus 17:12 NLT

A Mentor or Coach

You need a mentor or coach— and ideally both.

Mentors (traditionally an Eastern culture relationship) and coaches (typically more Western) can be found in any culture, and they don't have to be "professionals" or experts in disciple-making movements or national church-planting processes to help you and your team progress. You might, in fact, benefit from both a mentor, to help you continue to grow spiritually and personally, and a coach, to help you make wise leadership and management decisions. Your coach or mentor can be a personal friend, someone who lives either near you or outside your nation, or a professional fee-for-service coach with a strong track record.

Just as church planters who have a coach are more effective than church planters on their own, so also national SCP process leaders are more effective with the support of a coach. In fact, this support can be the difference between reaching the goal and falling short.

I have benefited from both mentors and coaches. An early mentor was a soft-spoken, gentle man thirty years older than me. My most recent coach was an ex-military man—strong, bold, direct, and about my own age. Despite their vastly different personalities and styles, I have learned much from each of these men.

The key is a willingness to listen with one's heart.[166] It's not that we do everything a mentor or coach suggests, because we remain responsible to the Lord for how we live our lives and conduct our ministry. Rather, we listen with an ear to hear God's still, small voice behind and beside the voice of a mentor or coach who seeks the Lord's guidance with us and asks key questions to help us break free from personal and servant-leadership problems to advance and accomplish all that the Lord has for us to be and do. Humility, not subservience, is key to seeing new options and gaining courage to take wise next steps.

Coaching Circles

National SCP process leaders can be aided in their desire to maintain momentum and overcome challenges by initiating or participating in coaching circles with peers. The central idea was developed by mission colleagues serving in an Asian Muslim nation in which disciple-making small groups are reproducing so effectively that leadership development for subsequent spiritual generations has become a challenge. In an adaptive solution, four leaders serving separate CPM streams meet regularly to coach each other through problems they face in their unique contexts. None claims to be an expert, but all are learning and benefiting

---

166 The first word in Benedict's Rule is *listen*, because only in listening can we discern God's guidance. Esther de Waal, *A Life-Giving Way: A Commentary on the Rule of St. Benedict* (Collegeville, MN: Liturgical Press, 1995), 46.

from this micro-community. The essential process is that one leader participating in the peer-coaching group each month receives the benefit of the full attention of the entire group, using the following steps.[167]

1. Share one current core challenge he is facing in his leadership role or in the development of the movement. His peers help him lay bare the roots of the problem, for greater clarity.
2. The others in the group help the leader identify people in his team or even outside of his nation who could potentially help overcome or work around his key challenge.
3. The others in the group ask the leader to share his dreams of what could happen in his movement if the challenge he shared is overcome.
4. Before any advice is given, the peer group offers only questions. Good questions can help the leader who has shared a key challenge to gain further insight into his leadership approach or options. Finally, the group helps brainstorm action steps which might be taken in addressing the challenge. The leader then prioritizes the action steps he will apply.[168]

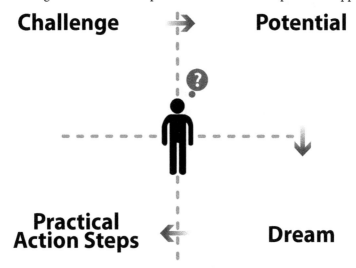

Figure 17: Quad Coaching Process (used by permission)

Let me describe an application of this format used by national SCP process leaders in four different countries, three of them Asian. An Internet video meeting allows one of the leaders to share the practical issue currently most challenging to him. The other three ask questions to help identify possible action steps.

---

167 With apology I use the male pronoun for simplicity in describing this peer coaching model, recognizing some cultures may cautiously include both sexes here or in coaching relationships.

168 www.gcpn.info/video/CoachingCircle-core-concept.mp4 provides a two-minute summary of the central process.

The group prays for that person, his situation, and his nation. The next month the leader who presented his practical issue shares an update. The rest of the meeting focuses on another member of the group. Thus each leader has an ongoing opportunity to receive the benefit of the questions, prayers, and insights of the other group members.

These relationships provide several benefits. In addition to personal support, each person is learning in some detail about the national SCP processes in three other countries. Although each context is unique, the discussions bring new ideas to the leaders in the other countries. This approach combines the support of peer coaches with that of a sense of community between leaders who share a common challenge.

In addition, this model is replicable. The four leaders commit to eight sessions. At the end of the eight months, they are given the option of ending their participation, re-upping for another eight months, or hosting a group of national church-planting process leaders who haven't had the support of a coaching circle. In any expanding movement, replicating leadership and coaching support for leadership is vital, particularly for growth beyond the fourth generation when relational ties to the first generation become impractical. An Asian friend serving in a higher-security environment pointed out to me that this practice moves leadership from a single effort to a plurality of elders, and then to teams of movement leaders. This allows geographically distant CPM expansion to continue without direct control of the initial leadership, but with residual influence.

I see parallels to my days as a young urban church planter when I invited other planters in the city to meet over a sack lunch each month. The details were different, yet equally simple. We divided ninety minutes into three parts: First, a planter shared a challenge he was facing. Second, the group discussed how they had dealt with a similar challenge. Third, the planters broke into groups of two or three to pray for one another. The group grew to ten or fifteen planters and met for years, many crediting it as the key element of support in their ministry.

This experience gives me confidence that the Lord works similarly among frontline disciple-makers, church planters, and national process leaders today.

Continental Conferences

In some continents, national church-planting process leaders gather in a conference-style learning community every year or two.[169] These can be greatly valuable in providing peer-learning personally and with leaders from other nations. These events also encourage an evaluation of progress in a context that stimulates creativity and goal-setting. If no one invites you to a continental gathering of national process leaders, consider convening one!

---

169 As I am able, I will post announcements of such gatherings. See Appendix 7 for links to forthcoming gatherings.

Sometimes such gatherings are stand-alone events. Other times, larger networks add a workshop track to focus on church planting in the context of a broader mission event. In such cases, the program design team may be open to the suggestion of adding such a track if accompanied by the offer of providing a team to prepare the whole-nation focus. Stand-alone events, however, are preferred for their sharper focus and especially for the larger block of time available, as compared with being a track within a larger event.

In a subset of continental gatherings in Europe, smaller groups of leaders in affinity clusters— such as Eastern Europe, the Baltics, or Scandinavia—meet online or in person from time to time. This is a great support option to be developed and hopefully replicated in other regions and subcontinents.

Group Conversations via Internet

In a variation of peer-coaching gatherings, for several years I hosted monthly Voice over Internet conversations in which practitioners from various locations share ideas and learnings about practical topics and the challenges they face. These have been supplemented by collaborative shared Google docs in which participants, or those unable connect at the group conversation time, add what they've been learning about the aspect of national-process leadership being discussed.[170]

Personal Visits

Just as church planters benefit from personal sharing and prayer with other planters working in similar contexts, national-process leaders can seek ways to visit peers in other countries for mutual encouragement. There may be opportunities to do so adjacent to a major international conference that would draw national-process leaders, or as part of an event key to a nation's mobilization process, which you can encourage a friend to attend. Sometimes an added leg to a flight made for another reason adds only moderately to the cost, thus enabling sharing time and prayer to lift the arms of a friend, as did Aaron and Hur for Moses in a critical season (Ex 17:12).

Collaborative Support Organization?

The heady days at the close of the last millennium saw a central organization solely dedicated to advance an inter-agency infrastructure supporting saturation church planning in every nation.[171] While this is no longer the case, a broader network is being developed. In 2017, Bishop Efraim Tendero, head of the World

---

170 Please email murraymoerman@gmail.com to participate in an Eastern or Western hemisphere conversation.

171 Mission history shows that the end of each millennium, and frequently also at the close of a century, the church is more optimistic about its mission and active in its obedience. The 1990s saw Dawn Ministries at its peak and the emergence of the AD2000 & Beyond Movement, which, illogically from my limited perspective, closed in 2000 while momentum was still building.

Evangelical Alliance, approached a friend whose organization had supported the DAWN process in the Philippines. He shared a vision which initiated a simple relational process, bringing together representatives of WEA, Lausanne, Global Church Planting Network, Global Alliance for Church Multiplication, and the OC Global Alliance for the purpose of seeing a vital national SCP process working effectively to accelerate church planting in every country on earth.

At the time of this writing, this SCP taskforce meets online regularly and is enlarging by continent. The Lord knows whether this simple relational structure between networks and organizations will advance as envisioned, but I am hopeful! Hopeful because I know that whether this or another collaborative relationship structure emerges, the Lord of the harvest continues to seek leaders who will heed his call to advance his mission in the spirit of his prayer as recorded in John 17.

You may be confident the Lord will support and empower your generation of leaders also, "for the eyes of the LORD range throughout the earth to strengthen those whose hearts are fully committed to him" (2 Chron 16:9 NIV).

If you are such a leader, don't be satisfied with trust in your gifts and intuition, however strong, but seek out a mentor and a learning community by some of the means I have suggested. You may well become a spiritual father or mother to others who need the support and encouragement of an Aaron and Hur, or of a Naomi or Abigail.

Next Steps
- Reflect on a key point that stood out to you in this chapter.
- What are some practical ways you can apply or adapt these insights into your context?
- Which of these points do you need to lift up to the Lord in prayer?
- What will your next steps be?
- Are there teammates or others you need to talk to about these action steps?

CHAPTER 18

Good Etiquette for Guests

MY VIEW of the potential and application of 1 Corinthians 12 and 13, particularly 12:12–26 and chapter 13, has grown over the years.[172] Let's step back to look at our goal of an effective national church-planting process in every nation. From this vantage point we can see both opportunity and challenge. Let me suggest, from my perspective and experience, several ways in which we can better learn to function as a global body.

The first challenge to coordinated impact is rooted, in fact, in a strength. We live in the day of a vigorous global mission community in which there are many strong and gifted organizations, many from the West and a growing number in Asia. In the last thirty years, more and more denominations, mission agencies, and networks have defined themselves to be global in scope and intent.

"The human body has many parts, but the many parts make up one whole body. So it is with the body of Christ."
—1 Corinthians 12:12 NLT

---

172 As a church planter I viewed the selfless cooperation for the building up of the body only in its original context: the local congregation. Later, when I was involved in a network of several hundred churches in the Fraser Valley of Canada, I came to see the appropriate linking of the unique strengths and giftings of many congregations essential for vital ministry to the needs of this larger piece of geography. Then, as Church Planting Canada was founded in 1996 and I discovered the strengths and giftings of denominations and mission agencies, alongside of critical needs in various ethnic, geographic, and social needs in the nation, I saw again how the church at the national level is a body—with "hands, ears, and eyes"—which must link and cooperate in such a way as to manifest and glorify the Lord of the harvest for maximum impact in the nation. In later stages of my life I came to see the diversity of the body in larger areas of geography to hold the same lessons.

> Our strategy *entering* a nation must complement—and not weaken—the strategy of the organizations *already in* the nation.

These organizations and networks are generally empowered with biblically inspired motivations and significant resources; their staff members are hardworking, passionate, and prayerful. The broad vision of these organizations frequently involves noble plans to recruit local leaders and set up structures to implement plans in large numbers of nations in response to the Great Commission. This is almost entirely a positive good.

It must also be noted, however, that many of these excellent organizations devote comparatively little of their time to discern how to integrate their unique contribution effectively with the contributions of other mission organizations, global and national, in the spirit of John 17. This can be overcome, although doing so requires a very deliberate decision at each level of the organization—and in my experience, probably more than once.

(Think Twice Before) Setting Up an Organization with Global Intent

It is comparatively easy to set up a global network or organization. This assertion may seem overstated to some. But because Christians are people of vision, mandated by the glorious risen Christ who has given us a global commission, it is not overstated to say global aspirations are increasing. I've been present in the founding days of two such organizations and not far distant from the formation of another such global network.

From a prayer circle, meeting room, or conference begins a visionary conversation about a dream that will circle the earth. It begins at the thirty-thousand-feet level and plans are quickly developed to establish a regional or national ministry presence everywhere. I've been part of these heady conversations and passionate times of prayer. Adrenaline runs high!

Months later when we descend from thirty-thousand feet and our wheels touch the runway in a specific nation, we are sometimes surprised to find other organizations with similar lofty goals and visions parking in the terminal at an adjoining gate. We don't always hear one pastor or national leader saying quietly to another, "Oh, here come the Americans (or Chinese, Africans, or Koreans). Will they be able to hear us better and serve actual needs better than the last well-meaning visiting group?"

This may be a hard question to hear (and usually it's spoken out of our hearing!), but our answer must be yes. To make it so takes much more than a translator to explain what we've come to contribute. It requires ears and hearts on our part, seeking to listen deeply and learn how best to contribute to the national process already underway in that nation.

To be sure, the national process in the country we are visiting or in which we are serving as an expat worker may not be highly organized. There may not be unity. There may not even be adequate vision. But be certain that God *is* already strongly at work in the hearts and minds of national leaders whom you can assist.

> ***Coming to* a national church-planting process is similar to *joining a local church*.**

I'm *not* suggesting that you set aside your global organization, if you are part of one. But you might want to think twice and pray hard before beginning another church-planting organization with global intent. It may well be wiser to coordinate efforts with another high-integrity global or national organization already in existence.

Whether your organization is a global household word or a small local church, your task is the same—to discern where you fit in the body and to do your part with all your strength in the spirit of John 17. Let me suggest some ways to discern the way forward.

Fully Trust and Leave Decision-Making to National Leaders

God is already at work. The Lord of the harvest has already begun work in the heart of an Ethiopian national (Acts 8:26ff), a Macedonian woman (Acts 16:14ff), and, in fact, nationals from every nation (Acts 2:9–11). Those whom he loves and trusts we are to love and trust also. The question for those who are part of international organizations is whether we in fact trust, respect, and carefully listen to the national leaders whom God has raised up.

As equals in Christ but well-meaning outsiders, are we to contribute vision, prayer, research, training, encouragement, or frontline planting? What is the need? What are our gifts?

When we come to the table of a national church-planting process, the progression is similar to joining a local church. We look and listen to see if we are an ear, hand, foot, or towel, and take our place in God's plan.

An Asian leader shared his observation that in one country in which he ministered most churches in the national SCP process were being planted by expat workers. In another country, most churches were being planted by churches led by indigenous pastors. He viewed the former model as a less helpful functioning of the body—a less mature model in which external NGOs plant most of the new churches and support many of the pastors. "But this is not sustainable," he said, "and tends not to multiply. In the next phase, NGOs should consider training mother churches, and then encourage mother churches to plant."

Help "globals" to think like nationals.

Learning to function as part of the global body, regardless of self-perceived strength or superior resources, means learning how to cooperate on the ground with the local body in humility and grace. Specifically, this means drinking tea with leaders of an existing national church-planting process, listening to their perspectives and concerns, and asking, "How might I (we) serve?" Remember you are a guest in the home of another. Good etiquette is not only polite but an expression of brotherly love (Rom 12:10 KJV).

If a national SCP doesn't yet exist, it means asking the Lord to lead you to national leaders whose hearts have been prepared to carry the vision of a whole-nation process, listen to their perspectives and concerns, and ask, "How might I (we) serve?" to help initiate the process. The answer in either case may be to assist with research, fundraising, infrastructure, prayer mobilization, or serving as someone's administrative assistant.

This does not imply that an expat cannot or should not initiate a national church-planting movement; only that he or she should look around and be equally willing to serve a national leader in this role. In my experience, it generally takes years for an expat to earn the trust of national leaders. He or she may, however, multiply the effectiveness of a national leader who is already trusted as catalyst of a national church-planting process, because such national leaders often also serve as full-time pastors. Until the national leader can raise support for a full-time national coordination role, an externally supported expat person in an administrative assistant support role can, in fact, make a difference greater than by attempting to lead personally.

Sometimes, however, an expat can lay the groundwork—initiating research, casting vision, and facilitating conversation among national leaders. When national leaders are ready to collaborate on a national vision, they are free to choose a leader for the coordinating team. That leader may be the expat who initiated the process.

Drink Tea with Other "Globals"

The Christian community in most countries is served, often in a small way, by one or more international denominations, networks, and organizations. At least some of these international groups are influenced by a broad vision which contains at least the embryo of a national church-planting process. But there need be only one national church-planting process in each country; indeed, it is best if there is only one. Best both for the sake of efficiency and relationships, as well as to honor and express Jesus' prayer in John 17.

In one country, several warmhearted, well-meaning, passionately-praying organizations envisioned a national process to serve that country. Each had in mind a national leader. This is encouraging, in that it confirms the time is right to advance the Lord's purpose. Yet multiple international organizations with the same vision for a single country can create an environment in which vison and resources overlap or even compete, requiring thoughtful and deliberate consideration of how each can best contribute, as a member of the global body of Christ, to a single national church-planting process.

> Just as a church can plant a church, a national church-planting process in one country can help start a national church-planting process in another country.

This involves drinking tea with "globals," other international leaders, to ensure love, trust, and appropriate collaboration between global organizations, combined with authentic love, trust, and respect for national leaders—and avoidance of inadvertently playing national leaders or organizations against each other, as well as any other sins of omission or commission.

Remember, the purpose of each denomination, network, and organization is not to set up a spiritual or organizational empire, even in our minds, but to contribute our part to the task of equipping and mobilizing the whole body of Christ for its calling to disciple the *ethne* of each nation.

Engage Nearby Nations

There is a second way in which we can function as a global body in developing a national SCP process in every country. Just as a human body and a local church have stronger and weaker members (1 Cor 12), the body of Christ in geographically adjoining or culturally near nations may well be experiencing SCP processes with different strengths or challenges. It may be that one nation is being blessed by a flourishing national SCP process, while an adjoining nation is without.

In this circumstance, leaders from the nation with the stronger or more unified Christian body can seek out leaders in the nearby nation in a spirit of friendship and encouragement. The nation with a national process can visit leaders in the nation without a national process to listen and learn how to serve. The nation with a national process can invite leaders from the adjoining nation(s) to observe or participate in a conversation taking place in a planning team meeting or training event. In Europe, South Asia, East Asia, and Southeast Asia, this process of supporting nearby nations and even those at some distance has become common.

May national process leaders everywhere ask how they can serve nearby nations also. May our understanding of the various gifts and strengths in the body of Christ increasingly be practically expressed in love for mission—globally and locally in every church in every nation!

Deploy Wisely

A third way that we, as the global church, can function with increasing effectiveness in the model and spirit of 1 Corinthians 12 and 13 toward the completion of the Great Commission is in the deployment of workers.

National goals set in the development of a national SCP process can include not only placing disciple-making communities where they are most needed in our *own* nation, but also sending workers to *other* nations. Not all national church-planting processes set goals for themselves or set goals for sending workers to other nations, but the value of the principle is generally agreed upon. The mission-critical question, however, remains: "But where should workers from our nation be sent, and what should they do?"

For a season, following the recognition of the need to engage unreached people groups, much of the global church's resources have been helpfully focused on the 10-40 Window, and yet many unreached people groups remain to be engaged. At the same time, there are many least-reached people groups to assist.[173] The needs of smaller-population people groups with very few disciples must be balanced with adjacent larger-population groups that are engaged but not progressing.

More recently we are also hearing the cry, "Mission is from everywhere to everywhere." We should affirm the measure of truth and positive intent of this slogan.[174] Certainly the church in every nation should be involved in sending workers as part of its contribution to the global task. Further, many nations need the benefits received from workers coming to assist with specific issues unique to their setting. Humility is needed to be able to see our own needs and give workers from other countries a genuine welcome.

Taken literally, however, the slogan "Mission is from everywhere to everywhere" can lead us to a cul-de-sac without thinking about what is most important, given limited time and resources. Unless the positive is nuanced wisely, one could wonder rather facetiously, "Is it wise to send preachers from the unreached to evangelize the Bible Belt, or ask the barefoot farmer to go and alleviate relative poverty in the West? Does it mean we're OK with taking skilled Bible translators away from their Bible-less languages for the sake of a new English-language Bible?"

This idea can become a recipe for a chaotic and unproductive mission. True, there are needs everywhere, but not all needs are equal. Therefore, the process of sending and receiving shouldn't be left only to emotion, whim, marketing skill, or personal interest.

---

173 The Joshua Project continues to provide invaluable help in keeping this priority before the global body of Christ; see https://joshuaproject.net/global/progress.

174 Patrick Johnstone, in *The Future of the Global Church: History, Trends and Possibilities* (Downers Grove, IL: InterVarsity, 2011), chapter 8, provides an excellent, detailed overview of the "From everywhere—to everywhere" deployment in the early twenty-first century.

Consider One Challenge's animated video "Understanding the Remaining Task" for a helpful review of the adequacy of an *unnuanced* "from everywhere to everywhere" approach.[175] Researcher Chris Maynard of Transforming Information and the OC Global Research Team has done us a great service in identifying where help is most needed, who should go, and what kind of role may best serve.

> It matters where we focus and put our resources.

Let's look at two such approaches as we consider how best to function within a global body as wise stewards of the harvesters God has given. The first resource is more general; the second is more specific.

In Figure 18 we see regions of the world marked in relation to two key factors—the region's comparative need for workers and the need for new churches to be planted.[176] Regions depicted to the lower-left should send their workers to regions to the upper-right where the harvest is comparatively more plentiful and the workers fewer. The chart warrants thoughtful study.

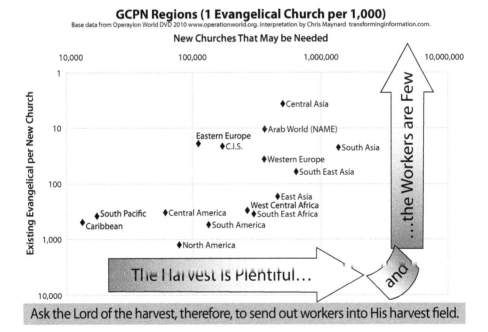

Figure 18: Deployment Priorities by Region (used with permission)

---

175 www.onechallenge.org/2019/02/19/understanding-the-remaining-mission-task-animated-video.

176 www.gcpn.info/regions/GCPN_Regions_Scatter_Diagram_potential_deployment_guidance_2011.jpg.

There are also variances in the harvest and available workers in specific nations. Because the level of detail required to depict the relationship between nations is too great for a chart fitting this page, please review an expandable PDF available to download.[177]

Both good research and the guidance of the Holy Spirit are needed in developing church-planting strategy and in mission strategy more broadly. Research is not to be followed woodenly, but neither is it to be ignored unless the Holy Spirit clearly directs us elsewhere for a season (see Acts 16). When the overruling assignment of the Holy Spirit has been fulfilled, it would be wise to return to the best research available until and unless the Holy Spirit clearly intervenes again.

Let's move now to a more specific resource, developed by Chris Maynard, which distinguishes among five kinds of assistance that a given nation might need. Some nations need help with pioneer church planting; others need partners to help them plant; others need support in church-planting initiatives already underway; others need encouragement to take on what they are able to do but aren't doing; others need challenge to refocus and engage more deliberately. The global body of Christ must not be fragmented or communicate, "You don't have a right to speak to me"—but we must, rather, recognize that we are one body and encourage the "eyes, ears, hands, and feet" of that body in every continent and country to fully contribute their strength and unique gifts to the mission of the whole body.

Let me introduce Maynard's thinking with this chart responding to the question, "How best can outsiders help?" Table 6 is best read from left to right.

---

177 A chart depicting all nations can be viewed in an expandable PDF by visiting this footnote number in Appendix 7.

How best can outsiders help?
We can provide church planting (CP) help to countries in different ways.
To keep it simple, we have chosen 5 types of help.

	To fill the earth with evangelical churches:	
If the country is like this...	...then this is a good plan for how outsiders work with in-country churches and networks...	...so let's call it...
We need more new churches than there are evangelical Christians in the country!	There is much CP work to be done and in-country evangelicals are few. Involve in-country churches in CP work if possible, but be careful not to overload them or put them in danger. Outsiders will often lead CP initiatives.	Pioneer
There are between 1 and 10 evangelicals in the country for each new church we need there.	Significant evangelical churches exist in the country. Try to include in-country evangelicals in every significant CP effort if it does not put them in danger. Sometimes outsiders may lead, sometimes in-country evangelicals will lead.	Partner
There are between 10 and 100 evangelicals in the country for each new church we need there.	The evangelical churches are numerically strong, although less than the global average. They may be able to do much (or most) of the CP work but will benefit from outside help, for example with training or strategy. Expect in-country evangelicals to lead major CP initiatives and to work with outsiders to define the types of support they need.	Support
There are between 100 and 1,000 evangelicals in the country for each new church we need there.	The evangelical churches are numerically stronger than the global average, but may still benefit from special kinds of support and encouragement to take on their share of global CP work. Expect in-country churches to do all their national CP work. Don't lead from outside.	Encourage
There are more than 1,000 evangelicals in the country for each new church we need there.	The evangelical churches should be taking a strong initiative in global CP – both in-country and outside. If they are not, then those outside may need to exhort them to action! We need them mobilized and fully engaged in the task.	Challenge

Table 6: How Best Can Outsiders Help? (used with permission)

This helpful conceptual framework is followed by a nation-by-nation analysis of the in-country challenge faced by the church, along with the most appropriate kind of response in three areas. First, each country has new churches to plant as indicated in the column with that heading. Secondly, every nation has the capacity to send workers to help needier nations as indicated in the middle section. Thirdly, every nation can benefit from outsiders coming to help in one of the five categories depicted in the right-hand column below. Table 7 has his current analysis of the needs and capacities of some of the world largest nations:

| IN COUNTRY | | SEND | | RECEIVE | | HELP |
| We need big national movements to pray & plant new churches here. | | We need big prayer & sending movements from here to help plant new churches abroad. | | We need a lot of prayer & help from elsewhere to plant new churches here. | | How can others help? |
Country	New Churches to be planted	Country	New Churches to be planted	Country	New Churches to be planted	
China, PRC	500K-2M	U.S.A.	500K-2M	India	1M-5M	Support
India	200K-1M	Brazil	200K-1M	Pakistan	100K-500K	Partner
Indonesia	100K-500K	Nigeria	200K-1M	Bangladesh	100K-500K	Partner
Ethiopia	100K-500K	Kenya	100K-500K	Vietnam	50K-200K	Support
Nigeria	50K-200K	Uganda	50K-200K	Japan	50K-200K	Partner
Congo, DRC	50K-200K	South Africa	50K-200K	Russia	50K-200K	Support
Tanzania	50K-200K	SouthKorea	50K-200K	Thailand	50K-200K	Partner
Philippines	50K-200K	Congo, DRC	50K-200K	Indonesia	50K-200K	Support
U.S.A.	20K-100K	Philippines	50K-200K	Egypt	50K-200K	Support
Mexico	20K-100K	Mexico	50K-200K	Turkey	50K-200K	Pioneer
Uganda	20K-100K	Ethiopia	50K-200K	Iran	50K-200K	Partner
Egypt	20K-100K	Ghana	20K-100K	Afghanistan	20K-100K	Pioneer
South Africa	20K-100K	South Sudan	20K-100K	Italy	20K-100K	Support
Myanmar	20K-100K	Zimbabwe	20K-100K	Yemen	20K-100K	Pioneer
Kenya	20K-100K	U.K.	20K-100K	Sudan	20K-100K	Support
U.K.	20K-100K	Guatemala	20K-100K	Germany	20K-100K	Support
		Chile	20K-100K	France	20K-100K	Support
		Angola	20K-100K	Morocco	20K-100K	Pioneer
		Argentina	20K-100K	Uzbekistan	20K-100K	Partner
		Tanzania	20K-100K	Iraq	20K-100K	Partner
See Table 6 on page 209 for category designations and definitions.		Venezuela	20K-100K	Algeria	20K-100K	Partner
		Australia	20K-100K	Poland	20K-100K	Partner
		Peru	20K-100K	Niger	20K-100K	Pioneer
		Zambia	20K-100K	Nepal	20K-100K	Support
		China, PRC	0-100K	Spain	20K-100K	Support
				Myanmar	20K-100K	Support
				Syria	20K-100K	Pioneer
				Sri Lanka	20K-100K	Support

Table 7: Largest Nations: Plant Internally, Send Workers, Receive Helpers (used with permission)

While further details of Maynard's work remain beyond the scope of this book, and the numbers involved will inevitably change over time, the comparisons and guidelines suggested are likely to remain of practical value for some time. I suggest you take a few minutes now to download this document and reflect on what it might mean for deployment of workers from your nation and the category of assistance you might look for from the global body of Christ, and specific nations in it.[178]

We've climbed to the thirty-thousand-feet level! Local decisions do not only affect our nation. We must keep the globe in view. This is true both for national church-planting process leaders and for those international workers who wish to assist. We must learn, both nationally and globally, to function in unity and humility as the body of Christ, as described in 1 Corinthians 12.

Eyes, ears, hands, and feet each make their unique contributions in a national church-planting process to mobilize and strengthen the church in our calling and process to disciple the nations. Likewise, international servants such as missionaries and organizations make their unique contributions to be coordinated and valued in serving the national process as needed. Finally, each nation should take its role in a global context to appropriately serve surrounding nations, especially those where the need is greatest and the workers are fewest, as suggested by the tables above.

May the Lord of the harvest mold every heart to recognize our best contribution in our context for the glory of his kingdom!

Next Steps
- Reflect on a key point in this chapter that stood out to you.
- What are some practical ways you can apply or adapt other insights into your context?
- Which of these points do you need to lift up to the Lord in prayer?
- What will your next steps be?
- Are there teammates or others you need to talk to about these action steps?

---

178 *To Fill the Earth with Faith*. A missiographic image and a document with detail by nation is available in color at www.gcpn.info/home/research/to-fill-earth. Used with permission.

CHAPTER 19

Joyful Redundancy

"Whatever is worth doing at all is worth doing well."
—Philip Stanhope,
4th Earl of Chesterfield

The 24:14 Network

SOME HAVE POINTED OUT that national SCP processes are not the only saturation strategy being engaged globally. This is joyfully true! The 24:14 Network also aims at gospel saturation, but with a methodology that focuses on the multiplication of house churches, CPMs, and DMMs to begin movements in unreached people groups as well as in each province or county. By the year 2025, 24:14 seeks to establish training hubs ("hot coals") in strategic locations and to identify people in every people group and location.

This shifts the research focus to finding and tracking networks of house churches, CPMs, and DMMs. In all this, 24:14 aims primarily not only to plant micro-churches but to initiate fourth-generation movements[179] in every place and people group. A further contribution is that 24:14 works hard to map movement progress globally. [180]

Is saturation church planting—working nation by nation through denominations and mission organizations—competitive with 24:14's focus on micro-church movements? Certainly not!

---

179 See the glossary for definition.
180 https://www.2414now.net/get-involved/movement-catalysts/the-task/.

SCP rejoices with 24:14 as each saturation strategy works to bring the gospel to the last of the least-reached, by many methodologies to produce movements, for one purpose—that none of those for whom Christ died might be overlooked, hastening the day of the Lord's coming for his own. [181]

In addition, there may be opportunities for collaboration. You may wish to seek out expressions of the 24:14 network in your nation to explore and assist.

The Complimentary Contributions of DMMs and SCP

Some have suggested there is competition between disciple-making movements and the saturation church-planting model, or even that one could make the other unnecessary. Such thoughts, however, are based on a misunderstanding of the unique contributions of each. The contributions can be compared as follows.

Context and Work: Using a now-familiar graphic, SCP can be seen as the broad mission context, as depicted in the four components below that are introduced in chapter 8. DMMs may then be understood as key *systems* in that component, along with prayer mobilization, coaching, and other empowerment, termed by some as tools and training.

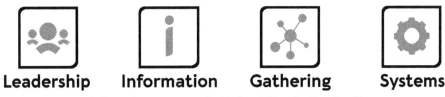

Leadership   Information   Gathering   Systems

Figure 9: Four Components of a National Church-Planting Process

Strategy and Tactic: Saturation church planting is a comprehensive *strategy* for discipling a nation by placing churches large and small into proximity of every community, people group, and high-rise apartment in the nation. By contrast, a disciple-making movement is a *tactic* within the overall strategy. Conventional churches, digital communities, and house churches are additional complementary tactics to complete the Great Commission.

Goal and Means: Our *goal* call be termed saturation church planting—a winsome church for every 1,000 people (or 1,500 or 500, depending on the size and effectiveness of the disciple-making community). Disciple-making movements are seen by many, including myself, as the most effective currently known *means* of introducing people to Christ and making disciples who can and do in turn make disciples who make disciples to the third and fourth spiritual generation. Because this multigenerational means of disciple-making is not commonly found in conventional churches, disciple-making movements are by most standards among the most effective *means* of reaching the *goal*.

---

181 https://www.2414now.net/get-involved/movement-catalysts/resources/.

Big Picture and Subsets: Another way of looking at this relationship is to see saturation as the *big picture* and disciple-making movements as *subsets* within it, as depicted in Figure 19. The number and size of disciple-making movements within the saturation church-planting framework will vary by nation, but will tend not to fill the entire circle because of the contributions of other tactics working alongside.

Figure 19: DMM as Sub-set of Saturation Church Planting (used with permission)[182]

Figure 20 depicts the way the broad *strategy* of saturation church planting works with the *tactics* of church planting, disciple-making movements and initial engagement with unreached people groups. Each can be viewed as a *subset* of the *strategy* toward the penultimate *goal*.

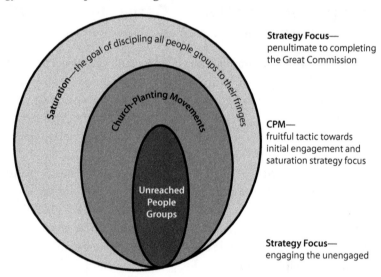

Figure 20: UPGs and CPMs En Route to Saturation

---

182 Provided by One Challenge colleague David White.

Returning to the image of the body of Christ, these collaborative approaches have working together in common, with each part contributing the tactic that it is best suited to help. And if there is, perchance, overlap, it is a joyful redundancy!

Next Steps

- Are there practical ways you can apply these insights in your context?
- Is there anything you need to lift up to the Lord in prayer?
- Is there a next step you are drawn to take?
- Are there teammates or others you need to talk to?

CHAPTER 20

The King Is Coming

"Be on the alert then, for you do not know the day nor the hour."
—Jesus, Matthew 25:13

WHEN I WAS A CHILD, I had a remarkable dream that has not left me to this day. The dream began with me on a street in a busy commercial section of an unknown city. Looking around, I noticed that people had stopped their bustling activity, standing now in twos and threes, speechless, all looking up in amazement and pointing toward the sky. At first, I saw nothing more than a small unidentified point of focus, which steadily grew larger. As it neared, it became evident that it was an image of Jesus returning—calm, composed, and purposeful—a stark contrast to the frenetic panic on the street. In how such things are possible in dreams, Jesus continued to draw near and become larger and larger to human sight, literally filling the skies from horizon to horizon.

Christ's appearing (Greek, *parousia*) will catch many off-guard. Most of Jesus' teaching regarding the coming of the Son of Man focuses on our need to be alert and ready, since only the Father knows the time.

Today's Challenging World

The banner of my website reads, "Following Christ in Today's Challenging World …"[183] I am keenly aware that this world is a difficult place for ministry. I am aware that the devil prowls like a roaring lion seeking to devour the distracted (1 Pet 5:8). History, both recent and ancient, reveals dynamics that we would prefer to forget. Giambattista Vico, an eighteenth-century Italian philosopher, used a series of loops enlarging through time to depict historical progression. The line following the top of the loops, appearing to ascend, represented improvement in technology that made life easier in many ways. The line following the bottom of the loops represented human nature, which did not follow suit. History has a way of appearing to advance (e.g., science and technology), while in adjacent pockets, and at the same time, to regress—sometimes horribly (e.g., advanced weapons of war).

> Our time is not unlimited, and Christ's appearing will catch many off-guard.

For this reason, there could be a day in which you might read this book in a nation or circumstance of darkness and chaos that would bring you, like believers in virtually every previous century, to discouragement bordering on despair. You might say to me at that time, if we were seated with a pot of tea, "I can see how you believed national church-planting processes were possible in the world which existed when you were writing, but they no longer are. I don't see how a national process is possible in my world."

As a young child, I grew up hearing stories from my parents about their experiences of Nazi occupation and suffering. Jesus knew this experience also in the Roman occupation of his day. Jesus was fully aware that until his return, our lives would not be easy. For this reason he asked, "When the Son of Man comes, will He find faith on the earth?" (Luke 18:8).

Christ's Persistent Call

Yet the King continues to call. He has called in all circumstances of history, and his eyes will continue to "range throughout the earth to strengthen those whose hearts are fully committed to him" (2 Chron 16:9 NIV). May we be like my Ethiopian friend who breathed the prayer, "Dear God, help me to be one of them."

I remember well Christ's call to me when I was nineteen years old to follow and obey. That call changed my life! Jesus' call was renewed during a low period when I was a young church planter struggling with challenges, minimal training, and my own insecurities. One Sunday afternoon as I sat looking out of my window but seeing little, I heard Carol's voice behind me say, "He who calls you is faithful, and he will do it" (1 Thess 5:24 RSV). This has become my life verse.

---

183 www.murraymoerman.com

> God's call is not separated from his presence and sustaining strength.

Later, in a season of recovery after a painful experience of burnout, I heard Christ's persistent call. And again, ten years later, this time in a form that uprooted Carol and me from our family to move to another continent, broadening our hearts further than we thought they could be opened without breaking. Your call, too, may have had multiple stages and extensions.[184]

A broad reading of history shows God's relentless passion. From the promise to Abraham (Gen 13:3) to the fall of the Soviet Empire, through the greatest turning of Muslims to Christ ever seen, despite frequent persecution—the glorious and costly *missio Dei* presses on, against all odds humanly speaking. Yet the King's love and rescue mission advances—despite spiritual opposition.

Jesus said to his disciples, "No one, after putting his hand to the plow and looking back, is fit for the kingdom of God" (Luke 9:62 NASB). An Indonesian friend speaks of this missionary persistence with military illustrations. When inviting laborers into the harvest, he highlights three models of persistence. He recalls when Mongolian soldiers landed on Indonesian shores and burnt their boats so as not to turn back. A second soldier is the Roman who surveys the land resolved to advance the Pax Romana. The third solder is a Jew who is commissioned on Masada making the commitment, "Masada will not fall again."

Esther de Waal writes that military imagery is out of fashion today, and perhaps we lose something by that.[185]

There is an urgency to Jesus' words as he commissions his disciples for their task. Many Christians are surprised at the strength of the Amplified Bible, Classic Edition: "So pray to the Lord of the harvest to force out and thrust laborers into His harvest" (Matt 9:38 AMPC).[186] Yet the Greek *ekballo* has that clear sense.[187] The Benedictine Rule recognized the truth and necessity of the resulting resolved perseverance long before, simply and faithfully reflecting the struggle within—the first battle that must be won—with the support of disciples in community.[188]

---

184 See Appendix 7.

185 Esther de Waal, *A Life-Giving Way*, 8. Interestingly, this question is raised by a Benedictine author.

186 The only other version to pick up the strength of Jesus' intent is The Passion Translation: "As you go, plead with the Owner of the Harvest to thrust out many more reapers to harvest his grain!" (Matt 9:38 TPT).

187 See an overview of lexical studies at www.lexiconcordance.com/greek/1544.html.

188 Henri Nouwen expresses the means of gaining inner strength to persevere in a 15 minutes commencement address in an audio recording available from www.murraymoerman. com/2mission/renewing/Henri_Nouwen,_Communion_Community_Ministry.mp3.

As the work and the battle endure, so must we—with our eyes remaining fixed on our coming King.

> The local church multiplies to build disciples who change the world.

Christ in the Local Church Is the Hope of the World

Christ in us is the hope of glory (Col 1:27). Likewise, Christ in the church is the hope of the world for God's intended glory. God's eternal purpose is not Christ in the universal church abstractly, but Christ in the local church—street by street, apartment block by apartment block, slum by slum—physically present in loving, caring, and sacrificial ways—which bring to the world the hope of glory in Christ.

Some feel this high calling is too much for the local church. After all, everyone who knows and loves the local church also knows its weaknesses and shortcomings. Yet the Lord is continually at work refining and making holy his bride. God has no Plan B as partners in his work of extending Christ's salvation to all the earth. It is no less than the eternal, holy, risen and returning Christ who dwells in us, the local church, for his highest purposes.

Therefore, as we strategize for national processes, it is necessary to keep disciple-making, multiplication of disciples, and planting churches into the fourth generation—along with compassionate social engagement—in mind from the start. Our King is worthy of nothing less. Our broken world will be healed by nothing less.

It's Not About Your Adequacy or Your Success—so Relax!

When you feel stressed, keep three things in mind. First, this is God's mission. God's mission is sharply focused on every man, woman, and child but yet so immensely broad as to reveal his glory in all the earth. God is at work in every nation, and he will continue to work in every nation for his glory until his kingdom comes. He can accomplish his purpose on the earth, and he will do so.

Second, you are part of a team. You are one leader among many in your nation. Your team extends into heaven. Rely on the Father, rely on the Son, rely on the Holy Spirit. Yes, do your best, but don't take yourself too seriously. You are not alone, but part of a team that you continue to lean on, work with, and are blessed by.

Third, in the end it's not about your adequacy or your success. It's about your reliance on the Lord, your willingness to learn, your perspective on mistakes, and your perseverance in and around detours. A long obedience in the same direction has time for discovery, learning, adjustments, and reboots as needed. For you, as for me, "He who calls you is faithful, and he will do it (1 Thess 5:24 RSV).

> God's talents in your hand, unreservedly devoted to him, are great in his kingdom.

Strive for Approval from God, not Critics

As you pray and labor for God's glory, the perspective of your critics, or even what you think, is not ultimate. One leader pointed out to his students that monuments are never built in honor of critics, but for those who have borne the brunt of the critics. As Paul reminded himself, final evaluation belongs to the Lord (1 Cor 4:3–4), and the Lord evaluates by his standards—rather than by the world's standards or even our own. "Therefore judge nothing before the appointed time; wait until the Lord comes" (1 Cor 4:5 NIV).

The Lord desires only that we seek to please his heart. It is this single-hearted desire that will enable us someday to hear his affirmation: "Well done, good and faithful servant!" (Matt 25:21, 23 NIV).

What Is That in Your Hand?

Before I responded to Christ's call I was an average student, mostly for lack of effort. Thankfully, though, my parents were wise. When the time came for me to give them my report card, they generally perused it calmly. They rarely, if ever, asked, "Why did you get a C this term?" Often, however, they asked, "Did you do your best?"

God asked Moses, "What is that in your hand?" (Ex 4:2). It wasn't much, but it was the Lord's, and the Lord used it—whether it was Moses' walking staff, his voice, his writing quill, or his strength of days.

I've come to love four-talent people who faithfully give to the Lord what is in their hand. In fact, I find it easier to love limited-talent Christians than eight-talent Christians who prioritize their comfort or leisure over their obedience. If we could see behind the veil, I believe we would observe the Lord often calling an eight-talent person to a great task. If that individual doesn't hear that call, or perhaps another interest overrides, the Lord may well then call a six-talent person or even a four-talent person, sometimes calling several before a faithful son responds (see Matt 21:28–31).

I've made a practice of asking the Lord each New Year, "What do you want to do through my strengths, weaknesses, gifts, and inadequacies this year, if all that is in my hands is entirely yours?" On each occasion, I've found the Lord faithful to give me fresh vision, and often strategy for the year ahead.

I use an Excel spreadsheet to track my time, priorities, and projects. I named that file "The Rest of My Life." It speaks to me daily of the Lord's gracious and purposeful calling on my all too brief life.

To serve the King in our national context is to give whatever the Lord has placed in our hand, in spite of the challenges and complexities, for his eternal purposes.

The King Is Coming

Christians have debated what exactly Jesus meant by his words, "This gospel of the kingdom will be proclaimed throughout the whole world as a testimony to all nations, and then the end will come" (Matt 24:14 ESV). For example, does "all nations (*ethne*)" mean every "people group," as we've come to understand the sociological reality? Did Jesus mean that every person will hear testimony to the gospel, or just that each *ethne* will be adequately engaged to have the capacity to share the gospel with every family in it?

I don't claim to know. I do believe, though, that the degree of our obedience to Jesus' Great Commission command may influence the Father's decision to speak the word and mandate Christ's return. If so, an earnest disciple-making and church-planting process of seeking first the least-reached segments of society—in every country, including yours—will hasten the day of his return.

Most of all, be confident of this: The King is coming! He calls us to ready his people as a bride for the bridegroom. He calls us to remain alert, "ready in season and out of season" (2 Tim 4:2 NASB). He calls us to disciple the nations.

May Christ's saving love be the measure of our lives![189] May he find us laboring faithfully in his harvest field. Look up! Christ's return is "nearer now than when we first believed" (Rom 13:11 NIV)

To God be the glory!

Next Steps
- Reflect on what the Lord may be saying to you in this chapter?
- What are some practical ways you can apply or adapt other insights into your context?
- Which of these points do you need to lift up to the Lord in prayer?
- What will your next steps be?
- Are there teammates or others you need to talk to about these action steps?

---

189 From the song "All to Us," by Chris Tomlin; copyright 2010, Sixsteps Music.

CHAPTER 21

Steps after the Penultimate

"Everyone now has a church within easy access both in a practical as well as cultural sense where he or she can attend and be further trained in discipleship should he or she become a believer. The penultimate step for making a disciple of every "nation" in a country has been reached."
—James Montgomery

"YES, BUT WILL planting disciple-making churches impact society?" "I want to see evidence that conventional churches bring social transformation." "Church planting isn't enough."

Critiques challenging the adequacy of church planting come in various forms. A common frustration for many pertains to their desires and expectations for social transformation. Underestimated in assessing the level of expectation in some discussions, I believe, is eschatology. The expectation for transformation was very high at the end of the nineteenth century, linked closely to postmillennialism, which was prevalent in the West at the time.

In recent years, there has been much emphasis on transformation. Documentaries produced by George Otis Jr., which encourage united intercession, have sparked popular interest.[190] Other leaders also rightly call the church to a more disciplined focus on community transformation.

---

190 www.sentinelgroup.org.

Multiplying disciple-making communities into every cultural and geographic space on the earth is not the final step of obedience to the Great Commission; but, as Jim Montgomery put it, such fruitful efforts are "penultimate" to God's redemptive purpose in Christ on the earth.

Saturation church planting is best seen as "second-last" in the *missio Dei*, as it is able to function as the salt and light (Matt 5:13–16) contributing to transformative gospel-impact to all societies. It seems the trickle-down process takes place more quickly than the trickle-up impact of the gospel, particularly where resistant, repressive regimes are involved.

Some expectations for social transformation flowing from a national church-planting initiative may not be realistic. For example, some point out that the church in Zimbabwe planted ten thousand churches in the 1990s, approximately doubling the number of churches in the nation, yet today corruption and political brutality remain. In my view, the faithful endurance of the suffering church should be celebrated unreservedly, without holding its members responsible for the dictatorship ruling the nation.[191]

Still, inspiring historical studies of the impact of the church, even upon oppressive governments, have been published. For example, George Weigel has written a gripping historical study of the victory of a "soft" (underground/ spiritual) power (Matt 10:16) against the brutal iron hand of Communism in *The Final Revolution*, providing practical insights for others under totalitarian regimes.[192]

Of course, discussion of the positive impact of the gospel on society extends far beyond the impact of national church-planting processes. This larger context is important and has, in my view, been well documented.[193]

At the Personal Level

Let's begin at the personal level, assuming social transformation to be the effect of many small contributions to a tipping point or, in a worst-case scenario, to progress in an uphill struggle.

Jim Wallis, in alignment with Catholic social philosophy on Christian responsibility for the common good, speaks of "10 Decisions You Can Make to Change the World."

1. If you are a father or a mother, make your children the most important priority in your life and build your other commitments around them. If you are not a parent, look for children who could benefit from your investment in their lives.

---

191 A report on the work of the Target 2000 campaign, along with the challenges of discipling Zimbabwe in a time of political turmoil, can be accessed in Appendix 7.

192 George Weigel, *The Final Revolution* (Oxford: Oxford Press, 1992).

193 See this footnote in Appendix 7.

2. If you are married, be faithful to your spouse. Demonstrate your commitment with your fidelity and your love. If you are single, measure your relationships by their integrity, not their usefulness.

3. If you are a person of faith, focus not just on what you believe but on how you act on those beliefs. If you love God, ask God how to love your neighbor.

4. Take the place you live seriously. Make the context of your life and work the parish that you take responsibility for.

5. Seek to develop a vocation and not just a career. Discern your gifts as a child of God, not just your talents, and listen for your calling rather than just looking for opportunities. Remember that your personal good always relates to the common good.

6. Make choices by distinguishing between wants and needs. Choose what is enough, rather than what is possible to get. Replace appetites with values, teach your children the same, and model those values for all who are in your life.

7. Look at the business, company, or organization where you work from an ethical perspective. Ask what its vocation is, too. Challenge whatever is dishonest or exploitive and help your place of work do well by doing good.

8. Ask yourself what in the world today most breaks your heart and offends your sense of justice. Decide to help to change that and join with others who are committed to transform that injustice.

9. Get to know who your political representatives are at both the local and national level. Study their policy decisions and examine their moral compass and public leadership. Make your public convictions and commitments known to them and choose to hold them accountable.

10. Since the difference between events and movements is sacrifice, which is also the true meaning of religion and what makes for social change, ask yourself what is important enough to give your life to and for. [194]

Small Groups of Christians Can Have a Disproportional Effect!

A survey of the social impact of a growing network of house churches surfaced encouraging outcomes. These included educating children, clothing the needy, adult literacy programs, helping people find jobs, professional job training, tutoring kids, giving out Samaritan Purse boxes, marriage counseling, counseling individuals struggling with depression, digging seventy water wells, filtering drinking water, scholarships for kids, going to hospitals to pray for the sick, teaching public health, feeding orphans in orphanages, helping widows and the homeless, helping to arrange marriages, building houses for the poor, providing uniforms for school kids,

---

194 With points like these ten, Wallis attempts to build bridges with the secular world; https://www.huffingtonpost.com/jim-wallis/10-decisions-you-can-make_b_3396921.html. Addressing Christian audiences, Wallis speaks of "10 Personal Decisions for the Common Good"; https://sojo.net/magazine/june-2014/10-personal-decisions-common-good.

painting government schools, providing blankets and bed sheets to poor people, clothing widows and orphans, eye and medical clinics, assisting in government programs, animal husbandry, agricultural help, and small business help.[195]

Many in my generation in the West have been influenced for good by the model of the Church of the Savior in Washington DC.[196] In the same way, my children's generation has been influenced by the community led by Shane Claiborne.[197] Inspiring and impactful models can be found in every nation.

The point is that national social impact does not require a national program or organization. Organic is good.

Broader Impact

Others will want and are called to lead for broader impact. Let me share an example from the nation of my roots.

Abraham Kuyper, prime minister of the Netherlands from 1901 to 1905, advocated for Christians serving in the spheres of their competence and responsibility to reflect a godly social order. In this model followers of Christ collaborate with other Christians in education, worship, civil justice, agriculture, economy and labor, marriage and family, artistic expression, etc. Kuyper recognized that Protestants, Catholics, and humanists would approach this task differently, but he called Christians to make this effort their highest priority in the area of their primary expertise and influence—aiming not at a theocracy but at a godly pluralism. Professor Herman Dooyeweerd provided philosophical underpinnings in his premise of fifteen spheres, or "modalities," of society in which Christians should seek to advance the kingdom.

Those who know the Netherlands will recognize that this model of Christian social impact also contains a cautionary tale of the necessity of the gospel being embraced in each generation anew. No transformation remains unresisted by subsequent unconverted generations.[198]

Nevertheless, and perhaps for that reason, Bill Bright, founder of Campus Crusade for Christ, and Loren Cunningham, founder of Youth with a Mission, met to share what they believed the Lord had called them to. And to their amazement, each had the same message, independently given to them by God, to give to the other. The call was to use their organizations to equip people to go into seven spheres of influence: church, family, education, government, media, arts and entertainment,

---

195 Shared during the 2018 Forum of the Global Alliance for Church Multiplication: see the link in Appendix 7.

196 I first read Elizabeth O'Connor's *Journey Inward, Journey Outward* (New York: Harper & Row, 1968) as a young Christian, and I believe the book remains equally powerful and relevant today.

197 Shane Claiborne, *Irresistible Revolution: Living as an Ordinary Radical* (Grand Rapids: Zondervan, 2006).

198 See my article "Social Outcomes of the Gospel," www.murraymoerman.com/2mission/social_impact.asp.

and business—"seven mountains," or mind-molders, in culture to bring to bear kingdom values. Francis Schaefer soon joined forces.[199] Their influence continues to mobilize, including the founding of schools like Regent University in 1978, which uses the strapline "Christian Leaders to Change the World."

The AD2000 & Beyond Movement, developed in the 1990s, sought functionally to influence the nations of the world with a similar collaborative vision that serves the *missio Dei*. The basic approach involved recruiting leaders in each nation to serve in one of nineteen collaborative in-country resource networks or tracks to bring to bear Christian unity and the power of the gospel toward the movement's vision— "A Church for Every People and the Gospel for Every Person by AD 2000." [200] I saw the value of this framework in providing impetus for several tracks in Canada under the Evangelical Fellowship in Canada including church planting, evangelism, ministry to Muslims and Christian higher education.[201]

The strategy appeared to be developing well in multiple nations, showing great promise. Sadly, however, the seed of the AD2000 & Beyond Movement's demise appears to have lurked in the date incorporated in its logo and goal statement: AD 2000. While working to help apply the collaborative track strategy for national impact in Canada, I fully expected the AD2000 & Beyond movement to refocus its mandate on the task remaining after the AD 2000 focus date passed. Sadly, the organization closed its doors on schedule.[202] The vision and strategy are still needed and could, in my view, be not only viable but greatly fruitful.

The following two initiatives, different in expression but similar in vision, seek to rally global collaboration of the church called to the *missio Dei*.

The remarkable visionary, Luis Bush, has gone on from AD2000 & Beyond to develop Transform World, holding consultations and leadership summits around the globe. [203]

In addition, two long-term DAWN workers in Asia, Jun Vencer and Steve Spaulding, seek to rally the church for "the phase after the penultimate." Both call the church to focus on the final goal of obedient nations in which Christ is ruler of the kings of the earth (Rev 1:5). Jun Vencer has attempted to

---

199 https://www.ywamers.community/7spheres. Some critique the post-millennial eschatology of Jonathan Edwards or political agendas of control, but these miss the point. The point is not when Jesus will return or control but letting our light shine, not just Sunday mornings but everywhere, for the common good. See https://rayedwards.com/the-seven-mountains/

200 The AD2000 & Beyond website is no longer active. A static version can be viewed at www.ad2000.org/tracks/index.htm.

201 Church Planting Canada, the DAWN initiative in Canada, was birthed in the context of the AD2000 & Beyond Movement. At the time of publication, several branches developed at the time remain active.

202 Organized labor problems in the host nation made AD2000's closing conference untenable.

203 http://www.transform-world.net.

summarize his thinking in a chart revealing some of the complexities of holism.[204] Following his mentor, Steve Spaulding's purpose in his book, *Obedient Nations*, is to help the church move from being overly *ecclesiocentric* to more *basileocentric*, which he defines as kingdom-centered.

Bekele Shaniko, before moving to his role as VP of Cru, led and modeled an exceptionally strong national church-planting process, aiming well beyond the penultimate, in Ethiopia. Take a few minutes to watch his account.[205] Inspiration for transformational impact beyond church planting will flow well into the future in highly practical ways.

From multiple streams have developed expressions of missional living and the missional church, often focused on the Western postmodern world.[206]

Also important to note are international movements within the Catholic community to restore missionally committed lay communities to roles historically held by clergy. Prominent among these is the Catholic Fraternity of Charismatic Covenant Communities, which aims at multiple local levels for a healthy balance of spiritual formation and social impact.[207] I first met Matteo Calisi, then president of the fraternity, as part of a Catholic delegation to an evangelical church-planting conference in Rome. While later attending one of his organization's annual gatherings in Assisi, I was encouraged by Matteo's practical model and serious efforts to think and live biblically with missional impact. The gap between Catholic and Protestant was smaller there than in any other setting I've experienced.[208]

How Will You Proceed?

Beyond the personal, local church, or missional community levels that I just addressed, you can develop a team or track at a city or regional level before pursuing national impact.

---

204 www.murraymoerman.com/mm (downloads/'Obedient_Nations' JV diagram.pdf. Glenn Smith of Christian Direction in Montreal developed a similar approach at the city level, seeking to demonstrate the values of the kingdom of God in concrete areas of transformative engagement; http://direction.ca/wp-content/uploads/2016/11/Key_indicators_for_a_transformed_City.2.pdf.

205 www.gcpn.info/regions/nations/Ethiopia_National_Initiative.mp4.

206 See reading list: www.tyndale.ca/seminary/mtsmodular/reading-rooms/missional.

207 http://www.catholicfraternity.charis.international/history.php?lang=en.

208 The relationship between Catholics and other communions remains a controversial topic among some evangelicals. The important area of ecclesiology certainly continues to be a major theological gap between the two bodies, despite Catholic agreement with Lutherans on justification by faith.

The range of potential engagements can be intimidating. Remember, however, that the Lord is at your side.[209] Because of his strength, our God needs only one Gideon to trust and lead with vision and power.

The following list can be considered a sampling to which the Lord may call one man to champion one track, a woman to champion another, and a missional community a third. In seeking to develop a team, the order in which the Lord calls leaders may produce a progression we might not have chosen. Remember, our gracious God is more committed to marking our nation with the grace of his salvation than we are, so rather than despise small beginnings, we may praise him for every step.

Consider the use of the "seven mountains," or spheres of influence, with the following sub-teams:

1) Church

    Prayer Mobilization
    Biblical Literacy
    Planting Churches
    Healthy Churches

2) Marriage and Family

    Developing Godly Men
    Developing Godly Women
    Discipling and Mobilizing Youth

3) Education/Academia

    Teachers
    Students
    Policy

4) Government

    Military
    Political Officials
    Police and First Responders

5) Media
6) Arts and Entertainment
7) Business

---

209 This is no platitude. The dangers of burnout or loss of faith among transformational ministries are real and frightening when the loss of intimate daily spiritual disciplines are permitted. Read soberly the thoughtful article in www.christianitytoday.com/ct/2017/july-august/fight-for-social-justice-start-within.html.

Other important needs could also be included as sub-teams or organized separately:

- Reaching the Least-Reached (in-country)
- Missions Mobilization (out of country)
- Caring for the Poor
- Serving Children in Distress[210]
- Sports
- Science and Technology for the Kingdom
- Intra-Cultural Relations (race and religion)
- Serving in Situations of Crisis (natural or man-made; national or international)

In addition, broader support teams can be envisioned to accelerate the effectiveness of those mobilizing the church through any of these teams:

- Evangelism Training
- Disciple-Making Movements
- Partnership Training and Coaching
- Communications
- Resource Development

Although this list is not in any order of importance, note the high priority on character development (marriage and family; godly men, women, and youth), which is in line with my view that no institution or nation will rise above the moral character of its leaders. In any case, I'm hopeful for prayerful consideration and purposeful engagement, initially with limited goals, rising as the team or network grows in strength and vision.

As you proceed in any of the next-step possibilities above, please review the incremental progress principle of appendix 5. The purpose of doing so is both to clarify first steps and, rather than feeling overwhelmed, to rejoice in God's grace on your labors devoted to him, whatever the early fruit.

The final goal remains unchanged—the Lord's glory seen and worshiped in all the earth!

The following overview may help stimulate your prayer life and planning as you or a team of friends envision the "steps after the penultimate" of a national church-planting process.

---

210 There are so many directions in which a "4-14 window" (see glossary) initiative can go: developing godly children at home and in the community, aiding in the adoption process (e.g., https://en.wikipedia.org/wiki/Lion_(2016_film), improving the conditions of orphanages, challenging the structures which produce trafficking and other such evils.

Prayer-Saturated Overlapping Next Steps Anticipating Christ's Return

◊ Maranatha!

◊ *"The obedience of the nations shall be his"* (Gen 49:10; see also Rom 16:26).s

◊ Add components where needs are evident.

◊ Form national tracks that work toward climbing the "seven mountains" in the nation.

◊ Mobilize every church to serve needs in its community holistically.

◊ Develop whole-nation partnerships to ensure that all people have a vital disciple-making community within geographic and socio-cultural reach, giving full and equal opportunity to know and follow Christ.

◊ Plant churches within reached people groups >2%.

◊ Plant churches among least-reached people groups <2%.

◊ Engage UPGs / Pioneer work.

Table 8: Steps after the Penultimate

Next Steps

- Reflect on what the Lord may be saying to you in this chapter.
- What are some practical ways you can apply this in your context?
- Which of these points do you need to lift up to the Lord in prayer?
- What will your next steps be?
- Are there teammates or others you need to talk to about these action steps?

APPENDIX 1

It's a DAWN Project If ...[211]
by Dr. James H. Montgomery

The Great Commission to us literally is to make disciples of nations. God's interest in nations is made abundantly clear throughout the whole Bible. The current reality is that there is a stirring in nations all over the world.

One of the means God is using to maximize these opportunities is what we call a DAWN or DAWN-type strategy. A true DAWN project is a saturation church planting process carried out at a national level and includes eight steps and ingredients.

1. *It is a DAWN project if* there is a national leader and a national committee with a firm resolve and commitment to work at mobilizing the whole Body of Christ in a whole nation in a long-term repeating strategy that leads most directly to the discipling of the nation including all the people groups within it. Such a leader, along with the national committee, is sometimes referred to as a John Knoxer, a man or woman or small group who embody the prayer of the reformer in Scotland whose life-long cry was "Give me my country or I die."

This leader must not only have the passion and calling but also the spiritual gifts, the experience, the respect of national Church leaders and, significantly, the organizational structure necessary for mobilizing the Church of a nation in a DAWN project.

As DAWN has developed around the world, we have seen an honor roll of such godly men and women rise to the occasion. At least one DAWN project leader has been martyred as a direct result of his role in the growth of the evangelical church in his nation.

Others have risked jail, sold their homes, left their jobs and otherwise sacrificed their security and tranquility in order to be involved at some level of the process of filling their country with congregations of new converts.

---

211 James H. Montgomery, "The Ideal DAWN Project," *DAWN REPORT* Issue 21, Nov. 1994: 11. See Appendix 7 for a link to the text. This issue was published in preparation for the AD2000 & Beyond Movement's "Mid-Decadal Global Strategy Meeting on World Evangelization," held in Seoul, Korea, May 17–26, 1995.

These godly men and women have emerged to take up the cause of the discipling of their nation under a great range of circumstances. The size, strength and spiritual dynamic of the Church varies from place to place. Likewise, the receptivity to the gospel or the degree of repression and persecution is different in each situation. For these creative and persistent leaders, however, a way is usually found to keep the movement alive.

2. *It is a DAWN project if* it is built on the premise that the most direct way to work at the discipling of a whole nation is to fill it with evangelical congregations so that there is one within easy access both practically and culturally of every person of every class, kind and condition of mankind in that nation. This includes all "reached" and "unreached" people groups.

As explained in detail in the book *Dawn 2000: 7 Million Churches to Go*, the core idea of the DAWN strategy for world evangelization goes like this:

> DAWN aims at mobilizing the whole Body of Christ in whole countries in a determined effort to complete the Great Commission in that country by working toward the goal of providing an evangelical congregation for every village and neighborhood of every class, kind and condition of people in the whole country.

> It is concerned that Jesus Christ become incarnate in all his beauty, compassion, power and message in the midst of every small group of people—400 or so to 1,000 or more in number—in a whole country including all its "reached" and "unreached" people groups.

> When this is accomplished, it is not assumed the Great Commission for a country has been completed, but that a practical and measurable goal has been reached toward making a disciple of that country and all the "nations" within it.

> With a witnessing congregation in every small community of people, it is now possible to communicate the gospel in the most direct, contextualized and productive way to every person in that land.

> Every person now has a reasonable opportunity to make an informed, intelligent decision for or against Jesus Christ.

> Everyone now has a church within easy access both in a practical as well as cultural sense where he or she can attend and be further trained in discipleship should he or she become a believer.

> The penultimate (next to last) step for making a disciple of every "nation" in a country has been reached.

> When this happens in every country in the world, we can almost hear the trumpet sound. The primary task the Lord gave his Church is close to completion and the Lord can soon return for his bride.

Of all the many affirmations of this DAWN strategy we have heard from around the world, I still like best the comment of a former Methodist bishop in Zimbabwe. "DAWN is a one-word summary of the Great Commission," he said to Dawn missionary Ted Olsen. "Jesus told his followers to make disciples of all nations. DAWN is the essence of our Lord's command."

3. *It is a DAWN project if* there has been adequate research that determines:
   a) the number of denominations in a country,
   b) their respective number of local churches and members and/or average attendance,
   c) the average annual growth rates (AAGR's) of each denomination,
   d) the methodologies being used by various groups that are producing the best growth,
   e) the ratio of churches to population for the whole nation and for every sub-group of the nation, and
   f) such contextual factors as the history, economy, religion, culture, politics, natural disasters and other societal forces that tend to indicate the relative responsiveness of the population and the methodologies and themes that might best see a response to the gospel.

Xolisani Dlamini of Zimbabwe is representative of that special breed that, in some circumstances at least, risks life and limb to get the data needed for a successful DAWN project.

In completing the research for one region of Zimbabwe, Xolisani hiked hundreds of kilometers, wore out five pairs of shoes, interviewed scores of Church leaders and spoke with dozens of government officials. In the process he encountered lions, deadly cobras, angry elephants and even killers wielding machetes and witches breathing satanic curses.

But even more important, Xolisani helped gather the data that led the participants in a DAWN Congress to set a goal of planting 10,000 more churches, a goal that many are successfully working toward.

On completion of his first round of data gathering, Xolisani said, "Now I know that the research I undertook was a divine appointment. Research is a most important thing! Without it, we simply will not know how strong or how weak the church is or where we need to plant new churches."

Or, as Ross Campbell, now with the AD2000 Movement, said after their first round of research in Ghana, "Nothing was the way we imagined it. We have had to change our whole strategy for 'churching' this country."

4. *It is a DAWN project if* a national Congress is held where the primary leaders of all denominations and other para church organizations along with leading pastors gather to consider the discipling of their whole nation and analyze the data that has been collected.

This is, obviously, the most visible aspect of a DAWN-type project. It is the event where anywhere from 50 to 1,500 delegates representing every stripe of evangelical are gathered in unity and commitment to a long-range strategy of working toward a common goal.

Putting together such a Congress requires great persistence in finding and gathering just the right mix of leaders, brilliance and spiritual insight in developing the prophetic message and a program to communicate it, skill in gathering and supervising a strong team of workers, ability to cut costs and raise large amounts of money—and much more! Committees are needed for selection of delegates, finances, site selection and arrangements, housing of delegates, Congress program, communications and so on.

Tom Houston, International Director for the Lausanne Committee on World Evangelization, warns that it will be disastrous "… to move ahead before the whole Body is ready." The unity of the Church in some countries makes it possible to start a project almost as soon as it is presented. In Finland it took eight years before such unity came. In Japan, at this writing, there is such division between Pentecostals and non-Pentecostals that the time is still not ripe for a true DAWN project.

Sometimes there is need for a major spiritual breakthrough. Such was the case in Argentina in September 1994, when leaders were gathered for an initial meeting to consider whether to proceed with a DAWN project or not. Bob Smart, who first experienced DAWN in his native England, broke down all barriers with his humble approach.

"I come in the name of the English Church to apologize for what my country did in the Falklands war," he said. "I confess also the pride that we as a Church felt."

At this point, Dawn missionary Berna Salcedo heard someone cry. It turned out to be one of the pastors who had participated in that hostility. Soon other pastors were weeping all around the room. Someone asked Alberto De Luca, leader of the meeting, to give brother Smart a hug as a sign of forgiveness. From that point on, it was not difficult for the Church to come together for a DAWN Congress and national strategy.

5. *It is a DAWN project if* the delegation gathered at the national Congress collectively commits itself to a specific number of churches to be planted by a specific date. This goal can either be suggested by the national committee based on the research done or can be the collective goal of all the denominations, missions and other para church organizations. (See next point.)

One of the best ways to set a national church-planting goal—and get commitment to it by all denominations in a country—is the way they did it in England.

In England, the national Challenge 2000 (DAWN) committee spent many hours praying and poring over the data that had been gathered through their research project. They concluded that a goal of 20,000 new churches by AD 2000 seemed to be what the Spirit was saying. But they shared this goal with no one. Instead, they had each denomination set their own goals at the Congress held in February 1993. When these individual goals were added together, the total came to almost exactly 20,000!

It was great confirmation to all that this represented the mind of Christ. With this conviction, the multiplication of churches throughout England is overcoming many years of decline.

6. *It is a DAWN project if* each evangelical denomination, mission agency and other group sets its own goals for number of churches to be planted by a certain date and develops and implements plans to reach that goal. It is expected that all para church organizations that do not plant churches themselves will so orient their ministries that they truly work "alongside" churches and denominations in their church-multiplication projects.

All the activities of a DAWN process are useless if the participants do not make specific commitments to national and organizational goals for massive church-planting efforts.

In Guatemala, for example, 15 individual denominations set goals and developed plans for church multiplication efforts. Under such names as "Vision 90," "Faith Projection," "Advance," "One by One by One," and so on, goals were set to double or triple their number of churches, have each church start a new church or reach a total of 1,000 churches. Most of these were five-year goals.

These individual denominational efforts kept a growth movement alive without a national focus and strong committee. Effective denominational projects of this nature include the same components as the national DAWN project.

7. *It is a DAWN project if* there is a national committee formed to keep the movement alive. One of the most crucial tasks of a DAWN committee is the continual communication of the vision to saturate a nation with churches. This committee sees that the research process continues, helps denomination leaders develop their plans for church multiplication, sees that regional DAWN seminars are held throughout the nation, encourages continued prayer for the movement, plans for the second DAWN Congress and in general keeps the vision alive.

Many committees are finding that they can keep in contact with large numbers of Christian leaders through the regular distribution of a publication. Through this they are able to foster interest in and commitment to the national church-planting strategy in all its many facets.

A good communication model is the newspaper-style publication called the Philippine Challenge, published by Philippine Challenge. With a circulation of 9,000 going to pastors and lay leaders throughout the Philippines, it has been chronicling the development and growth of the Philippine DAWN movement begun in 1974.

This publication is full of good news—churches being planted, new strategies being tried, denominational growth programs that are underway. You catch the encouraging flavor when you read some of the headlines: "Local church plants 13 churches in 1992;" "Foursquare plants 126 churches in '88;" "Mindanao owns half of DAWN 2000 goals;" "Cebu church sends missionaries to Thailand;" "23 thousand churches found;" "Church planting institute opens in '92."

This kind of reporting gives readers a bigger picture of what's going on in their nation. As they read issue after issue about what God is accomplishing through the church, it also becomes a source of vision and creative thinking. People have models to follow and adapt to their situation.

8. *It will be a truly powerful DAWN project if* it is undergirded by effective prayer movements on national, regional, denominational and local church levels.

As the current proliferation of books on world revival emphasize, prayer is the key. "The evangelical scholar J. Edwin Orr," writes David Bryant, "summarized into one simple statement his sixty years of historical study on great prayer movements preceding major spiritual awakenings: 'Whenever God is ready to do something new with his people, he always sets them to praying.'"

If God indeed is "about to do something new" in mobilizing his Body in nation after nation and in the whole world to complete his 2,000-year-old command, surely this also will come about as he sets us to praying.

Where would we be without intercessors like Jean Lim?

God raised her up from a family of idol worshippers in Indonesia and from a life of gambling and greed. She came through a series of deaths of loved ones, attempted suicides, enslavement to Japanese Buddhism and attendance with mediums and witch doctors.

"Now," she says, "I just love to pray and wait upon the Lord in His presence for hours and hours."

God has also used her to lead one of the most powerful prayer ministries connected with any DAWN project in the world. Her extended times of intercession, her small prayer group, her constant travels around the nation to organize prayer cells and her organizing of special seasons of prayer all mightily empower the Malaysia DAWN vision of planting 4,000 new churches.

I think there are two sides of the prayer coin that need equal emphasis. One is the spiritual warfare aspect of breaking down strongholds of the enemy in individuals, in cities, in people groups, in nations or wherever they occur. When satanic forces are bound or scattered, there is then entrance for the gospel. This, rightfully, is receiving a lot of attention and is another indication of the world-wide revival we are in. It is a significant factor in being able to complete the Great Commission in our time.

APPENDIX 2

13 Steps to a Successful Growth Program[212]
by Dr. James H. Montgomery

At the heart of the DAWN strategy for saturating countries with evangelical congregations until there is one for every small group of people in every ethnic and cultural setting is the Church denomination. It is the denominational growth programs in the Philippines, for example, that have brought about the doubling of the rate of growth for that whole nation in the past ten years and has kept them on target for the goal of 50,000 churches by 2000 AD.

A study of those denominational programs—and those in other nations as well—reveals at least 13 common denominators that seem to be essential ingredients for any successful growth program.

Though addressed to denominations, it is assumed that these same 13 factors apply for growth programs in local churches or groups of churches in a regional setting.

Here are the 13 steps to a successful growth program:

STEP ONE

Dream great dreams; see large visions. The first common factor is that growing denominations have a vision larger than themselves. They have a driving concern to see their whole region, their whole country, won for Christ. Such a challenging goal as a church in every barrio appeals to them. They want to be part of something bigger than themselves.

"Where there is no vision," the Proverb says, "the people perish" (Proverbs 29:18). The verse reminds me of one denominational leader who said, "We are the largest denomination already. We don't have to grow." The result was very slow growth. And, by the way, they are no longer the largest denomination either.

---

212 James Montgomery, *Dawn 2000: 7 Million Churches to Go*, appendix 1, "13 Steps to a Successful Growth Program"; adapted from an address by Jim Montgomery to the delegates of the 1985 DAWN 2000 Congress in Baguio City, Philippines.

Another denominational leader, on the other hand, had a burning desire to see his whole province filled with churches. The result was hundreds of churches planted and thousands of converts being discipled.

When you dream great dreams and see large visions, you are driven to work persistently toward seeing them accomplished.

STEP TWO

Develop, maintain and use a solid base of data. The Living Bible translates Proverbs 18:13 this way: "What a shame—yes, how stupid!—to decide before knowing the facts."

The second common denominator in successful growth programs is that denominations not only have their heads in the clouds but their feet on the ground. They see that the way to accomplish their dreams is not through sentimental, emotional fantasizing but through a concrete understanding of their situation.

These denominations study their context to see who is responsive to the gospel and how to best reach them. They study their own resources to see how big they are, how fast they are growing, what their effective and ineffective methods are and so on. They study other growing churches and denominations to find good ideas for their own programs.

I have a whole seminar I give on this topic, but I think you already have a growing appreciation of the importance of keeping detailed records on each aspect of your church, of gathering and analyzing that data, and of using it to set goals and make plans.

STEP THREE

Set challenging, realistic and measurable goals. This I believe, is at the heart of effective denominational growth programs. Challenging goals stir up and mobilize the people. Laymen and women get involved to an extent that surprises even themselves. It is exciting to work together toward a worthwhile and challenging goal.

Realistic goals are set so as not to discourage the people. If goals are not based on previous experience (the facts) and in terms of what is possible, they can be worse than no goals at all. Goals should be set large enough to be challenging, but realistic enough to avoid discouragement.

Measurable goals are set so the people can rejoice in their achievement. Specific numbers and specific dates get members involved.

I am frequently told that people in non-Western nations do not respond to goals, that they are more relational in orientation. But setting goals worked, I believe, because it is biblical and therefore above culture. Goals set under the guidance of the Spirit are "the substance of things hoped for, the evidence of things not seen (Heb 11:1)."

In other words, goal setting by the Christian is an act of faith, without which "it is impossible to please God (Heb 11:5)."

STEP FOUR

Achieve goal ownership. In one very large denominational program with which I am familiar, the foreign missionaries got together and set their 10-year goal. Then they had a very difficult time getting the Church to work toward it.

In their second program, however, everyone had a say in what the goal should be. They argued and wrestled with each other until everyone was satisfied it was the right goal. Since everyone now "owned the goal," they all worked hard to achieve it.

This is a very crucial step in a successful growth program and can be skipped only at great cost.

STEP FIVE

Give a name to your program. The denominational programs mentioned above give evidence of creative thinking in this area. The best names are not only colorful but also descriptive of what the goal is. "Strategy 1085 by 1985" and "Expansion 100" are good examples.

How would your children feel if they were given no names? Lost, ignored, unimportant! So a program needs strong identity if it is to be supported and completed. Give it a good name.

STEP SIX

Develop a functional organizational structure. As we see the Church enjoying explosive growth in the book of Acts, we find that many changes had to take place. One of these is recorded in the sixth chapter. As the Church increased in number, there developed a problem in administration. This was solved by the development of a new layer of leadership and giving a whole group of lay leaders more responsibility.

As one denomination after another developed growth programs and actually experienced increased growth in the Philippines, we found that they also had to redesign their organizational structures. Leaders had to be found to oversee the total program, take leadership in a host of committees, oversee prayer programs, supervise the recording and reporting of statistics, develop and produce various publications, handle training programs and so on.

For your growth program to succeed, you will have to break out of some of your traditional organizational structures. In the process, you will also have the joy of seeing many more laymen and women switch from being bench warmers to active participants in the church. And your denomination will grow spiritually and numerically.

STEP SEVEN

Depend on prayer and the power of the Spirit. Critics of the type of movement in which you are involved sometimes have the impression that concern for numbers and the wisdom of men are substitutes for the work of the Holy Spirit.

My observation is that just the opposite is true. Denominational programs that are truly successful are those that have been solidly backed by prayer.

The Target 400 program of the CMA is a good example. They appointed a national prayer chairwoman and made her a member of the executive committee. She helped organize hundreds of prayer cells in their churches and kept them supplied with a stream of prayer requests for the movement. The result was thousands more laymen actually involved in group prayer than they ever had before.

The book of Acts certainly models this need for dependence on prayer and the power of the Spirit in relation to the growth of the Church. The 120 spent many days in fasting and prayer before the advent of the Holy Spirit and the first 3,000 converts. Then it was a miracle of healing that led to the conversion of the next 2,000 men.

Acts 16:5 says "The churches were strengthened in the faith, and they increased in numbers daily." Both from the Word of God and the present experience of His Church we must conclude that spiritual dynamic and growth of the Church go hand in hand.

STEP EIGHT

Keep your members motivated and informed. In growth programs I have observed, I have found many creative ideas for keeping people from losing interest. First and foremost is a steady stream of announcements, reports and related sermons from the pulpits of the local churches.

Almost all have found it necessary to put out a regular publication that reports outstanding results, answers to prayer and progress toward goals. Such periodicals include articles on the biblical and practical foundations of the movement and feature men and women who have made outstanding contributions.

Added to these basic tools of communication are a host of other motivators such as annual rallies, special sessions and annual meetings, yearbooks with pictures of each church, seminars, and even such things as printed T shirts and book markers.

Denominations need to give much thought, planning and prayer to the teaching and activity necessary to keep the program moving forward month after month and year after year. Of course, the greatest motivator of all from a human standpoint is the thrill of actually reaching the goals that have been set.

STEP NINE

Train your members. This has been an indispensable part of any significant growth program, as might well be expected. The biblical strategy is to equip (train) the saints (laymen and women) for the work of the ministry.

In successful denominational programs members are trained for every aspect of the program. This includes training for starting and pastoring churches, starting and leading evangelistic Bible study groups, leading committees for record keeping and for data gathering and analysis, prayer groups, finances, executive leadership, communications and so on.

Training is given in every type of situation from Bible schools and seminaries, to short term and TEE (Theological Education by Extension) training programs, to informal and apprenticeship programs. Equipping and training are the basic ministry of the Church. No program will reach its goals without effectiveness in this area.

STEP TEN

Create sound financial policy. Denominations creating strong, new growth programs are forced to evaluate their whole financial structure.

For one thing, they need to evaluate just how they are spending their money. Frequently, funds can be diverted from lower priority items to the challenging evangelistic thrust before them.

Another matter is developing methodologies for promoting the program, training the workers, starting new churches and so on that are effective, yet within the means of local churches and national denominations.

A third matter is effective fund-raising programs. No denomination or church I know of is seeing their members come anywhere near a standard of a tithe of total income. Good teaching and creative planning are needed in this area.

No growth program is going to reach its goals without an overhaul of its finances in these three areas.

STEP ELEVEN

Send out missionaries. When the Conservative Baptists saw their annual growth rates fall from above 20% in 1974 to 12.1% and 12.8% the next two years, they realized the program was in trouble unless some firm action was taken. Among other things, they sent out missionaries.

Vic Andaya went to the province of Nueva Ecija and saw 84 converts enter his new church the first year. Dave Billings pushed this work out to include Nueva Viscaya and Isabela provinces. At about the same time, Robert Skivington was developing a thorough plan for a responsive tribe way off in Mindanao. In the first year alone they saw about 400 come to Christ and into new churches.

This missionary thrust re-established strong momentum for their ongoing program and is a beautiful example of how local churches and denominations must see beyond their own circumscribed areas for continued growth. Every church needs to be challenging, training and sending out missionaries to neighboring barrios and more distant provinces and peoples. A vast new emphasis on missions, which is actually now developing, is crucial to reaching local, denominational and national goals.

STEP TWELVE

Regularly evaluate progress. The strength of having measurable goals is that it is always possible to see just where you are in relation to those goals. In the illustration just mentioned, the Conservative Baptists might never have developed such a strong missionary emphasis if they had not known they were falling short of their goals. After all, they were still adding new members and new churches at a rather good rate. How would they have known they were slowing down if they had not set a goal and evaluated progress in terms of that goal?

Leaders of each program must constantly be aware of progress being made toward goals, problems that are arising in any of these 13 steps we are presenting and new opportunities and trends in their community, region and nation.

An annual evaluation with data in hand and lasting two or three days is the twelfth essential ingredient in an effective growth program.

STEP THIRTEEN

Make new plans. By far, one of the most heartening aspects of the 50,000 by 2000 movement in the Philippines is the sequence of growth programs. Scarcely is one goal reached and one program successfully completed when another grander goal is set.

I remind you of the CMA "Target 400" program being followed by the "Target 1000,000" plan which gave way to their "Two, Two, Two" project: 20,000 churches and 2,000,000 members by the year 2000. Several others could be cited.

In this way evangelism and church planting become a regular part of the church life rather than an activity engaged in only at long, irregular intervals. In this way, and only in this way, will the goal of 50,000 by 2000 be reached.

Each year as the current project is evaluated, new plans must be made for the coming year, made in light of the evaluation. As each five or ten-year project nears completion, it too must be evaluated and new plans made based on this evaluation.

The Church of the Philippines will make a great leap ahead in discipling its nation and in the cause of world evangelization with this good habit of making and carrying out plans, evaluating progress, and making new plans in light of the current situation.

These, then, are the 13 common denominators I have discovered existing in successful denominational programs in the Philippines as well as other nations.

Study them, pray about them and develop your program incorporating these 13 essential steps.

Jim Montgomery
Dawn Ministries

APPENDIX 3

Best Practices from Europe
(NC2P.org)

Reflective practitioners in Europe meet annually to give concerted thought to best practices as national church planting process leaders. The following emerged out of conversations in Oslo, Riga, Prague, and Amsterdam between 2011 and 2014. The document is not complete and perhaps cannot be. It is offered in that form with an invitation to engage in the conversation and bring improvements from your own experience.[213]

Toward Fruitful National Church Planting Processes

Definition: What do we mean by church planting? Functional descriptors for "church" (Craig van Gelder):

We are *called* by Christ to be people of God in the world,

We *gather* around our calling and values and shared practices (confessional affirmation, spiritual disciplines, hospitality, generosity, service to our community),

We are *connected* with our context *within our Christian tradition,*

We are *sent* into society with a calling for which we will be held accountable, including serving among the real needs of the community and knowing how to speak in the public square reflecting our shared values and practices expressing the Kingdom.

What then is conversion-based church planting? Conversion-based church planting is Gospel-sowing that will lead to Christian community/formation of disciple-making communities, expressing the descriptors above.

Definition: What is a national church planting process? As far as we can observe, a national church planting process works toward a reality when the majority of the body of Christ cooperates with one another for the purpose of seeing churches multiplied in all the nation's geographic and ethnic and cultural spaces.

---

213 Best practices shared in other settings can be found at www.gcpn.info/home/regions/national-initiatives.

A national church planting process is usually propelled by relationship and vision casting moving toward collaboration and momentum in new strategic activity (e.g., prayer, training, etc.) until it reaches a tipping point and results in measurable progress in church planting through evangelism winning people for Christ.

Tipping point takes place when:

1. A process is underway involving collaboration and momentum.
2. Church planting is helping cause net growth in a) new evangelical churches and b) total evangelical attendance nationally and in each of its geographic, ethnic and cultural spaces. Measurement requires an ongoing national research process.
3. Cooperation of the majority of evangelical denominations, agencies, etc. involving mutual learning, sharing training materials or experiences, and/or benefiting from common information, research, etc.

Why is a national church planting process valuable to discipling a nation? Why not let things just happen (or not)? Because the power of vision, the power of information and the power of unity and synergy make a national discipling process more effective than when they are absent.

Mission-Critical Components: As far as we've been able to observe, the following puzzle pieces are vital to a national church planting initiative:

- *Leadership:* a committed national church planting process leader for whom the initiative is a top priority. A person with high integrity, person with Kingdom vision, who loves and relates to the whole church and reflects values broader than any single organization or model of church plant. Able to keep peace with gatekeepers and continue to move forward with younger leaders (bridge the generational gap). A person with personal church planting experience.

  Continuity of leadership is essential, rather than by a committee with annually rotating leadership.
- *Motivating information and communication.* Components include:
  - A national research process identifying priority locations and people groups in the nation for church planting.
  - Some kind of mapping that gives a picture to the nation, stirring the need for church planting. This process measures net growth in churches and total attendance.
  - Communication which provides encouragement and motivation through shared stories showing the human dimension of changed lives and working models is also important.
  - *A gathering place:* a recognized forum, network or place (national and regional) where people come to learn and be encouraged. This gathering function:

> › *Builds toward a national consensus* that more churches are needed in the nation to accomplish the task of making disciples in every geographic, ethnic and cultural component.
> › *"Nested"* within an existing recognized body broader than any denomination or single organization.
> › *Mobilizes prayer:* connecting with new and existing prayer networks seeking spiritual breakthroughs in the nation.
> › *Ongoing systems* for recruiting, assessing, training and coaching planters—principle driven, accessible to all.

Best Practices *Toward* a National Tipping Point

- Gather strategic information and present it in a way that is prophetic, compelling and motivating to action.
- Gather denominational and mission leaders, share the research and ask for blessing/mandate to serve a national movement to meet the need.
- Form core team and gathering places to serve the national process.
- In the process, move with the movers (early adopters) while welcoming all (later adopters) as they engage.

Best Practices *After* the Tipping Point

Keep the vision on winning people to Christ and forming new disciple-making communities and fostering multiplication DNA and movements. Aim *at the start* for reproduction within 3–5 years. (If it's not multipliable, it is too expensive.)

- Develop and work with core leadership team, composed largely of practitioners, recognized by denominations.
- Meet two or more times annually in person and additional times by Internet.
- May need to become legal entity to handle finances (if no suitable "nesting" organization is available).
- Continually monitor national progress: measure the remaining gap (between reached and unreached) by updating research.
- Keep peace with gatekeepers (providing blessing); work with younger leaders (providing vision and energy).
- Meet for coffee, invite gatekeepers to share their vision for church planting in the next 10 years, honor them by inviting them to open public meetings in prayer and to offer closing benediction.
- Invest in selected younger leaders, for example:
  - 24-hour forum twice a year, sharing stories as a learning community.
  - Mentoring individually and in small groups.

- Avoid:
  - Promoting one model or style of church.
  - Setting unrealistically high goals (this is not to avoid setting goals per se).
  - Adding church health or other good things to church planting. Doing so diffuses the focus. Stay sharp on church planting.

If Possible, Provide These Ideal Practices

Provide training in a de-centralized way; bottom-up, non-linear:
- Church planter assessment tools available to assist in identifying high potential planters.
- Church planter training accessible to all planters.
- Church planter coaching provided to all planters.
- Church planter peer-learning communities accessible locally.

Gain consensus on an overall "game plan" designed to maximize assistance to denominations and church planting leaders. These could contain elements denominations would need to develop individually but recognize that these could be equally or more valuable if done in synergy with others.

Rhythm of leadership gatherings: Planning meetings of smaller core team (e.g., quarterly); larger national conference of key leaders (e.g., every two years).

Process and/or end goals: Process goals are objectives useful in the service of a national process (e.g., training, coaching, peer-learning communities). End goals are outcomes of a national process (e.g., a national church-to-population ratio, number of churches planted, people won to Christ). National end goals can be the sum of denominational goals or that sum plus a bit more to encourage further dependence on the Lord. National end goals can have a timeframe or not have a timeframe. Process goals should have a timeframe and be clearly defined. National goals can include only process goals or end goals or both.

- Quarterly newsletter or website, or both.
- Exploration of low-cost church planting approaches.
- Administrative staff to assist the process.
- Tell the best founding stories of the past to inspire hope and courage for the future.
- (Optional: acknowledge present dissatisfaction.)
- Cast vision of preferable future.
- Don't bypass denominational leaders/official channels. Discover the door openers in each denomination. Build relationship and unity—repent of mistrust where needed.
- Provide possibility-thinking leadership.
- Do research and mapping.

- Be devoted to prayer.
- Hold to perspective.
- Highlight good local models—give leaders opportunity to see and experience these, not only hear of them.
- Expose younger leaders to effective seasoned leaders—e.g., via lunch, internships, visits, mentors.
- Develop communication system—e.g., newsletter, web—to keep vision, stories, models, encouragement, etc. alive and growing.
- Develop learning communities—for planters, perhaps also for denominational leaders seeking strategic denominational change.
- Develop a "leadership pipeline" process—help leaders develop from "novice 15-year-olds" to "effective seasoned mentors."
- Share resources among denominations—e.g., training events, fruitful models and practices, research, etc. Open-handed and open-hearted sharing raises trust and synergy.
- Learn to do effective planter assessment and coaching (these two may be 80% of the battle for initial survival and success).
- Find ways to welcome parachurch organizations to work with denominations in resourcing church planting, or to church planting directly, with the blessing of denominations.

Keep Balanced

Set a reasonable pace—not too fast so as to discourage, or too slow, so as to be disobedient to our calling to disciple the nation.

Pursue wise goals—not too ambitious, not too vague.

Don't get sidelined with definition of "church" or discussions about which is the best church planting model. Rather allow diversity of understanding and practice within biblical perimeters.

Contributors to this document:

Raphael Anzenberger (France)
Øivind Augland (Norway)
Richard Hultmar (Sweden)
Martin Robinson (United Kingdom)
Peteris Sprogis, Kaspars Šterns (Latvia)
Jiří Unger (Czech Republic)
Peter Dyhr (Denmark)
Reinhold Scharnowski (Switzerland)
Murray Moerman (Canada)

National Team Self-Evaluation[214]

"How are we doing?" is an important question for every national team. Our criteria for annual self-evaluation should be neither too simple nor too complex. The process suggested by Jim Montgomery in appendix 1 is worthy of annual review.[215]

Let me suggest that each national team update its unique "dashboard" annually and make subsequent plans based on what they find.

Vital Component: How are we doing? (Place an "X" in the appropriate box)	In place; working	In Process	Yet to Come
National Team:			
National team leader, committed and capable			
National team, right-sized and effective			
Team meets regularly (four or more times a year)			
Strategic Information:			
Strategic information, updated in last three years			
Widely distributed			
Stimulating discussion and action			
Leader Gatherings:			
National gathering, key leaders in last three years			
Regional gatherings; discussion and collaboration			
Support Systems:			
Widespread training in church planting, disciple-making, multi-generational movements			
Coaching			
Communication—website or newsletters, regular, effective			

List up to five priorities, based on our self-evaluation, for the next year ...

1.
2.
3.
4.
5.

---

214 Downloadable from www.murraymoerman.com/mm/downloads/SCP-Dashboard-for-National-Team.pdf.

215 Available from www.gcpn.info/resources/it_is_a_dawn_strategy_if.pdf.

APPENDIX 5

Encouragement for Incremental Progress

Servant leadership of a national process can be difficult, particularly because of the length of the process. The perspective contributed by James Engel therefore can be helpful. Engel came to value incremental progress, applied in his work in evangelism, as a person—unaware of or even hostile to the gospel—takes gradual steps toward fruitful life in Christ.[216]

Simplified Engel Scale

-10	No God framework
-9	Experience of emptiness
-8	Vague awareness of Christianity
-7	Interest in Christianity
-6	Awareness of the Gospel
-5	Positive attitudes to the Gospel
-4	Experience of Christian love
-3	Aware of personal need
-2	Grasp of implications of the Gospel
-1	Challenge to respond personally
0	Repentance and faith
+1	Evaluation of the decision
+2	Learning the basics of the Christian life
+3	Functioning member of local church
+4	Continuing growth in character, lifestyle and service
+5	Effective sharing of faith and life

Table 9: Simplified Engle Scale

---

216 James F. Engel and H. Wilbert Norton, *What's Gone Wrong with the Harvest?: A Communication Strategy for the Church and World Evangelization* (Grand Rapids: Zondervan, 1975). Another approach to understanding stages in spiritual development is offered by Les Goertz in *Not-Yet-Christian: The 10 Stages of the Spiritual Journey* (Abbotsford, BC: Mile Marker Press, 2013).

This way of thinking is both helpful and encouraging in other important areas over which we have no control or limited influence, such as the development of national processes.

You may find encouragement in developing your own adaptation of Engel's approach.

Here are just a few ideas to get you started as you develop your own list that envisions incremental progress (read from bottom to top):

- A vigorous national process of planting new disciple-making communities at an accelerated rate, bringing local transformation to tens of thousands.
- 75 percent of denominations are focusing on planting among the least-reached.
- 50 percent of denominations say they are giving high priority to mobilizing church planting.
- Only 25 percent of organizations are willing to participate in a national gathering to commit to the task.
- An initial national gathering is convened to share national research on the least-reached and cast vision for a discipled nation.
- A small coordination team agrees to plan an initial national congress.
- Only a few national church leaders will meet to discuss church planting needs in the nation.

Research is difficult to complete, but a start has been made. Don't be discouraged. The Lord of the harvest is at work. Focus on one incremental step, pray, persist, and seek the Lord for fresh insight. He will move his redemptive purposes forward!

APPENDIX 6

Setting Priorities

Within your country are many people groups. How can you help church and mission leaders focus most fruitfully?

Your research team can aim to learn whether specific people groups and geographic locations contain more or less than 2 percent of evangelical Christians, and also the percentage of professing Christians who are not evangelicals.

This chart, developed by the Joshua Project, offers categories into which you can then place people groups to help denominations and mission agencies understand how they can set church-planting priorities.[217]

Mission Progress Level	Description	Criteria	People Groups	% of People Groups	Population (in Millions)	% of World Population
1	**Unreached:** Few evangelicals and few who identify as Christians. Little, if any, history of Christianity. Frontier Peoples are a subset of unreached.	Evangelicals <= 2% Professing Christians <= 5%	7,408	42.5%	3,230.2	41.7%
2	**Minimally reached:** Few evangelicals, but significant number who identify as Christians.	Evangelicals <= 2% Professing Christians > 5% and <= 50%	1,179	6.8%	278.7	3.6%
3	**Superficially reached:** Few evangelicals, but many who identify as Christians. In great need of spiritual renewal & commitment to biblical faith.	Evangelicals <= 2% Professing Christians > 50%	1,821	10.4%	536.3	6.9%
4	**Partially reached:** Evangelicals have a modest presence.	Evangelicals > 2% and <= 10%	3,786	21.7%	1,954.4	25.2%
5	**Significantly reached:** Evangelicals have a significant presence.	Evangelicals > 10%	3,252	18.6%	1,752.5	22.6%
	Totals:		17,446		7,752.2	

Table 10: Level of Progress in the People Group with Whom You Are Working

217 https://joshuaproject.net/global/progress.

APPENDIX 7

Further Resources and Author's Website

This appendix has additional links and resources. The following footnotes from the text of the book have external links. Please see the author's website: **http://www.murraymoerman.com/mm/more.asp** or scan the QR code above for clickable links, updated information, new research, and downloadable video/Powerpoint links.

Footnote 2: David Garrison's booklet, *Church Planting Movements* (Richmond, VA: International Mission Board, 1999), can be downloaded from www.murraymoerman.com/mm/more.asp.

Footnote 11: John Wesley's encounter with Moravians is reported in *The Guardian* (https://guardian.ng/sunday-magazine/ibru-ecumenical-centre/the-influence-of-the-moravians-on-john-wesley/) and in *Christian History* magazine (https://www.christianitytoday.com/history/issues/issue-1/moravians-and-john-wesley.html). William Carey was likewise influenced. See https://www.youtube.com/watch?v=DSWwgIdWamc&feature=youtu.be.

Footnote 33: If uncertain where to start, consider the classics listed here: www.murraymoerman.com/3downloads/prayers/books_on_prayer.asp.

Footnote 44: Russ Mitchell's paper, "*The Vital Role of Church Leadership in Advancing a National Church Planting Process,*" presented at the eighth Lausanne International Researchers' Conference, in Nairobi, Kenya, May 2018, is available for download from www.murraymoerman.com/mm/more.asp.

Footnote 62: If you would like to begin in your nation or assist in beginning such a process in other nations, please contact the author at: murraymoerman@gmail.com.

Footnote 69: Here is an early sample from Canada prepared by Lorne Hunter of Outreach Canada: http://www.murraymoerman.com/2mission/Initial-Research-Survey,Canada1996.pdf.

Footnote 75: Sample of denominational breakout worksheet: http://www.murraymoerman.com/mm/downloads2.12 Denominational Breakouts.doc.

Footnote 86: Top sixty nations in descending population size in 2020: http://www.murraymoerman.com/mm/downloads/60 most populous nations.xlsx.

Footnote 94: Team manual for implementation of "four components" strategy: http://www.murraymoerman.com/mm/downloads/NationalChurchPlantingProcess-4ComponentsTeamManual.pdf.

Footnote 96: Movement for African National Initiatives can be downloaded from http://www.murraymoerman.com/mm/downloads/MANI Overview 2007.doc.

Footnote 108: Should restrictive trends develop, it may be necessary to make leadership networks smaller in geographic coverage or ask the Lord for greater means of creativity: http://www.murraymoerman.com/mm/downloads/Creativity%20in%20restrictive%20settings.docx.

Footnote 112: See here for Bob Waymire's downloadable scan of *National Research Mobilization Handbook* manual: https://www.ocresearch.info/sites/default/files/National%20Research%20Mobilization%20Handbook%20Bob%20Waymire%201994.pdf.

Footnote 114: "The Harvest" video is more difficult to find recently; see a version with Dutch subtitles here: https://drive.google.com/file/d/1Y61o8HDNKj3ddaM3tiqHLZW-KoSi6KFO/view?usp=sharing, or find a clickable link at this footnote number at www.murraymoerman.com/mm/more.asp.

Footnote 116: Downloadable examples of additional static maps can be found at this footnote number at www.murraymoerman.com/mm/more.asp.

Footnote 119: A good example of how data can be presented in visual form was prepared by Lorne Hunter of Outreach Canada for Church Planting Canada in that nation's church-planting mobilization process. PPTs can be downloaded at this footnote number from www.murraymoerman.com/mm/more.asp.

Footnote 123: Software can help track church planting field progress by generation and nationality (https://disciple.tools/ is software for DMM practitioners). GenMapper (developed by IMB) helps track church planting movements. iShare (developed by Global Church Movements of www.Cru.org) works with GenMapper to paint a picture of national priority needs. To connect with personnel, contact murraymoerman@gmail.com.

Footnote 145: Conversation between denominations and mission agencies to empower mission agencies: http://www.murraymoerman.com/NCPP/downloads/Partnership%20Models.ppt.

Footnote 155: To be connected to an intercessors' network that focuses on disciple-making movements and national church planting processes, contact murraymoerman@gmail.com.

Footnote 169: At time of publication Covid restrictions are delaying or moving to virtual format planned gatherings. You may, however, be interested in a video summary of the NC2P 27-nation gathering in Berlin, October 2018: https://www.facebook.com/NC2PEurope/videos/2532032000355743. When restrictions are lifted, I intend to post details of regional national church planting process leader gatherings, as they resume, at this footnote number on www.murraymoerman.com/mm/more.asp.

Footnote 177: Research by Chris Maynard comparing each nation relative to harvest need and workers available is available at:

http://www.gcpn.info/regions/Church_Planting_Model_version_7.1_A3_Chart_2012-05-14.pdf

http://www.murraymoerman.com/mm/downloads/Church_Planting_Model_version_7.1_A3_Chart_2012-05-14.pdf.

Footnote 184: Leadership is challenging. My favorite leadership sites include www.healthyleaders.com and www.arrowleadership.org. See also https://www.linkedin.com/pulse/eight-things-you-need-know-gods-calling-your-life-dmin-6068954640634961920.

Footnote 191: Zimbabwe DAWN process. Download "Target 2000 Congress Handbook," a celebration of ten thousand churches planted and the challenges of discipling a nation in turmoil: https://www.ocresearch.info/sites/default/files/Zimbabwe%20Target%202000%20Manual%202001.pdf.

Footnote 193: See http://www.murraymoerman.com/3downloads/effects_of_gospel_in_history.asp and this footnote number at www.murraymoerman.com/mm/more.asp.

Footnote 195: Shared during the 2018 Forum of the Global Alliance for Church Multiplication. Photo of PPT slide: http://www.murraymoerman.com/mm/downloads/GACX2018Forum-study-of-social-impact-of-housechurches.jpg.

Footnote 211: The DAWN strategy as originally presented. Montgomery, James H. *Dawn 2000: 7 Million Churches to Go.* Pasadena, CA: William Carey Library, 1989. Text only: https://www.gcpn.info/resources/dawn2000_seven_million_churches_to_go.pdf.

Scan: https://www.gcpn.info/resources/Dawn2000%28scan%29.pdf.

Footnote 218: See www.murraymoerman.com/mm/more.asp.

Footnote 220: Several resources for prayer mobilization are downloadable at this footnote number from www.murraymoerman.com/mm/more.asp.

Footnote 221: Several resources on the social impact of the gospel downloadable at this footnote number from www.murraymoerman.com/mm/more.asp.

Footnote 222: Several resources for strategic information are downloadable at this footnote number on www.murraymoerman.com/mm/more.asp.

FOR FURTHER READING

Church Health

Schwarz, Christian. *Natural Church Development: A Guide to Eight Essential Qualities of Healthy Churches*. St. Charles, IL: ChurchSmart Resources, 1996.

Silvoso, Ed. *Ekklesia: Rediscovering God's Instrument for Global Transformation*. Bloomington, MN: Chosen Books, 2017.

Warren, Rick. *The Purpose Driven Church*. Grand Rapids: Zondervan, 1995.

Church Planting

Cole, Neil. *Church 3.0: Upgrades for the Future of the Church*. San Francisco: Jossey-Bass, 2010.

Mannoia, Kevin W. *Church Planting: The Next Generation: Introducing the Century 21 Church Planting System*. Indianapolis: Light & Life Communications, 1994.

Van Engen, Charles, "Why Multiply Healthy Churches? Biblical and Missiological Foundations." In *Planting Healthy Churches*, edited by Gary Teja and John Wagenveld. Sauk Village, IL: Multiplication Network Ministries, 2015.

City Reaching

Dawson, John. *Taking Our Cities for God*. Lake Mary, FL: Creation House, 1989.

Dennison, Jack. *City Reaching: On the Road to Community Transformation*. Pasadena, CA: William Carey Library, 1999.

Montgomery, James H. *I'm Gonna Let It Shine: 10 Million Lighthouses to Go*. Pasadena, CA: William Carey Library, 2001.

Silvoso, Ed. *That None Should Perish*. Ventura, CA: Regal Books, 1994.

Collective Impact Literature

Crutchfield, Leslie R., and Heather McLeod Grant. *Forces for Good: The Six Practices of High-Impact Nonprofits*. San Francisco: Jossey-Bass, 2007.

Hanleybrown, Fay, John Kania, and Mark Kramer. "Channeling Change: Making Collective Impact Work." *Stanford Social Innovation Review*, January 2012.

Kania, John, and Mark Kramer. "Collective Impact." *Stanford Social Innovation Review*, Winter 2011.

———. "Embracing Emergence: How Collective Impact Addresses Complexity." *Stanford Social Innovation Review*, January 2013.

Turner, Shiloh, Kathy Merchant, John Kania, and Ellen Martin. "Understanding the Value of Backbone Organizations." *Stanford Social Innovation Review*, July 2012.

DAWN Literature

Mitchell, Russ. "DAWN 2.0." Paper written for a gathering of international church-planting catalysts in Berlin, February 2018, http://ocresearch.info/sites/default/files/DAWN%202.0.pdf.

Montgomery, James H. *Dawn 2000: 7 Million Churches to Go.* Pasadena, CA: William Carey Library, 1989.[218]

———. *Fire in the Philippines.* Rev ed. Carol Stream, IL: Creation House, 1975.

———. "The Ideal DAWN Project." *DAWN REPORT*, Issue 21, November 1994.

———. *Then the End Will Come: Great News about the Great Commission.* Pasadena, CA: William Carey Library, 1996.

Montgomery, James H., and Donald A. McGavran. *The Discipling of a Nation.* Milpitas, CA: Global Church Growth, 1980.

Steele, Steve. "A Case Study in Cooperative Evangelism: The Dawn Model." Prepared for the Billy Graham Center Evangelism Roundtable "Toward Collaborative Evangelization," October 4–5, 2002.[219]

Disciple-Making

Eastman, Dick. *Beyond Imagination: A Simple Plan to Save the World.* Ada, MI: Chosen Books, 1997.

Moran, Roy. *Spent Matches: Igniting the Signal Fire for the Spiritually Dissatisfied.* Nashville: Thomas Nelson, 2015.

Peterson, Eugene H. *A Long Obedience in the Same Direction: Discipleship in an Instant Society.* Downers Grove, IL: InterVarsity, 2000.

Robertson, Patrick, and David Watson. *The Father Glorified: True Stories of God's Power through Ordinary People.* Nashville: Thomas Nelson, 2013.

Sergeant, Curtis. *The Only One: Living Fully In, By, And For God.* Littleton, CO: William Carey Publishing, 2019. (For a free ebook, see missionbooks.org/products/the-only-one)

Shipman, Mike. *Any-3: Anyone, Anywhere, Anytime—Lead Muslims to Christ Now!* Monument, CO: WIGTake Resources, 2013.

Smith, Steve, and Ying Kai. *T4T: A Discipleship Re-Revolution.* Monument, CO: WIGTake Resources, 2011.

Trousdale, Jerry. *Miraculous Movements: How Hundreds of Thousands of Muslims Are Falling in Love with Jesus.* Nashville: Thomas Nelson, 2012.

Watson, David, and Paul D. Watson. *Contagious Disciple Making: Leading Others on a Journey of Discovery.* Nashville: Thomas Nelson, 2014.

---

218 See this footnote number in Appendix 7.

219 http://docplayer.net/25520846-A-case-study-in-cooperative-evangelism-the-dawn-model.html.

Discipling Nations

Cahill, Thomas. *How the Irish Saved Civilization: The Untold Story of Ireland's Heroic Role from the Fall of Rome to the Rise of Medieval Europe*. New York: Anchor Books, 1995.

Cunningham, Loren. *The Book That Transforms Nations: The Power of the Bible to Change Any Country*. Seattle: YWAM Publishing, 2007.

Miller, Darrow. *Discipling Nations*. Seattle: YWAM Publishing, 1998.

Spaulding, Stephen. *Obedient Nations: What's So Great about the Great Commission?* Sisters, OR: Deep River Books, 2020.

Leadership Literature

Johnson, Barry. *Polarity Management: Identifying and Managing Unsolvable Problems*. Pelham, Massachusetts: HRD Press, 1992.

Kounzes, James M., and Barry Z. Postner. *The Leadership Challenge: How to Get Extraordinary Things Done in Organizations*. San Francisco: Jossey-Bass, 1987.

Senge, Peter, Hal Hamilton, and John Kania. "The Dawn of System Leadership." Stanford Social Innovation Review, Winter 2015. https://ssir.org/articles/entry/the_dawn_of_system_leadership.

Movements

Addison, Steve. *Pioneering Movements: Leadership that Multiplies Disciples and Churches*. Westmont, IL: InterVarsity Press, 2015.

Brafman, Ori and Rod Beckstrom, *The Starfish and the Spider: The Unstoppable Power of Leaderless Organizations*. New York: Penguin Group, 2006

Garrison, David. *Church Planting Movements*. Richmond, VA: International Mission Board, 1999.

———. *Church Planting Movements: How God Is Redeeming a Lost World*. Monument, CO: WIGTake Resources, 2004.

———. *A Wind in the House of Islam: How God Is Drawing Muslims Around the World to Faith in Jesus Christ*. Monument, CO: WIGTake Resources, 2014.

McGavran, Donald A. *Bridges of God: A Study in the Strategy of Missions*. Eugene, OR: Wipf and Stock Publishers, 2005.

———. *Understanding Church Growth*. Grand Rapids: Eerdmans, 1970.

Reach, Robert M., *Movements That Move*. Bloomington, MN: ChurchSmart Resources, 2016.

Simson, Wolfgang. *The Starfish Manifesto*. Adelaide, Australia: Starfish Bay Publishing, 2009.

Wagner, C. Peter. *Our Kind of People*. Atlanta: John Knox Press, 1979.

Prayer[220]

Anderson, Kirk. *City Prayer: Using the Lord's Prayer to Pray for Our Cities*. Digital, 2013. www.ocresearch.info/sites/default/files/City%20Prayer%20Research%20Questions%20based%20on%20Lords%20Prayer%20Kirk%20Anderson.pdf

Greig, Pete, and Dave Roberts, *Red Moon Rising,* Colorado Springs: David C. Cook, 2015.

Mills, Brian. *DAWN Europa Prayer Manual*, England: self-published, 1994.

Wagner, C. Peter. *Prayer Shield: How to Intercede for Pastors, Christian Leaders and Others on the Spiritual Frontlines*. Glendale, CA: Regal Books, 1992.

Social Impact of the Gospel[221]

Carroll, Vincent, and David Shiflett. *Christianity on Trial*. San Francisco: Encounter Books, 2002.

Claiborne, Shane. *The Irresistible Revolution: Living as an Ordinary Radical*. Grand Rapids: Zondervan, 2006.

Johnston, Jeremiah J. *Unimaginable: What Our World Would Be Like Without Christianity*. Grand Rapids: Baker, 2017.

O'Connor, Elizabeth. *Journey Inward, Journey Outward.* New York: Harper & Row, 1968.

Schmidt, Alvin J. *How Christianity Changed the World*. Grand Rapids: Zondervan, 2004.

Stark, Rodney. *For the Glory of God: How Monotheism Led to Reformations, Science, Witch-Hunts, and the End of Slavery*. Princeton, NJ: Princeton University Press, 2003.

Weigel, George. The *Final Revolution*. Oxford: Oxford Press, 1992.

Spiritual Formation

De Waal, Esther. *A Life-Giving Way: A Commentary on the Rule of St. Benedict*. Collegeville, Minnesota: The Liturgical Press, 1995.

Engel, James F. and Norton, H. Wilbert. *What's Gone Wrong with the Harvest?: A Communication Strategy for the Church and World Evangelization*. Grand Rapids MI: Zondervan, 1975.

Foster, Richard. *Celebration of Discipline: The Path to Spiritual Growth*. New York: Harper & Row, 1978.

Goertz, Les. *Not-Yet-Christian: The 10 Stages of the Spiritual Journey*. Abbotsford, BC: Milk Marker Press, 2013.

Medefind, Jedd. "The Fight for Social Justice Starts Within." *Christianity Today*, June 21, 2017.

Willard, Dallas. *The Spirit of the Disciplines: Understanding How God Changes Lives*. San Francisco: Harper & Row, 1988.

---

220 Several resources for prayer mobilization are downloadable at this footnote number in Appendix 7.

221 More resources on the social impact of the gospel are available at this footnote number in Appendix 7.

Strategic Information[222]

Allison, Thayer, and One Challenge Research Team. *OC International Research Manual*. http://www.ocresearch.info/sites/default/files/OC%20International%20Research%20Manual%201990s.pdf, 1995.

Kraft, Larry. *Your City for Christ: How to Understand Your City*. http://www.ocresearch.info/sites/default/files/Understand%20Your%20City%20Kraft%201995.pdf, 1995.

Waymire, Bob. *National Research Mobilization Handbook*. LIGHT International. http://www.ocresearch.info/sites/default/files/National%20Research%20Mobilization%20Handbook%20Bob%20Waymire%201994.pdf, 1994.

Waymire, Bob, and Peter Wagner. *Church Growth Survey Handbook*. Overseas Crusades, 1988.

Wingerd, Roy. *Dawn Research Handbook*. Colorado Springs: Dawn Ministries, 2001. www.gcpn.info/needs/wingerd_dawn_research_handbook.pdf.

Other

Datema, Dave. "Defining 'Unreached': A Short History." *International Journal of Frontier Missiology* 33, no. 2 (2016). https://www.ijfm.org/PDFs_IJFM/33_2_PDFs/IJFM_33_2-Datema.pdf.

Georges, Jayson, *The 3D Gospel: Ministry in Guilt, Shame, and Fear Cultures*. Timē Press, 2017.

Johnstone, Patrick. *The Future of the Global Church: History, Trends and Possibilities*. Downers Grove, IL: InterVarsity, 2011.

Nida, Eugene. *Customs and Cultures: Anthropology for Christian Missions*. Wahroonga, Australia: Joanna Cotler Books, 1954.

Terry, John Mark, and J. D. Payne. *Developing a Strategy for Missions: A Biblical, Historical, and Cultural Introduction*. Grand Rapids: Baker Academic, 2013.

Winter, Ralph D., and Steven C. Hawthorne, eds. *Perspectives on the World Christian Movement*. 4th ed. Pasadena, CA: William Carey Library, 2009.

---

222 Several resources for strategic information are downloadable at this footnote number in Appendix 7.

Web Resources
Introduction

http://www.missionfrontiers.org/issue/article/glimpses-through-the-fog

> *Glimpses Through the Fog: Multiplying Movements,* by Robby Butler who served at the U.S. Center for World Mission from 1980 to 2004 and is an occasional writer for *Mission Frontiers.*

https://www.youtube.com/watch?v=pJq1N4PiH28

> "What are disciple making movements?" is a 4 minute overview of DMM by www.cityteam.org/international, which has since become https://newgenerations.org.

http://dbsguide.org/

> David L. Watson and Paul D. Watson, authors of the book and website www.contagiousdisciplemaking.com, provide multiple resources for Discovery Bible Study, a key tool for disciple-making movements.

Training

https://zumeproject.com

> Curtis Sergeant, who currently serves with www.2414now.net and https://e3partners.org, has developed a remarkable series of spiritual disciplines leading to disciple making. The website guides small groups through a ten-week process.

www.FocusOnFruit.org

> The above site provides the detailed practical learnings of a remarkably fruitful CPM practitioner in a non-Christian majority nation. His name is not included for security reasons.

https://www.missionfrontiers.org/issue/article/any-3

> "Any-3: Lead Muslims to Christ Now!" by Mike Shipman is published in *Mission Frontiers.*

Dissertations

Anzenberger, Raphael. "Whole-Nation Saturation Church Planting: Towards A New Dawn?" PhD diss., Columbia International University, 2020.

> http://scp.outreach.ca/Portals/scp/SCP%20Towards%20a%20New%20Dawn%20Final.pdf.

Carlson, Dean. "Target 2000 & Beyond: The Impact of Saturation Church Planting on the Discipling of Zimbabwe." DMin diss., Fuller Seminary, 2003.

> http://www.murraymoerman.com/mm/downloads/DeanCarlson,Target2000&Beyond,2003.pdf.

Moerman, Murray. "The 'Discipling a Whole Nation' Challenge for Canada." DMin diss., Fuller Seminary, 1991. http://www.murraymoerman.com/2mission/dissertation.asp.

INDEX

About
the Author

MURRAY MOERMAN has been married to Carol for forty-five years. They are parents to five married children and enjoy God's gift of eleven grandchildren.

Murray started church planting in 1976 and served as pastor and daughter-church planter in the Vancouver area until 1995. During this season he earned a DMin. from Fuller Seminary. He joined Outreach Canada to initiate a national church planting process, Church Planting Canada, and led the movement for ten years. He and Carol then moved to Europe to serve the mission, One Challenge, as Area Director. For five years Murray led an intercultural partnership to train Muslims coming to Christ in Europe and North Africa. During this time, he helped found the Global Church Planting Network, which he led from 2009 to 2016. He currently leads the national initiatives team in GCPN and serves several partnerships, globally and locally, including the SCP Taskforce and Pray Ridge Meadows. Contact him at murraymoerman@gmail.com or visit www.murraymoerman.com.

CPSIA information can be obtained
at www.ICGtesting.com
Printed in the USA
FSHW021127250321
79734FS